Yours, from Wyoming

Letters and Stories about People and Other Wildlife from the Cowboy State

Robert W. Howe

*Yours,
(Rw Howe*

Illustrated by Vel Miller

Published by Morningsong Publishing, International
Encampment, Wyoming, U.S.A.

Published by Morningsong Publishing, International, P.O. Box 247, Encampment, Wyoming 82325

Manufactured in the United States of America

Library of Congress Cataloging in Publication Data: ISBN # 0-9678267-0-5
Library of Congress number 00132088

Thanks...

*To all our wonderful friends, who shared their stories
about this wonderful part of the Old West.*

*To Bill Brockner and Oakleigh Thorne, II, for their manuscript checking,
technical advice, and friendship.*

*To Herb Kelleher, chairman and CEO of Southwest Airlines, who wrote me,
"Thanks for your great letter. You oughta write an outdoors/wildlife book!
From your eloquent description of "springtime in the Rockies,"
not only was I antsy to get back to the ranch, but I could see, smell, feel,
and hear it all!" Well, Herb, we did it. Thanks for your encouragement.*

*To Barbara Scott, whose editing and encouragement went beyond making sure
commas, dashes, and other punctuation were in their right places.
The book owes its greater strength to your helpful comments.*

This book is dedicated to...

*Margie, whose encouragement and love have been to me
as springtime is to a gnarled, old apple tree.*

Introduction

A famous naturalist lived alone in the mountains for most of his years, but sometime in the 1920s he went to the city for a brief visit. His friends and admirers wanted to show him a good time, so they took him to a night spot with loud music, laughter, and dancing. Although gracious and smiling, it was obvious the man of the woods was uncomfortable. Suddenly, his eyes opened in surprise, and he turned to face a wall ten feet away. "Listen," he said, "a cricket." None of the others could hear it, so he got up and went to a window, where, with a pen knife, he gently poked out a small, brown cricket. His friends were incredulous. "What phenomenal hearing," they said. But the naturalist was modest. To teach a lesson, he took a silver dollar from his pocket (it *was* a long time ago) and tossed it onto the floor. It clanked and rolled as coins do, and everyone from the nearby tables looked. Above the din they'd heard the money fall. Smiling, the naturalist returned the cricket to its perch and said to his friends, "You hear and see what's important to you."

When I first came to southern Wyoming and the ranch that would become our home in the Medicine Bow Mountains, all that most of our visitors knew about the winter here was, "It's cold. Really cold." On their summer visits they met new friends and, if they were lucky, had some encounters with nature, then hurried back to the cities, where they dreamed of Wyoming throughout the winter and wondered what winter was really like, "out there."

As an amateur naturalist, I was delighted with the biological diversity in the Medicine Bow Mountains and at the ranch, which has been a protected area for almost forty years. To add to the guests' experience even after they were back at home, I began to write them letters with a special format. The first part of the letter was the business section and the last paragraph became a sort of image, a sharing of something we had seen or experienced at the ranch that day or week. This book grew from those letters to friends who had come to Wyoming to listen to their crickets and other things.

They came for reasons as varied as the families but usually discovered the truly valuable elements of life: the friendship, appreciation for quiet moments, participation in the natural events. They began to see the beauty of the year and to feel the warmth of experience with nature.

In modern America we're often separated from nature by glass and steel and wood; the lack of open space means fewer places for natural acts to take place, severely limiting our opportunities to feel connected to nature. On the other hand, it's our nature as a species to be a part of the land. We're out of practice when it comes to observing nature because, as we hide in our homes and offices, we seem less affected by it. After all, most of us don't have to hunt or fish just to live. If there's a drought or flood that destroys crops in one place, we get them from somewhere else in the world that isn't buried in water or dust.

We've become so busy being busy that we seldom take time to look and listen, truly look and listen. My parents always felt it was important to "keep the kids busy." Even today I have this annoying habit of trying to do two things at once, like watching television and reading a book. Once I sat drawing a gnarled, old tree at timberline. As I sketched the lines on the paper, I watched a spider patrolling the weathered and gray limbs, listened and watched as a nuthatch picked around the bark, felt and heard the wind soughing lightly through the needles, smelled the light scent of drying sap. I was amazed at how much I'd been missing. I promised myself to be better at what Sherlock Holmes called perceiving, not just seeing, to concentrate on one thing at a time.

A walk through a forest, a horseback ride over a sage-covered hillside, wading in a stream (either with or without a fishing rod) are all times for discovery. At every step something beautiful — at our feet, in the air, or in the distant view — screams quietly for attention. Occasionally, though, a person can return from such a mini-trek without any new experience; there was too much to absorb, and they traveled too far.

One of my particular joys has been to go slowly, to pause in my walk or ride or wade, and let each of those elements converse quietly with my senses. To focus even a few moments on what I'm hearing, smelling, seeing enhances my experience of nature. The closer I look the more I see and feel. If I have several hours free, I'd rather walk a mile or two than five or ten. The longer trek becomes a blur for me, while the shorter walk becomes a view through a magnifying glass.

Most of us humans can't look at a sunset or the fiery colors of an autumn aspen without being stirred. A sunset is, after all, music for the eyes. Far fewer, however, turn to the east at sunset and marvel at the dove-soft hues of the clouds and dusky light, or pause in wonder at the silvery touch of sunlight on aspen bark. My goal has been to look at the little things, for they, together, make up the big ones and help me appreciate and understand the grander picture. Our world is, as M. Luckiesh noted in his book, *Light and Shade*, "a picture gallery containing an infinite number of canvases." One of my nature mentors lived in the same house for more than thirty years. From his living-room picture window, Stan had an imposing view of Mt. Princeton. Over the years, he took dozens of the same picture and built an album. Each picture was the same, insofar as it was a portrait of the mountain from the same place. But each picture was different in that no two were really alike. The light or snow or greenery or clouds or elk prancing across its face or wind chasing the elk — every picture was another sample from that infinite number of original canvases.

It seems that every part of the country says about itself, "If you don't like the weather, wait a few minutes." In Wyoming it's true. Old Wyoming residents claim there are only three seasons, summer, winter, and mud. Fall is in September, bright gold and breathtaking, but it lasts only a few weeks or days, and then the trees are bare. Spring is so short that one rancher told me, "Ye don't want t' sleep too long in May. Y' might miss spring."

About 25 miles from us, the Continental Divide cuts across the mountain peaks. It's more than just a separation of waters, determining whether the rain and snowmelt go to the Atlantic or the Pacific. The Divide defines our landscape. Just to the west of it, where most of our weather comes from, the mountains receive huge volumes of snow and rain that create lush vegetation and undergrowth — as well as some of America's best ski areas. But, when the moisture is dumped on the western side of the mountain, our eastern side is drier. Spring snowmelt though, creates clouds that bring rain, which waters our meadows and the ponderosa and lodgepole forests. Then the air dries out again, and for the next 800 miles across the Great Plains few trees grow. In fact, when the Transcontinental railroad was built in the late 1860's, the Medicine Bow Mountains were the first source of timber for the crossties. Until that time the forest had only been visited by Arapaho, Ute, Cheyenne and Sioux, who came to get lodgepoles for their tipis.

Hundreds of white men came into the forest to cut trees. They discovered the beauty of the area and stayed to start ranches, learning to deal with the harsh weather of mountain country.

The sudden changes of weather can be fun, and generally I enjoy those changes but mostly when our guests aren't here. Back in the early days of guest ranching, friends gathered for a month or longer and expected the weather to vary. Now families take only a week and hope for sunshine every day. Most of the time here it works out. Others....So I watch the sky like a city person all summer long, hoping our guests will have "pretty days," feeling tense and a bit like I've let them down when clouds hang low. Then, the day we close, I return to "rancher think" and again appreciate the rain and snow.

Wyoming is the Cowboy State, and cowboys love what they do. A bumper sticker on one of my friend's truck says, "Cowboys never die. They're already living in heaven." Generally they love their solitude, but they also like company, often for friends to "tell lies" to. When they do gather, there's a definite code of etiquette. For instance, if you drop by someone's "place," you stay on your horse until invited to "git on down." When shaking hands, remove your glove. Keep your hat on, unless you're meeting a lady, then remove it and place it over your heart, delivering a little tip of the head and saying respectfully, "Ma'am."

To some extent our non-Wyoming friends' conceptions of our state are true. Winter here is long, often lingering into May. Surprisingly, though, there isn't all that much snow — because of that Divide I mentioned before. I recall one cold-warm-snowy-clear day in March when an old cowboy friend rode into the ranch. He'd been out since before dawn, looking for some lost heifers, and hadn't shaved before he left, or for that matter before he'd left home four days before. In the breeze, his Stetson lifted slightly, revealing a bit of fish-belly white skin in a line on his forehead. He was dressed in a fleece-lined jean jacket and long batwing chaps. He was in a hurry, so politely refused getting down and remained perched on his sorrel gelding. He sipped the coffee I offered and smoked a Marlboro (even cowboys are taken in by the advertising).

"Looks like more snow," I said. He squinted at the incoming cloud bank and gave me a patient look.

"Nope," he said. "'T ain't more snow. 'T's more o' th' saime. 'T only snows once each winter, then blows 'round th' countryside 'til it's plumb wore out. Thisn's gettin' pritty thin."

On the other hand, the county road crews, who drive six-wheel-drive graders to muscle the snow off the road, have another outlook. They say, "Anything less than a foot of snow is a skiff."

It *does* get cold here. In December and January it's common to get down to twenty below, and I've seen it as low as minus-fifty-two degrees Fahrenheit, without the wind chill. Most of our trees are evergreens, with waxy-surfaced leaves (needles) that are green year-round. The waxiness helps prevent the leaves from drying out, and the green lets the tree photosynthesize through much of the year. Even the sap has an anti-freeze, so it won't turn to ice until very low temperatures.

Spring plays with us, brightly warm and sunny, sunburn weather one day, freezing-cold dripping-snow weather the next, or changing from one hour to the next. The most notable element is mud. The roads become deepening ruts, as the frost metamorphoses to mud, and low cars bottom out to become high-centered, teetering in the middle of the road, wheels spinning hopelessly like a turtle on a pinnacle with its legs moving frantically.

September may bring a golden color from the aspen trees, but summer is golden in the way it warms our souls. We love both, perhaps in part because they are so brief and filled with dozens of new and old friends coming to visit.

So I wrote the stories here, to share with people I thought would appreciate them. Friends began to tell me that these little stories in my letters were special to them. I was grateful to hear they enjoyed them, often sharing the stories with their children, and that through the images they gained a clearer understanding of how to look at nature, whether at the ranch or driving through a suburb or city.

Many of these images are from those letters. You'll notice that I've sometimes included the closing. Generally it's, "Yours, from Wyoming, where...," which is the way I normally close my letters.

This book is a compilation of images, both those experienced by me and those shared with me by friends. Some relate to the plants and animals. Others tell how various "city slickers" met the Medicine Bows. The years have been blended into one, so the reader can appreciate the feeling of being in the mountains over time, but understand what a year is like here on the frontier.

You'll notice that my year is divided a bit differently. For instance, I think of October as the changing from one year to the next. It isn't a sudden change, as the countdown on December 31, rather it's a gradual, month-long process. At the ranch we have guests throughout September, but that month is as different from August as April is from June. The changing aspens linger for a couple of weeks, and the air itself changes. We breathe more deeply — I often find myself sighing in appreciation of the beauty — and look back on the year, which somehow seemed to have started this time last year. So I hope you'll excuse my calendar adjustment and that you'll enjoy participating in the Wyoming year.

The Wyoming Year

I grew up in a city of 60,000, with vacant lots interspersed among the houses. We children prowled the open spaces daily and began to learn about nature. Our favorite lot was two blocks square, wild with tossing grasses at the top, wetland cattails and sedges at the bottom of a long, sloping hill. In the summer we'd wrestle or roll down the hill or lie on the grassy slopes and play the cloud game. Other days we'd slog around in the marsh (no boots of course) and gather brown cattails or sneak up on the *oak-a-leeeeing* redwing blackbirds. In winter we'd sled down the hill on Flexible Flyers or toboggans or other devices of our own invention, the sale of which would most likely make us rich if we were old enough to patent them, or so we dreamed.

It was during this time that I began to grasp a sense of the seasons and how people fit into those changes. Humans do make changes in their environment, some from bad intentions, some from good intentions or even fear.

Other than birds and insects, the first wild animal I knew about was an unfortunate opossum. Late one night, when I was about five, gunshots awakened me. The opossum had been on our porch, and my parents, fearing rabies, had called the local deputy, who came armed with a .22 pistol. They dispatched the poor animal quickly, a victim not of something it had done wrong, but of its own "ugliness" and my parents' unreasonable fears for their children.

American city dwellers, child or adult, often have a considerable amount of disconnection from, or "fear and loathing" of, the natural environment. A friend operated a camp near a large city. Each July and August inner city children came to the camp for an outdoor experience. When the director discovered that most of the children had never seen a live cow, he arranged with a local dairy to send one out for a few days. The children could try milking her and learn about where milk comes from. It was a mistake. When the kids discovered that milk didn't come from those nice plastic containers they saw in the store, they refused to drink another glassful. Early next morning the cow was returned to the dairy, and the camp staff began a milk-drinking campaign. Counselors drank glasses, full and bubbly, at each meal, smacking their lips and exclaiming how good it was. Meanwhile, most of the campers ate their cereal dry. Then, ice cream sundaes were served at each night's dessert, and a few couldn't resist. Finally, a bedtime milk and cookie event won them over, and nearly all returned to their favorite beverage.

I was nineteen before I first saw the West, when I drove from near Chicago to Buena Vista, Colorado, a village of two thousand in those days and not much bigger today. Before departing Illinois, I decided I wouldn't just speed to Colorado but would see the trip, not just the destination. I made good on that promise, and those memories continue to reward me. One day in Kansas (I'd never seen such flat country or so much sky at once, even being from the prairies of Illinois), I drove only a hundred and ten miles. I still think this is the best way to travel.

Children and adults love natural areas. I've always been glad for the foresight of park makers in saving those more natural zones that give us a chance to refocus. Even small areas of nature are important, as, for example, in the crowded culture of Japan, where mini gardens delight the eye and please the soul.

When I became a parent, I wanted to share a love

for the environment with my children. Even when our daughter, Heather, was very small, my wife, Margie, and I would take her into the forest. She'd play among the trees, and we'd discover through her eyes the newness of squirrels and robins. Later, when we moved to the country, she'd "help me" as I worked around the ranch. In winter she'd jump from porches into snow that was chest deep on me, laughing with joy and burying herself so only the glow from her orange snow suit was visible. One cold, moonlit evening when she was about six, we went outside. In the bluish light we watched a stardust of ice crystals falling gently and caught them on our tongues, enjoying the tiny bits of cold.

One of my friends teased me recently, saying, "Walking in the woods with you is like walking with a kid." Thanks. Wouldn't it be wonderful if we all approached life and the things around us with the same sense of wonder as a little child?

When my grandson, Dallas, was four, he shared his excitement with me and his family. It was toward evening in late March, after a long spell of unusually warm weather. The porchlight switched on, and a moth came to investigate. Dallas was elated; it was the first moth he'd seen since last year, and he wanted to look at it closer. We caught the moth in a jar and spent half an hour watching it before releasing it to the light.

There's at least some aspect of beauty in all of nature, and a true outdoors lover works to see it. For instance, a leach, or the thought of one, is repulsive to most. Yet, when one stands in a pond and watches them cruising, swimming in a porpoise-like way, their slender beauty is appealing. I suppose it's mainly their attach-and-suck-blood lifestyle that repulses. But they need only one or two blood meals a year (for protein, to reproduce); the rest of the time their meals are snails and little crustaceans. Hunting through the water plants, they remind me of a stretchy rubber snake without the flicking tongue. They attach one end of their body, stretch out two or more times their length and attach the other. Sometimes the critter goes forward, and sometimes the rear end goes forward. Which end is which is hard to tell, but the grace of movement is interesting to watch.

I understand how difficult it can be to connect with wild things when you're surrounded by the different wildness of a city street. Still, almost every city has its parks and open spaces, where nature-under-control is still a wonderful experience and where one can commune with nature. There are advantages to living as we do here on a ranch. It's easy to strap on skis and go out, if only for half an hour, but even in the city you can find a touch of nature that will nourish your spirit.

I was delighted when my daughter, Jennai, wrote an essay for college and described our early times together, looking at nature and trying to discover its secrets. Looking closely at things in nature continues to be important to both of us.

I enjoy living in smaller towns, and Wyoming has some of the best. You can always find a parking space, and our town is so small that more than once I've stopped my car in the middle of Main Street to have a conversation with a neighbor.

Driving along the highways of Wyoming is interesting, and not just for the expansive views. People usually wave, or at least lift their fingers from the wheel in a small salute. Even if you aren't sure you know someone, it's normal to return salutes. A couple of times, when I was wrapped in thought, I failed to wave.

Later, in town, a concerned friend will ask if everything is okay.

Mostly, I like the intimacy of knowing the people I see, to lock eyes and share grinned greetings, with a friend we'd seen just yesterday or with a stranger. In the city I notice that people almost never make eye contact, for, I've been told, that can be dangerous. I guess that explains one reason so many city dwellers walk looking down or with eyes locked straight ahead.

It's generally safer here, too. I watched the news from Denver last night, then turned to the local newspaper that covers this area of Wyoming. There were some interesting articles, as usual, but one caught my attention because of the contrast to what I'd just seen. Our big cities do seem to be violent places, or at least parts of them. The article I mention was the monthly report from our chief of police. It stated that, during the year, there had been all of 356 police calls. In the month of November — a virtual crime wave — there were two animal calls (dogs wandering without a license), one criminal arrest, one assault, twelve speeding tickets plus nine warnings, thirteen calls for community service (including to open a door), one case of vandalism, and two domestic disputes (amicably settled). Andy Griffith would have been happy here.

Fulfilled. It's a lovely, double-dipped word — full-filled — and when I look back on my life I think for the most part it fits. The truest joys haven't been in the "toys" I've bought with my money — boats, snowmobiles, cars, gadgets. The best memories are in my family and friends and the times I've spent being a part of our outdoor world.

I always felt I needed a connection with nature to be fulfilled. Some time ago, when I had to live in the city with my family for six months, I discovered how very much I needed that contact, and I believe that most of us have that same need. We just don't realize what it is and feel somehow disconnected. Perhaps a more regular nature fix, would help everyone. Nature programs are popular on public television. They help us understand more about our environment, but they just aren't enough. We need the real thing. When a guest tells me a story about an animal they've enjoyed that day or asks me questions about a flower or, "Why do the trees grow so thick only on one part of the mountain and the other's so bare?" it makes me happy. Why? Because they've just imaged their own mental photograph, and taken another step toward understanding the mountains and the nonhuman world.

I used to be a hunter, but not anymore. Frankly, I don't have anything against hunting. Some of the most committed conservationists are hunters. I cringe a bit, though, when someone calls them "outdoorsmen" (or women). Hikers, bikers and campers all fit into that category of outdoorsmen. Nevertheless, I do appreciate all that they've done as a group to enhance the environment. I'm just not one of them anymore.

I have a mental photograph of the day I decided to stop hunting. The day was cold but clear and calm as I headed to an area where I thought the elk might be gathered. I'd walked for several hours through the woods and mountain meadows and was ready to rest a bit. There had been a few tracks but not much else, so I climbed a small ridge for a look around. At the top I paused in awe. From the crest of this small peak, I looked down into a hidden valley I'd never seen. The beauty of the place overwhelmed me, and I had to sit on a boulder, and stare. Bright snow covered the tops of each boulder, and at the bottom of the valley a little emerald-green lake was beginning to freeze around its edges. Almost noon, the sun was high. Sparkling reflections bounced up at me from dozens of points in the valley, and the land below looked at the same time both cold and warm.

It was then I realized that this was why I hunted, not just for the meat, but to enjoy this kind of place and this kind of feeling. If I were to leave the gun at home, I'd have much less to carry. So I started a little fire, brewed a pot of coffee, and sat back to memorize the scene. Two hours later, I unloaded my rifle and returned home. That was more than twenty-five years ago, and although I've never seen it again, I "visit" the place often. When the pressures of life become too much, I'll sit in a quiet place, close my eyes, and I'm back on the ridge top.

How many times have I seen something so beautiful I felt I just had to capture it on film, snapped the shot, and then went on without truly looking? When the film came back and the picture somehow didn't match the reality, I realized something was missing. Even an excellent photograph lacks something. A while back I began leaving my camera home more of the time, using it merely for recording details or taking pictures of friends. I decided instead to take a different kind of photograph.

I would really look at something I thought was beautiful, or sad, or interesting, or just stirred me in some way. Using a notepad and pen, I found I could just memorize certain details and then retrieve the picture for my own enjoyment any time I wanted. That works for me. It's really maximizing the present. If we really think about it, except for snapshots of other people, most pictures we take are for ourselves. It's the rare individual who really wants to see someone else's vacation pictures. More cases of insomnia likely have been cured by vacation slide shows than sleeping pills. But, like a song we can sing or hear over and over, a description that includes all the senses — and involves the reader or listener — allows us to share the experience.

Here's what I've found works for me. I sit on a comfortable rock or in the shadowed area below a tree, settling in so I don't have to shift around a lot. Then I just try to memorize or absorb the scene, using all of my senses. Sometimes I'll focus on what I'm smelling for five minutes, then what I'm hearing, and so on. Not only is a thing beautiful because of what we see, feel, etc., but because we are at that moment awash in the joy of living, and we reach out to experience that joy. Taking "foolproof" photos has, for me, been a way to experience more of life and build a very special picture album. Give it a try.

Whether in the mountains, forest, or desert, I enjoy knowing the plants and animals I see. They are the friends along the way, which change by the season. I love the early mornings of May, when the songbirds wake me as they sing from the edges of their dozens of territories. One July I walked through an aspen grove and surprised a mule deer buck. Velvet antlered, cautious but unafraid, he paused in mid-bite. A phosphorescent orange fairy trumpet flower dangled from his black lips, and I knew he'd become used to me when he finished chewing the pretty snack. In early August the pikas (tiny members of the rabbit family) *eep* from their hay stacks on a sunny rock. By September they're hidden, and their crops are packed into their rock homes for food and warmth over the long winter.

I try to be like a child, asking questions, then seeking answers. That's why my friend was kidding me about my approach to a hike. While he goes for hikes with double-digit mileages, I consider mine "nature strolls." For me, it's better to go through life asking questions and looking closely, participating in the natural scene and not just viewing it.

The year follows changing yet unchanging patterns, and I enjoy being a part of them. Living in the country, we pay more, or at least different, attention to the things around us. A lousy, rainy day in the city can be a wonderful day in the country, if your land is parched and your grass won't grow so you can make hay to feed your livestock in the winter. Of course it can be a lousy, rainy day to a rancher who's trying to make that hay and needs sunshine to dry the grass.

How we make our living can make a difference too. While a trucker usually can't stop at a scenic area to enjoy the view, ranchers often stop their tractors or pickup trucks to soak in the glories of where they live.

In April I watched a black cow licking her bald-faced blacky calf (an animal with black body and white face). By late September, that calf was beginning the weaning process. It was gathered in a corral with hundreds of bawling others, while the mothers trotted nervously around the enclosure, adding their own deeper bawls.

When a raven struggled to land on a power pole one January day, it had to turn and face the wind to brace itself. Once settled, it let the wind flow around its streamlined body without fear of being blown off. I thought about another raven on a very warm day in July. That one perched atop a power pole and faced the breeze to cool off. The raven's beak was partly open, and it held its wings slightly spread from its body, panting to cool from the inside out.

On a snowy March day I peeked into an early robin's nest. The bird's eyes followed me, but she remained to protect her eggs. The eggs were cozy and warm under her, although melting snow formed shiny beads on her glossy, gray back. She'd been unmoved for so long that her tail held a two-inch-high dollop of snow. By late April her spotted-breasted babies were on their own, scurrying across the lawns and probing for worms. The October robins, probably including her and her offspring, gathered in loose flocks and left one night, appearing again in late February.

In early spring the grass begins to green at the sun-warmed edges of the asphalt roads. Within a few weeks the green spreads until it fills the meadows. About this time the aspen buds begin to swell, and the trees disgorge catkins — clusters of flowers that cover the tree like hundreds of dangly brown earrings. By late May the groves fill with a pale green haze, which becomes deeper green each day as the tiny leaves gradually expand and chlorophyll deepens their color.

Summer brings the magic of a kestrel, hovering over a likely meadow, then "stooping" (diving) onto a mouse or fat grasshopper. In the fall I watch it hunt the edges of glowing gold aspen groves for a few days, then they, like the robins, are gone for the winter.

The ever-present element in all seasons is, of course, the wind. Winter's wind blows the snow from our peaks into banners a half mile long then deposits it in "cornices," huge overhanging snow cliffs. Eventually they crumble, unable to support their own weight, and roar downward in grinding avalanches.

Sometimes, especially in February and March, our

valley fills with the howling warmth of a "chinook," and the snow melts or sublimates, almost disappearing as we watch. Summer wind can be warm or cold, depending on the minute. In June it does its pollination work, both in the meadows and around the ponderosa forests, where clouds of yellow pollen drift through the trees. If the wind brings rain, the puddles are yellow-edged and thick with drifting pollen. In fall, the wind blows lightly one day, hard the next, rattling the changing aspens until their leaves tear free and lie scattered on the ground. The dead leaves blacken quickly, but for a few days a hiker feels as if they were walking atop gold coins.

As we cleaned one of the barns, Margie discovered an original oil painting. She cleaned it up and hung it in one of the cabins. A few weeks later, as new guests arrived, the new occupants rushed into the office very excited. They recognized the signature and told us that the painting could be worth tens of thousands of dollars. I left it in the cabin for them to enjoy that week, then displayed it in the office for everyone to enjoy. Now it's in our new dining room/lodge.

The true value of a thing, however, isn't in what it costs, but in how it affects us. I have a shadowy-bright image from my childhood of an oil painting owned by my grandfather. The picture was probably a romanticized painting. It featured an Indian with a single feather in his hair, wrapped in a blanket and standing on the shore of a lake. The background was a snowy mountain, shining in the dusky blue light of a full moon. All of my growing up years that painting overhung the mantel of our home. I must have stared at it for hours over those times, for it is permanently engraved in the recesses of my memory. My grandfather is gone now, and the picture sold, destroyed, or simply lost, except in my memory. Even today (is it really more than fifty years ago?) a snow-filled moonlit night always returns me to that childhood home and to the painting over the mantel, my treasure without dollar value.

A couple "cowboy" and raise their children on a little ranch about forty miles from any town. She looks at their yard and its view and sighs, "It's like we're living in a painting." Some doctors believe that a sense of beauty in our lives is important for good health. When we discovered the dollar value of that painting from the barn, I realized how often the greatest treasures are hidden from us, in plain sight. Unfortunately, they're often hidden because we simply depreciate the value of a thing, which includes an appreciation of its beauty. It can take someone with more experience or a different perception to point it out to us. Then we realize that we, too, live in a painting.

October

Seasons and places change so quickly. Last week riders explored on horseback, and hikers strolled through miles of golden aspen trees. One evening I watched a lone fisherman in the dying light, casting into an iridescent pool and pulling out a living splash of color, a rainbow trout. Now, the ranch is closed, and where there were two hundred people, now there are seven.

It's a busy time though, and we're well begun on some projects to be done before winter sets in. We're busy painting the bridge over the North Platte, reroofing six cabins, building one new cabin, and preparing to paint another six. It's October, and fall's about over now, but the glory remains.

Fall, after the leaves are gone, can be depressing, or just another stage of beauty — it all depends on how you look at the scene. All the aspen, for instance, are bare, but their stark grayish-white bark seems to glow in the sunlight. Whole groves look that way. A week ago they were brilliant gold, but it changed quickly after three days of wind. Now the leaves on north slopes lie in shadow, moist and scented with mold as they turn black. In the sunlight the dry leaves fly over the grass with a light rattling/rushing sound, like distant waterfalls.

This morning, six-foot-long silvery threads of spider web drifted from hundreds of branch tips, dancing lightly in the sun, like thin plumes of smoke. For the last several nights, a bull elk ravaged through the meadow and around the house, bugling in that eerie/beautiful, grunting/whistling sound of fall. I wrapped one very nice tree with a wire cage, to discourage him from tearing at the bark. Now the bent cage lies on the ground a dozen feet from the tree, but

at least its bark is intact, so far. All the flowers are gone except outside my office window, two yellow coneflowers with black centers and wilting yellow petals. Indian summer is here.

And the grasses? They're a pale whitish brown most of the day, but at dawn and sunset they change. They are about knee high and wave in the sunlight in a hundred shades of fading green, gold, tan, brown, black, and silver, swishing brittlely in the wind. Quito, the border collie, romps through a dozen times each day, sniffing out the exciting new things that have come through since his last visit. We've had a couple of weeks with perfectly clear skies and colorless sundowns, but last night high cirrus clouds moved in, and the sunset turned fiery in the still air. The meadow by our house changed to amber with overtones of russet, then as the sun dropped lower, it became deep, golden red-brown, with each kind of grass a different tone. I climbed atop a corral fence to watch. But it only lasted a few minutes as the light faded to blue gray and then black. So many colors. So short a time. The clouds are still here, and I can't wait until tonight.

I'm often asked, "What do you do the rest of the year, after guest season is over?" Some think we settle down by the fire and read, travel to exotic places, generally forget about the ranch until it's time for people to return. Ha. We're about to enter two really busy months, where we'll race against winter to see if we can get the outdoor projects done. We generally make up a "to do" list for the winter, and it's often five or six single-spaced pages of projects. Some will be completed quickly: "Oil the hinges on cabin 7," for instance. Others will take more time: "Build a new bridge over Mullen Creek." Or, "Paint the bathrooms in cabins 2, 7, 15, and 16." So, our days are still full. They're just different. Instead of spending time with groups of friends that change each week, we're working with only four or five.

So it's still busy but in a different way. One of the things I promised myself 35 years ago was to stop each day and look around, to appreciate what I was doing and where I was privileged to live. It's not always easy.

For instance, one day I was digging a ditch, literally. A water line broke. We'd dug as much as we could with the back hoe and were cleaning the muck out by hand. The day had been long, frustrating, cold, definitely muddy, and we still hadn't solved the problem. Then, about 4 o'clock, I paused to stretch my stiff back and looked up just as a flight of geese honked overhead, so close I could hear the swishing of their wings. They flew upriver under a bank of thickening clouds that were already beginning to deepen to a rosy color. Each time I pause now, whether at my desk or in a ditch, I look around and appreciate. Other times, it's easier, like when I'm on horseback, hiking, or cross-country skiing, all of which I like to do in my free time.

So, we'll take a stroll through a year at the ranch.

Animals aren't afraid of us here because the ranch has been a wildlife sanctuary for so long. We get to see them going about their business in some often unusual ways. One bright day at noon, I watched a jackrabbit sneaking across a sunny, shortgrass pasture and into the knee-high brome grass. Even in the two-feet-high brome I could trace his steps, for the brown stalks rustled and shook stiffly, waving their seed heads gently in the calm air. When the rabbit, I think a male, came to the edge of a horse-cropped area, he paused. His ears and head looked first in one direction then another as he listened and watched. Mother rabbit must have warned him, "Be sure to look both ways (and up) before crossing an open spot." Sensing danger, he slowly flattened his enormous ears against his back and lowered himself to a crawling crouch, like a cat on the hunt. But this was the miracle. He disappeared as I watched. Of course he was still there, but his mottled brown coat blended so well with the plants that even through the binoculars I could barely see him. Then he began to move, crawling slowly. In about five minutes he crept like an Indian scout across an opening as long as three cars and into a shady spot. Reaching the shade of a willow, he pulled his legs up tight — as if ready to leap to safety — and seemed to doze.

Other animals are less careful. A crew moved in to renovate our swimming pool. Jackhammers rattled against stone as they tore at the old pool surface; half a dozen men carried equipment and shouted instructions to each other. Most wore ear protection, for the sound carried a quarter mile or more. As I watched the fall colors, I noticed a small movement in the willows about 150 feet from the pool. It was a line of ten deer, led by a young buck. They sauntered out of the bushes, then one-by-one they leaped the fence across the golf course and continued uphill into the cottonwood trees. They weren't at all bothered by the noise and confusion. In fact they weren't even interested in us.

Horses are always thinking. If you give a horse ten miles of fence with one weak spot, she'll find it and invite the rest of the herd to join in an escape. One such day we had the whole herd scattered across a 2,000-acre meadow along the river instead of the smaller pasture that had more and better grass. I rode out to gather them and put them back where they could get more to eat. It was a clear, calm day, and I was enjoying the sun's warmth on my neck, the soft purling of the river and the clop-clop of my horse's unshod feet on the moist ground.

When I noticed a field of gray, beach-ball-sized boulders, I rode down to check them out; I hadn't recalled their presence before. Suddenly each "rock" sprouted a long black neck and head, and dozens of Canada geese leaped up. Their calling and running with flapping wings startled my horse, and he started to buck as the geese flew up in a noisy cloud, circled us, then honked their way upriver. As they disappeared, my horse snorted a few more times, then calmed, as if embarrassed. In a minute the only sound again was the purling river.

Deer-crossing signs are endangered species now that it's hunting season. You've probably seen them, showing a buck deer silhouette in mid leap. Almost every one of them carries round pockmarks, bullet holes from frustrated hunters. Most of the holes miss the outline of the leaping deer — which obviously wasn't

even moving. Perhaps their poor marksmanship is why the hunters are frustrated.

"Goat roaming" is an interesting way one local high school makes money and gets the community involved in the fun. If you want to have a big and smelly billy goat "visit" someone, you can send him for $5. If you are concerned that someone's going to send *you* the goat, you can buy goat insurance for $5, ensuring that the billy will never, ever come to your door. When the billy arrives at a house he's required to stay ten minutes, I imagine looking over the various edibles in and around the house. But there's a way out. If you forgot to buy goat insurance, for $5 you can have the goat leave right away. Because in addition to being big and smelly, he's also messy. So, it's probably worth the $5. I'm told that the *Eau de Billy* lingers for an hour or more, even if you have the house open and breezes pass through. It's a weeklong riot of fun, with everyone trying to sneak the billy (actually, there are several) in on their friends at the most unexpected moments. Last year the graduates took their senior trip courtesy of the old goat(s) — and the rest of the townspeople.

But you really know you're in cowboy country when the local high school raises money by having a pickup truck and saddle wash.

It's an almost-winter kind of day. The whole landscape is gray on gray, from the pale clouds filling the sky to the lowering charcoal clouds that spit "graupel" (ice pellets that look like tiny, styrofoam balls) on the feathery seed heads of the rabbitbrush.

Reflecting the cold sky from its polished steel surface, the river flows quietly through the dying autumn. A few aspen groves glow brilliant orange-yellow, especially in one place at the foothills, where a shaft of sunlight pierces the cloud cover and pours into the trees.

Black cattle lie among the sage, where the wind whistles less, but still shiver as they chew their cuds and wait for the sun to return. Two vultures drift on the wind, their wings and bodies motionless and their heads swiveling, eyes searching as they soar low over the hillsides, looking for night deaths.

Tomorrow, the weather predictors promise, will be sunny and warm again.

In the cottonwood grove the trees are almost bare, their castoff leaves rattling off on their short-term adventures away from the home tree. Most will end up piled against bushes or the tennis-court fence. A few will dive into the swimming pool and float from shore to shore for a few days before sinking. The white puffs of salsify flowers are sending their downy seeds drifting away, swirling on breaths of wind as slow as one mile per hour.

We've moved the horses to the fall pasture; each night they graze on the warmer tops of the hills on Savage Ridge, overlooking the ranch. Not only is it warmer, but they can see us coming from a long way off and trot away quickly if we even think about bringing them in. They *are* on vacation.

The river continues to drop toward its low point. Geese, ducks, and mergansers gather in quiet, mixed parties. At dawn, dozens of birds paddle or wade in the shallow pools or perch atop low rocks, sitting on their feet to keep them warm. As the day warms, so do the birds, and by 8 a.m. they are flying noisily up and down the river, searching for food.

Our bighorn sheep have gradually been dying off. The herd, which had numbered almost sixty-two years ago, is now down to twenty-four. A wildlife biologist has been studying them for almost a year and thinks they have a blood disease called "Chlamydia." Rams, which move from herd to herd, spread it among the ewes. When the ewes are infected, most abort their fetuses and become sterile. The few lambs that are born seem healthy until early October, when they quickly sicken and die. One herd only, which has a very large-horned and powerful alpha male, hasn't been affected. He chases all potential suitors (infectors) away. Still, the sheep continue to die in the other three herds.

But because the territory historically was sheep range, and because no one wants the sheep to disappear, the Wyoming Game and Fish Department plans to transplant twenty new sheep to the area. Not only will the new animals be vaccinated but they'll bring in a supply of new genes. Perhaps, the biologists theorize, the problem is made worse by inbreeding.

We're also going to see what we can do to help reduce stress by building a "guzzler," a little covered pond that holds about 3,000 gallons of water. Its roof is about twice the size of the hidden pond and diverts rain and snowmelt into the basin. Covered and protected from the winds that would steal the water, it lasts for months. By reducing the bighorns' need to go to the river three times a day (1,200 feet down and 1,200 feet up), they can spend more time relaxing and feeding.

The bull elk are bugling in the meadows around the ranch. I woke yesterday to one calling just outside our bedroom, rather more effective than an alarm clock. I dressed quickly and sneaked around the corner to see if I could catch a glimpse of him. It was 5:30 and still dark but calm and cold. At first I couldn't see much because my eyes weren't used to the dark. Then, as the irises opened, I saw him, or them. One huge-racked bull and a half dozen cows grazed at the edge of the lawn. Every once in a while the bull would raise his head so his antlers almost touched his back; then, as his breath poured into the cold air, he'd let out that weird, whistling, snorting, grunting call. My chills were from more than the morning cold.

It's good to be a mammal. I do love milk, and ice cream, and yogurt, and sour cream, and a big glass of cold chocolate cream, which lifts the spirits and tastes better than a shake. This morning I was reminded of this again as I downed a foamy glass of cold milk with a stack of hotcakes and began to think about the milk cows we've had.

Our first was Ethyl, a beautiful fawn and white Guernsey. We got her in the days when high-test fuel was called "Ethyl" and the kids decided it would be a good idea to name her that, so they could sit at the table and "fill 'er up with Ethyl." She arrived at the ranch about a month after she'd "freshened" (had her calf and started her milk flow), and she came with a handsome bull calf that stole our hearts. We named him Buster. Each day Ethyl gave us four gallons of rich milk (two in the morning and two in the evening) and still fed Buster.

One of the boys, Gregg, milked at night, unless he had commitments at school, and I milked in the morning. The whole family knew how to milk, but somehow, Margie never quite got the hang of it. "If you get good at something," she said, "you just might have to do it." Nonetheless, it was a quiet ritual I looked forward to. Our milking barn was about the size of a box stall with a shed roof and a door so low that even I almost had to duck to get in. At least thirty years before, it had been a blacksmith shop. The old crank bellows and forge stood in one corner and retained the scent of coal and smoke. Even on a windy, wintery morning the shed was moist and filled with cow-breath warm air. As Ethyl ate her way through a bucket of grain — and her rumen began its grumbling, gurgling work — I'd brush her, wash her udder, and settle onto a three-legged milking stool. We put hobbles on Ethyl, not because she would kick but so I could tuck the end of her tail into the clip and prevent being swatted by its perpetually wet end. Three ranch cats generally appeared about then and sat down at just the right range for a quick squirt or two into their waiting mouths, then they'd lick their faces and wait for another squirt.

At first, the milk came in thin streams that sprayed against the bottom of the stainless-steel pail with a high metallic note. Then as the bucket began to fill with milk and five inches of foam, the note changed to a deeper, richer tone. On cold days vapor rose gently from the foamy bucket and surrounded me with a sweet milk scent. After taking our share I'd let the calf in with Ethyl (Buster was kept apart in his own big pen but was always glad to see her) until he'd cleaned out the rest of the milk. Then I'd wash Ethyl again, massage a thin coat of Bag Balm onto her teats (my hands were strong from milking in those days, but oh, so soft), turn her out, and take the milk to the kitchen to be strained and pasteurized.

Our pasteurizer was a Sears model ordered out of the farm catalog. Filtered milk was poured into the aluminum container. The machine heated from both top and bottom until the milk reached 180 degrees and a buzzer announced it was ready to cool. Guernseys produce wonderful, rich milk. After it sat in the pasteurizer in the cooler for a few hours, the lighter cream, about a quart per milking, floated to the top. We'd skim off the cream with a ladle and pour the milk into pitchers for milk and cookies when the kids returned from school.

All summer, when the grass was green and filled with Vitamin A, the butter we churned from the cream was warm yellow. In winter it tended to be pale, the color of morning sunlight through thin clouds. Of course we used the cream in our coffee and cranked homemade ice cream. Later, we experimented with yogurt, cottage cheese, and sour cream, making them by the gallons, using recipes that I found in that old standard cookbook, *The Joy of Cooking*. We really did fill up with Ethyl.

Then one morning in August, I found Ethyl lying in the corral; she couldn't get up. We called the vet, who came within an hour. He gravely listened to her heart and her rumen, sniffed her breath, then stood up to stretch and shook his head.

"She's got acetonemia, [Ketosis]," he said. "It sometimes happens with high-producing cows after they start milk flow, even if they seem like they're getting enough to eat. Basically, she's used up her energy reserves to produce the milk, and her blood sugar level has crashed severely. Worse, I'm not sure if we can get it back up." He gave her glucose and a transfusion of ethylene glycol spiked with cobalt, magnesium, propionic acid, niacin, and vitamins A, D3, E, and B12.

The whole family sat beside her for several hours, stroking her, encouraging, and letting her know we were

there, that she wasn't alone. Then, about noon, she took a final sighing breath and died.

Most ranchers just drag dead animals into a meadow well away from the house and let the vultures and coyotes clean things up, burying them only if they have a backhoe, which we didn't. My family wouldn't hear of leaving her unburied, so I had to bury her. (Note the emphasis on the word I). And, they told me they just couldn't bear seeing her dragged behind a tractor, so I had to figure out how to pick up a 1,000-pound cow. Several hours later, using three, twenty-feet-long lodgepoles and rigged a very tall tripod over her. Then I tied her stiffening legs together, and used a "come-along," a kind of ratcheting device, to lift her into the air. In another half hour I laid her gently in the bed of the pickup, which I'd maneuvered under her. It was now mid afternoon.

Next I had to find a soft spot below a hillside, where the sand had deposited deep enough that I could dig. After another hour of bouncing around one pasture and then another, I found a good spot. Two hours later I'd hand-shoveled a hole seven feet deep and eight feet long. Setting up the tripod again, I lowered her into the hole. By that time she was getting pretty stiff and it was a struggle to fold her legs to fit into the space. Finally, as the sky filled with sunset colors, I filled in the hole. When I tried to leave, the truck tires spun hopelessly in the sand; another forty-five minutes passed as I jacked it up and laid sagebrush under the wheels to get enough traction. I drove home in the dark, glad I'd taken care of her properly, but Ethyl was the last cow I buried.

Ethyl's passing left another little problem. While Buster was eating grain and hay, we felt he was too young not to have milk, and I had to find another lactating cow to nurse him. Besides, we needed milk too. Margie bought a few gallons of whole milk at the store, but the kids hated it. They called it "city milk" and thought it tasted like water. Meanwhile, I networked with neighbors and, several days later, found a man eighty miles away who had a dairy cow to sell at a reasonable price. The next day, we tried to follow his directions, got lost, and discovered several dozen miles of new (to us) back roads before we found the ranch and inspected the cow. She was a full Jersey with flirtatious brown eyes and a deep fawn color. At home the kids, already in the naming mode, said she was "Nanny Cow," because she was going to be a nanny for the calf. Her flow, however, was only about three gallons a day plus calf milk. We had to put anti-kicking hobbles on her, so she wouldn't hurt Buster as he tried to suckle. All seemed back in order.

About two weeks later I went to the barn to do the evening milking because Gregg was at school. Nanny was standing by the gate, unusual because I normally had to chase her in. Then I looked closer and her whole body was swollen. She looked like a football on legs. Nanny had eaten something, probably she got into a patch of alfalfa, and it caused excess gas and horrible bloating. Her ribs were invisible, and the skin thumped like a drum when I tapped it. Over the phone the vet gave us a few things to try to relieve it but eventually I had to "tap her with a trocar," a tool no cattle ranch can be without. Essentially, it's a six-inch-long hole-punch that slides into a sleeve. You feel for the third rib, push the trocar through the skin into the hollow, air-filled space, then stand back as you slide the punch out of the sleeve. If you've done it right, the gas comes rushing out as from an opened valve.

It worked, and the crisis passed. I moved her to another pasture, but a few days later she bloated again, and I tapped the same hole. Eventually she'd bloat once a week, and the vet installed a relief valve, which stayed in permanently. Sometimes she'd waddle in for milking, her valve hissing!

The next spring I took her to a sale and bought another cow. This was a ten-year-old Jersey/Guernsey cross. She was in good condition, but her teeth were mere nubbins, from grazing in poor pasture and taking in sand with the grass. She'd recently freshened and came with a little bull calf. The two of them settled in quickly and again stole our hearts. We named her Muffin, for her golden brown color and sweet temperament.

She pastured in a rich meadow with one section of sagebrush about two hundred feet square. Although the grass was green and tall everywhere else, she preferred the sage. Why? I never could figure it out. Most days, that's where she'd lie to chew her cud, ignoring the shade of cottonwoods or the sunny, high grass. Now her udder was rather large and pendulous. Below that protruded the four extra-long teats. They made her easy to milk, because you could squeeze out about one-eighth cup of milk with each tug. But they were delicate, and many days Muffin reported to the barn with her teats scratched and several times with long cuts. Although I doctored them, they were still sore, and only the hobbles kept her from kicking her doctor.

Muffin loved to be with people though. She roamed freely, as the pasture wasn't fenced, and often laid down near where the kids were playing, or peered curiously under the hood when I was working on a truck. One day she appeared at the open kitchen door and was halfway in before Margie heard her and shooed her out, laughing. One day a herd of range cattle passed through, and Muffin joined them. It was three days before we found her. Normally, if she'd gone that long without being milked her flow would have begun to dry up, but she was so good natured that she'd allowed several other calves to suckle, which kept the milk good. She never wandered again, but I often saw her watching range cattle on the hills above the ranch and probably thinking about her big adventure. Muffin stayed with us for several years and gave us more than milk.

As I said, it's good to be a mammal, and to have such good friends.

Today has been a weather forecaster's delight. The day was alternately warm-cool-warm and with scattered clouds and "virga" (low clouds whose rain evaporates before reaching the ground). For about ten minutes, one cloud spat graupel, which bounced on the grass as if they were alive. It was a good day to be outside, and I rode my mountain bike up Mullen Creek, where I found a new beaver pond forming behind a dam of fresh-cut willows and mud. Could this be the same "passage beaver" someone saw strolling down Main Street at midnight a few weeks ago? They got that name because at this time of the year there always seem to be a few singles, passing through as they search for new territory to chew and flood.

Our guests often see the work of a beaver, aspen groves tumbled and looking as if an angry giant had just passed through. These visitors tell me of the beavers' "destruction" on such and such a trail. I agree, in the short-run things look bleak. But the beavers actually help the aspen. If an aspen grove is allowed to grow without beavers cutting them down, the grove may die of old age or be weakened and susceptible to molding. On the other hand, when a beaver cuts a tree down, its roots are stimulated, exactly like a house or yard plant that's pruned to give it extra strength. Where one tree stands before the beaver cuts, the next spring there may be dozens of seedlings, all sprung from the roots of the old, and the grove can continue.

Today, I'm off on an early morning ride to check for deer poachers. False dawn comes late this morning, about 7:30. The gray duskiness is heightened by low, veil-like clouds under the dark hulk of a fall thunderhead that covers the ranch like a lid. By 8:00 dawn is to my back and the sun is trying to melt holes in the clouds. The distant hills are bathed in a lemony glow, and brilliant vertical shafts of sunlight stab the earth. Opposite the sunny hills, a morning rainbow arches over the valley with a pale, color-inverted second rainbow above. The lower bow becomes stronger, and the hills, which had seemed flat, are now vibrant with 3-D splendor. As the clouds race past, the valley colors fade then deepen in color as if someone were operating a visual volume switch on the sky.

An hour later the valley is covered in tones of gray against a pale-blue sky. The air is smoky blue from two forest fires to the north, which probably added to the rainbow colors I just enjoyed. Beside the river, scattered cottonwoods cling to a few of their golden leaves; but on the slopes the aspens are white and bare. In both places the fallen leaves are already blackened, molding quietly and releasing a light, musky autumn scent.

Sage grouse are flat-breasted, short-winged, and normally given to brief, explosive, then gliding flights.

As I continue on my ride, I startle one big male. In his panic he climbs almost sixty feet into the air then turns and tries to beat into the wind, but it's too strong. In his fear he beats his wings harder but remains in place, almost hovering. Then, giving up, he turns. His powerful wing beats finally catch in the wind, and he slingshots downhill, settling in the sage again a half mile away.

It's time to gather cattle, and the cool breeze that ruffles the sagebrush carries the sound of a moving herd. They are a half mile away with a sagey ridge between us, and yet their bawling, tromping progress is clear. I imagine the bunched Herefords with cowboys riding back and forth slowly, keeping them together, the tailless dingo dogs nipping at stragglers' heels and watching the cowboys for instructions.

A fawn startles and leaps over the sage to escape. Its mother knows I'm no threat, but "pronks" after him and down a hill. (A pronk, or spronk, is a gait the animal uses when it jumps straight forward into the air and lands on all four feet, then jumps again, propelling itself easily over the sage and other bushes.) She leaps into the air and, when landing, her hooves strike the ground at the same time, making hollow thumps and spraying up bits of rock and dirt from the deep, wide-spread hoof prints. Then, two bucks, which are more careful because it's hunting season, join their retreat. Their powerful muscles carry them higher as they spronk over the sage, almost in slow motion as they seem to hang over the bushy growth.

Later that day two hunters came to the ranch. They'd wounded a three-year-old buck on the BLM land, near where I saw the deer, and it had crossed onto the ranch. The men forded the river to ask if they could track it. The blood spoor was heavy, and the animal was obviously in pain, so of course I agreed. I didn't see them again, but I assume they killed it.

A deck was my observation platform today, and I settled into a comfortable chair, thermal coffee cup and notebook in hands and bundled against the cold. After half an hour I'd seen nothing close. In the distance a chickadee called, and a woodpecker tapped lightly. I was half dozing when the juniper near the deck rustled lightly. Whatever was in there was invisible to me. Then the tree began shaking as if tossed by a breeze, and a dozen red breasts flashed from all over the ends of the branches. Robins were plucking up one after another of the silvery berries and tossing them down their gullets. In five minutes they were gone, and so were most of the berries.

Next a sapsucker landed on a gangly young cottonwood. He'd cut sap pits all round the trunk and was there to sip at them. Each day he's been here at about the same time, following a regular route I suppose, and may have been following his "sap line" all summer. Now, with winter approaching, the leaves are yellow and barely clinging. The sap is barely rising, and he struggles to get a beakful, when only a few weeks ago he had plenty and even enough to share with the occasional hummingbird.

A year or two ago, a passage beaver began cutting down a small aspen grove beside the road and near the river. The five trees were of equal height and about eight inches in diameter. Because they were at the edge of the road, I always enjoyed looking at them when I passed by, especially in fall when they were a spot of bright yellow in a tanning landscape. Then, one by one they began to be cut down. Each morning there was another drag mark across the road, where the little rascals had pulled a tree into the current and packed it into their dam.

Then, Jennai and her husband, Matt, went to the remainder of the grove and wrapped the two remaining trees with chicken wire. Next morning the guarded trees were still standing, surrounded by the webbed footprints of two or three frustrated beavers.

By the next July I noticed a difference. Where there had been five adult trees there were at least a hundred young trees that had grown from the roots of the cut aspen. They were already spreading out into a miniature aspen grove. Their color came and went rather early the next fall but we did appreciate the help the beaver gave. The little aspen were about two feet tall and packed so tightly together that I couldn't pass through them without damaging the young trunks.

That enlarged aspen grove has continued to grow. After three years the trees are chest high. Last winter elk or deer ate a few of the smaller ones, I suppose because they were more tender. The remainder seemed to gain strength from their loss, because the youngsters are looking more like a true grove, with their wire-wrapped parents nearby.

We had a light snow early last evening, which gave way to a cold and starry night. When I left the ranch early this morning, only two sets of tracks had preceded me, both made last evening as the construction workers on a project headed home for the weekend. I was surprised when one of the tracks veered suddenly, and gravel was sprayed as the driver sped up. Then I saw the young porcupine in the road. The tracks rolled right over the small of its back.

When I saw it was still alive, I stopped. His back legs were useless but scratches in the snow and road showed he had tried vainly to pull himself forward. The poor thing rested with its chin on the ground. In its pain it still struggled to rise when I knelt beside it and looked into its eyes. I was surprised to see tears running down its hairy cheeks. Because there was nothing else to be done, I ended his suffering as quickly as possible and laid the little body by a boulder, away from the road.

I've named that place on the road Porcupine Curve, in honor of the creature so thoughtlessly murdered.

It's that time of year now, with the aspen bare and nights in the twenties, to move the cattle. Because cold air is heavier and flows down into them, the valleys are generally colder than the hilltops. So, in the morning, the cattle crowd on each of the higher, warmer peaks, which makes them easier to gather, but there is a price.

Before dawn the cowboys are already on horseback and climbing the hills, moving the cattle toward winter quarters fifteen miles away. This morning I had to go to town; just as I started it began to rain. (We get only a few inches of rain all summer, so even though the growing season's past we still welcome it.)

I met a herd of cattle that had just climbed up a

steep embankment from the North Platte and were trotting down the road in the same direction I was going. They were pushed by a single cowboy riding a tall, lanky bay horse. It was alert and prancing, tossing its head and pressing its ears forward, almost daring the cattle to try to escape. The cowboy, an old friend, touched the sodden brim of his hat in greeting and grinned as I drove past. The water dripped onto his wet chaps, to his soggy boots, and splatted onto the hoof-churned mud of the road.

Because they were warm from exertion, each steer had a personal cloud rising from its back. The cattle trotted, milling and mooing, squishing and slipping along under a wet-hair-scented fog bank that moved along with them. For a mile or so they surrounded me and we squished our way through a gloomy, soggy canopy of Douglas fir. The tunnel of trees ended abruptly, just as the sun broke through the clouds, reminding the cattle that they were tired and hungry. The bunch broke apart and scattered into the sagebrush with a sound like distant, muffled thunder. At first one stopped to graze, then another and another. In less than half a minute the entire bunch was grazing, and the only sound was ripping grass. The cowboy who followed paused, too, banging his wet hat on his chaps and settling back for a little rest and sunshine.

Although most of the fall has been calm and almost hot, today was blustery. I rode out to gather the horses and move them to another pasture. One of my favorite spots along the way is a beautiful view from the crest of a hill that looks out across a broad, open expanse of sage, bitterbrush, and rabbitbrush, edged by more tall hills. Nearing this point I stopped to look and shared the view with a golden eagle. Although the wind was howling, the bird's feathers were unrumpled, and its golden head glistened in the light. It had found a perch in the wind shadow of the hill and could enjoy the warmth of the sun as it scanned several thousand acres for a meal. When I stopped, it turned its head slightly toward me, then returned to scanning the meadows, barely acknowledging me when I moved on.

I haven't seen or heard a marmot for a while, and they may have gone into hibernation already; surprising because it's been so pleasant. All summer they've been stuffing themselves, and by this time of the year most weigh in at a roly-poly ten pounds, almost waddling over the rocks. They sleep about six months, and that stored fat keeps their little hearts pumping, although very slowly. One man, who claimed to be an expert on marmots, told me that during some distant age in Europe the fat of a marmot was treasured as a cure for rheumatism. Since most everyone suffered from that malady, the marmots were trapped in early fall when they had the most fat. The man claimed that in the late 1800s, to ease the pain of rheumatics, 16,000 of the rock chucks were killed each year.

Marmots are fun to watch when they are at play, and I miss them during the winter. Most adult animals don't seem to play much, but I've often sat behind a rocky place and watched as the marmot families perform pushing matches or wrestle, rolling in the grass together between the rocks. Of course the youngsters play the most, and once I tipped them off to my presence when I couldn't control my laughter. They were playing king-on-the-rock, and it reminded me so much of eight-year-old humans at play. Seeing my gray hair behind the rock and not sure of my intentions, they hightailed it back to their den.

They seem to live in family groups in a rabbit-like warren, sharing escape holes. Under their chins they have a scent gland for identifying each other; when they meet they'll sniff throat areas. Instead of spraying their territory like a dog or cat, they rub their chins on rocks at appropriate intervals and at the entrance to their dens.

Our riding trails are busy places, and we enjoy the tracks of other creatures that use them. One day there may be only cows and splatted cow pies. Other days the dust shows mice, chipmunks, golden mantled ground squirrels, coyotes, and even cougars. We didn't make the trails ourselves, they just grew from forest highways the deer and mice have been making for centuries with their sharp hooves and tiny claws.

Delicately tapered cloven hooves leave their own distinctive story about the deer that passed by but sometimes also of other things. In mid-afternoon I came upon a set of tracks from a deer and fawn, pressed into the powdery tan soil. They were unusually clear, very fresh, and filled with tiny glitters of fool's gold.

Various minerals can masquerade as gold, but this was mica, a mineral so soft you can scratch it with your fingernail and so light that grains can swirl away in the slightest current of a stream. Mica is common in our volcanic rocks and breaks down into those light flakes that scatter through the soil. Many an early prospector

on first seeing the glittering mica thought he'd found gold. Unlike the gold, however, mica floats down into streams and away in the current. Heavier gold would settle into any crack or low spot.

Oh, there is gold here. At our main entrance there are two old mines. One's been abandoned a long time; but at the other, a man uses more modern techniques and mines the tailings (trash dirt thrown away after the original gold was taken) for gold the first prospectors missed. One summer I watched as two guests carried bucket after bucket of soil past my office window and to a stream. All afternoon they panned at streamside, happily swishing the soil and picking through the debris in their gold pan. By dinner they'd earned enough to help pay for part of their stay at the ranch. Two or three flakes would reduce their bill by about two cents.

Mid-October

Most of the aspen have been bare a couple of weeks now, except for a single grove where yesterday the golden remainder glowed magically in the gray light just before sunset. This morning an early snow has caught on the remaining leaves on the aspen and weighs the trees down, making the grove look like a ghostly battleground. It's a calm day, so the snow — and trees — will stay as they are until the sun melts the icy burden. That won't be long though, because the rocks, still warmed by months of sunshine, have dissolved the snowflakes as they fell, and they shine wetly above the snow-covered grass.

In the new snow I find the tail-dragging footprints of a beaver, made last night several hours into the snow storm. They are about half filled with the new snow. Their new pond, too, is gradually filling, rising each day to the new height of the dam the creatures built in the starlight.

Hunting season has begun all around us, and, although we're a game refuge and the animals are safe, there are changes taking place. By necessity we lock the gate at the highway and make daily patrols for poachers who have heard about the bucks living here. Even so, yesterday someone cut the lock and came in. We caught them and have pressed charges.

It's interesting to watch the various animals. A few days after hunting season began, we had a most unusual reaction between a group of seventy-plus elk and our horses. The elk were being especially hard-pressed by the hunters and discovered the meadow where our horses were grazing. For several nights the elk grazed in the meadow all night and spent the mornings lying in a tight cluster, chewing their cuds. What made it unusual was that the horses, all 120 of them, gathered around the elk like a wagon train around its people. A few horses nibbled grass, but most of them just watched the elk and the hills as if they were on guard.

At this time of the year our snow comes and goes. Now it's gone. Mullen Creek was a little trickle last week but is hurrying again as the snow melts off the "riparian zone" (the land near streams, which benefits from the moisture the streams hold). It floods through dry grass and thistles with heads brittle and brown, the seeds picked and blown clean. Leaves are piled and drifted around rocks now, sodden brown, where two weeks ago they were gold and three weeks ago green. Some form

rafts or islands three or four inches thick with bits of green or yellow leaves stirred gently by the dartings of silvery trout.

Brown trout are spawning, moving upstream. Their trek is made easier by the higher water, but they still avoid the sun-dappled areas, preferring the shadows where they are hidden from predators.

At 4 p.m. the sun is lowering, the light pouring onto the river in a shimmering, dancing light that seems to flow downstream with the water. In the last half -hour the ducks have been gathering in twos and sixes, and now dark squadrons fly upstream over the lighted water, quacking softly.

Antelope often doze by one or the other of our various "two-tracks," (roads through the pastures, created by driving trucks through the grass, creating two parallel trails). This morning I startled one, and it jumped up right by the door of my pickup. In two strides it matched my speed of almost 25 mph and was so close I could see the shine on his black horns and the fear in his eyes. We ran together for a hundred yards, then, springing forward in a sudden burst of speed, he crossed the road at an angle before me. I sped up, too, and just before he turned into the sagebrush I clocked him — 43 miles per hour!

Although the days are warm, in the high sixties, nighttime temperatures are down to the single digits. The river, however, is still rather warm, and this morning the fog was thick and cold. A moist, woodsy scent drifted with the fog as it frost-coated the aspen, cottonwoods, and willows along the river's edge. When the sun finally rose and shone through the trees, they appeared to be made of crystal, and when I walked into the forest I felt I was entering a cathedral. Walking through this glass chapel, I heard a gentle movement and half turned to see a mule deer and her still lightly spotted fawn press cautiously from the trees. They picked their way through the frozen grass and waded knee deep into the water to drink from the steaming river.

Here in Wyoming, we take a different view of yard sculptures. You won't see too many of those pink flamingoes, and I have to admit I think ours are rather creative. One retired rancher neighbor has a herd of fiberglass horses, including one frozen in mid-lope; a pair of Clydesdales at a bobsled, driven by a painted plywood cutout cowboy; and a big palomino gelding, wrapped in lights and tethered to two lighted jack-o-lanterns for Halloween. There is even a mare and her foal. Other neighbors create columns of cow and horse skulls, white in the sun- and moonlight. One yard artist made three hay-bale-bodied deer with rebar legs and antlered heads and has posed them feeding at another hay bale. One deer has several arrows stuck in it (it is hunting season now). Some of the folks hereabouts even claim that non-functioning cars qualify as yard sculptures too. As Shakespeare said so well, "Beauty is in the eye..."

The passage beavers are back. Each year our North Platte River is a highway for singles and young, looking for a place to spend the winter. We know they've arrived when we begin to see aspen tumbled over and stumps that look like pencils sharpened with

a giant penknife. They always try at one particular spot on the river but always fail. One morning, drag marks across the paths and into the stream show where the branches are hauled, to a ratty old derelict beaver lodge at a bend of the river. There it sits, a rumpled, conical structure wedged between rocks in an eddy. The little engineers must like the looks of the location because they've rebuilt the lodge each year for the past five. Each spring though, ice floes tear it away and the beavers move on.

Beavers like to work in the half light of dawn or dusk, and we try to watch them when we can. It's usual for several to be out at the same time. A couple might be eating the bitter white bark of the aspen they've cut, then littering the river with the peeled stems. Another might be swimming across the growing pond, its head at the point of a v-shaped wake. Still others might be scouting the riverbanks for more aspen or willows. Many times I've lain in the dry grass overlooking a pond and watched them for half an hour or more before they've seen me and disappeared with a series of tail-slapping "warning shots" followed by silence.

I stop at a small town in northern Colorado for lunch, in a nice little restaurant called the Cowboy Coffee Café. All round the room are coffeepots of all shapes. Even the menu and wall decorations are coffeepots. Hunters, with orange jackets and hats, have taken several tables and pore over maps or sit and stare, exhausted from the morning's hunt. At one table, two couples sit and visit, lingering over their coffee and discussing local gossip. Behind them, a stained-glass-window sign advertises the Gold Rusch Room.

The waitress is friendly enough but tired and distant. An older lady with her hair in a French twist, she complains to me, "I don't know where everybody is. It looks like it's gonna be a long winter." I try to draw her into a conversation, asking about some friends in the area, but she answers quickly and moves along — must be a bit tired of people, even if they *aren't* here.

At one table, a salesman type, dressed in a coat and tie, finishes a bowl of homemade vegetable soup from the salad bar and fills another.

Two hand-written signs are taped to the wall. One says, "$3.95 salad bar. Take all you want. Eat all you take. Extra charge for wasted salad." The second advertises "Good Luck Lunches" for hunters. The bag lunch is $5 and includes your choice of sandwiches, chips, a candy bar, and a "Good Luck Quakie Bun." I watched several hunters leaving with their bags full. Whatever works. If I were hunting today, I'd probably buy some buns.

Today, October 31, we're having a wonderful, strange day — what you'd expect for Halloween, actually. The coyotes woke us at 5:30, singing in the meadow by the house. We couldn't see them, but there were two or three shadows moving through the aspen and we sure could hear the wonderful high notes they were hitting. If I were superstitious, I suppose it would sound like werewolves howling out on the moors of Scotland. Dawn was white and misty. We were in a dense cloud, and I couldn't see a hundred feet across the meadow. It's very humid now and getting colder, so all the trees and pine needles and leafless branches are collecting white rime — crystals that are growing thicker every time I look out the window. In Laramie it's drizzling, but the forecasters expect that to change to snow soon. Yesterday's blizzard left us a foot and a half of snow, and Laine (the ranch foreman) is out with the snow blower, clearing the road for the first time this year. The little ghosties and goblins will be wearing parkas over their costumes tonight.

November

At dawn it continued cold and unusually humid so each tree, bush, and dried flower was again coated with gleaming, sunlit rime. The bald eagles have been back for several weeks. Each day they perch on branches and glare into the river, watching for fish. As I rode toward the rising sun, looking for yet another wandering horse, a flurry of ice crystals flew from a branch, and a dark shadow fell off, gradually spreading to become a white headed eagle flying toward me. It landed on another crystal branch a hundred feet away. At home in his kingdom and not afraid, his icy gaze matched his new perch as I continued.

Most of the migratory birds already have moved south but the Canada geese are still here. The river to us is cold, but when compared to the air, it's warm. I've seen as many as two dozen of the giant birds lately. They hunch down in the warmth of the water, making soft "ahink" sounds as they float with the trout in the eddies behind the rocks. Even the geese will be gone in a few days though, and mornings will be almost silent until they return in April.

At dawn, about fifty elk moved into our meadow. The "gang" (what you call a herd of elk) was made up of all ages and sizes and both sexes. It was a windy day, which made them edgy. They grazed about fifty feet from the house for half an hour or so, nervously watching each other and the forest nearby. If one startled at something, the gang gathered and ran, then stopped to see if the danger was real. Realizing it was safe, they returned to nibbling at the dried grass poking above the snow and very close to the young aspen I'd planted, but left them alone. They ate like horses, gathering the dried grass with their flexible lips then nipping it with their sharp incisors.

The gang gathered in a loose circle. About a dozen of them settled in the grass and began to chew their cuds, which bulged in their cheeks like quids of tobacco. Their long necks and the tops of their heads, both major heat-loss areas, were covered with long, sable-colored hair that was much darker than their buff-colored bodies. It looked like they were wearing neck muffs, which were probably good heat absorbers. Most of those not lying down turned sideways to the sun, soaking in the morning warmth after a cold night.

Then one of the big cows, which are the real leaders in a gang, began to move up the meadow. In a moment all of them began to follow and disappeared over the ridge into the next horse meadow, leaving only the lines of hoof prints crisscrossing through the snow as evidence they'd been here. Around 2 o'clock, about thirty of them returned and began to graze again, this time "browsing" (feeding on leaves and twigs rather than grass) on the aspen they'd passed over earlier. Ah, well, I guess it really is *their* meadow.

It seems that most people we meet pass through our lives quickly. This morning I was thinking of a lady I met some years ago, who I'd hoped would stay, but galloped through. Her name was simply Virginia, given to her in the same way that someone from Dallas might be called Tex. A ranch woman, she lived a man's life, alone but not hermit-like or without friends. At the time I met her, I was in my twenties and she was in her mid fifties, so she seemed old to me.

One of my cows was lost in the national forest, and, after several days of searching, I asked a neighbor if he might have seen her. He hadn't but suggested that I ask

Virginia, who seemed to know where everyone's stock was all the time. "She doesn't have a phone," he said. "Just drop in. If she's home, she'll be glad to help you."

Following his directions, I left the main road, turning onto an unpaved, snow-filled two-track that wound into the mountains half a mile or so, to a two-room cabin. In the yard was a woodpile — literally a pile of wood — the size of the cabin. It was mainly big branches of all sizes from a couple of feet to ten feet or more in length. Apparently she cut the wood as it was needed. At the end of the road I parked beside an old truck she seldom used. (Later, she told me that two tanks of gas a year were all she needed.)

When I parked and honked once, Virginia stepped onto the porch and waved me in with a friendly grin. She was smaller than I'd expected, probably only about five foot four. Her hands, too, were small and calloused, the handshake firm from strength and not from conscious effort. She was dressed entirely in faded and patched denim, worn thin where she sat the saddle and over the shirt pocket that held her tobacco pouch. She couldn't afford the store-bought cigarettes, or wouldn't spend the money, so rolled her own. Even with those work-worn hands, she could roll one pretty fast but always with great ritual. Her hair was still dark, except along the sides where a few grays showed silver under her cowboy hat. She wore the hair short. "I cut it m'self," she told me.

Virginia welcomed me into her sparse cabin, and we sat in front of her wood-fired stove, the only heat in the house. Almost as if she'd known I was coming, she'd prepared fresh, and thick cowboy(girl?) coffee and poured me a cup as I stomped into the room. It seemed colder in the cabin than outside, so we sat in chairs with our feet up on the stove door. Actually, she put her feet *into* the stove. Although the stove crackled warmly, our breath puffed into the air along with smoke from her cigarettes. The only other furnishings of the kitchen were a table, the two chairs we sat on, and a refrigerator. The windows had frilly curtains, a bow to her feminine side, but the windows were unwashed; there was no time for such things, she said.

She told me where my cow would most likely be hiding, then we hunkered down to some serious talk about the cattle business, about my family, and about her. Two hours passed quickly. She seemed a happy woman, even without family around. Virginia had been raised in that warmer eastern country and was well schooled. Moving west to be alone on a ranch was too much for her family, and she hadn't heard from or about them in more than twenty years, which suited her just fine. She chose the solitary life because she didn't want to get married and be a "cowbunny" (her term for the wife or sweetheart of a ranch man). Although she didn't have much, she was better off than some she'd met. Some were so poor, she said, that they "used their backs for mattresses and bellies for a blanket."

Big flakes began to fall onto the already-deep snow, and my truck's path was disappearing quickly, so I thanked her and left. Several times that winter and spring we saw her in the forest or passing through our ranch, and she always paused to visit. Even if she was with us an hour she sat atop her sorrel gelding, in her battered and smooth-worn "rough out" saddle. She'd drink the coffee we offered, laugh and visit, then flick out the remains of the coffee, hand me the mug with a nod and a grin, and trot on down the road. Then one day she was gone, really gone. She sold her cattle, closed up her cabin, left the country, and no one seemed to know where she went or why. Maybe it was back to Virginia.

The Platte is mostly frozen now. No geese wade in the shallows or pace the ice edges. No mallards quack in the grass at the bank. No trout leap at floating insects, but hide under the growing ice floes, their gills barely moving as they balance delicately in the icy current. Sometimes a bald eagle cruises overhead, searching for those unwary, slow trout. But not today. The air is still and cold; the only sound is the river, muffled under the ice.

Justin (my son) has a field trip today, and we leave the ranch at 5:30 a.m. As we grope sleepily for the car-door handles, it's twelve degrees. False dawn begins as we pass the guard house four miles from the main ranch, and a white jackrabbit skitters ahead, panicked in the triangle of our car's headlights. After a half mile of holding us to a slow pace, he leaps into the darkness and disappears. We'd been to the city a few weeks ago and seen speed bumps in parking lots, which act to slow drivers. Justin dubs this a "speed bunny."

One section of our road to the highway sits in the wind shadow of a small outcrop of rock and is drifted two feet deep. Instinctively I hold to the left then swing hard right, knowing the drift pattern. Even in summer, you can see the results of those snow piles, for this is the first place the road turns "washboardy." Today, the hilltop road above the drift is clear, except for baby drifts forming downwind of grass clumps that bend in the 20 mph wind. The animals are still lounging in their beds, the new snow is smooth, satiny white in the headlights — untrammeled in every direction — and at the top of the hill I can see the shadowy coming of dawn for thirty miles.

In the windy darkness, we wait for the school bus and enjoy the coming dawn. First the eastern sky becomes paler. Low clouds are black, but amid the darkness a subtle orange begins to spread. At first it's so subtle that merely glancing at it you wouldn't notice the color. But it's there, cast from the true dawn a hundred miles away and racing toward us at 1,000 mph.

Our pastures are very fertile and productive, providing high-protein grass all summer. In the winter, however, they get covered with deep snow, and the wind races across them so the horses need more shelter. All summer the horses are sleek and carry their hair short. By September it's begun to grow and by November it's two to three inches long. We tried stacking our hay in long rows at various places in the pasture and fencing it off so they couldn't eat it. The idea was to create wind breaks, and they worked well. On a windy day you could see a great teardrop-shaped group of horses on the downwind side of the stacks, out of the wind. Every so often the outer horses would shift inward, and the inner, warmer horses moved out. But our pastures were just too windy, so I decided to find a winter pasture for them, one with streams and willows throughout.

Our first winter pasture was in Colorado, about fifty miles away, and we decided it would be fun to drive the horses there. As a "big ol' kid," I'd worked at a summer camp that had a similar setup, and we drove 120 horses fifty miles in two days. We did it then so why not now?

Half a dozen guests and riding friends gathered at the ranch for a few days of fun and hard work. The night before we left, we sat in the cook house and talked about the drive, what to expect, what each should be doing, and where we were going. A foot of new snow had fallen but wasn't a problem because the ground underneath was damp and soft, good footing for the horses.

By 7 o'clock the next morning, about a hundred horses, headed for winter pasture, were gathered in the corrals. Three of the men rode out first, leading the boss horses as guides. They walked slowly out of the corral and crossed the river as we urged the others to follow, which they did willingly. It was a picture of what a drive should be. We snapped photos and pushed the bunch gently along. We'd gone about three quarters of a mile when everything fell apart.

The bunch was moving quietly up a hill when, about halfway down the line, one of the horses moved out on its own. It had spotted an open gate about an eighth of a mile away and trotted toward it, taking the last half of the herd with it. We tried to turn them back, but they began to trot, then lope. As the first part of the herd continued uphill and out of sight, the last half ran down the fence line. We turned them finally. But when they couldn't see the rest of their friends, they ran back to the corral and continued past it for a half mile.

It was then that we spotted Tom L. He was afoot with one arm dangling. The horse he'd been leading pulled loose but not before dislocating Tom's shoulder. Because it was too painful for him to remount, we drove a tractor across the river and brought him in then headed him to the clinic.

Meanwhile, the horses were finally brought back to the corral and didn't want to leave it. After letting them calm down for a while we tried again and managed to get them back across the river and up the path the rest had taken. This time the gate was closed, and they went uphill nicely. We'd gone about two miles when the rest of the herd came galloping over a low hill toward us. At their mixing they milled excitedly then galloped off in another direction.

Well, we gathered them again, and when I looked at my watch I realized that we'd gone about three miles in five hours. "Let's take them home," I called, and we did. Next morning I hired horse trailers, and we spent the day hauling them in the modern way.

So, for the next few years we did haul them, until we found a neighbor, just fifteen miles away, whose pastures met our criteria, and we decided to drive them again.

The next year's drive to the new pasture was only slightly less eventful. In a letter to a friend, I wrote:

Winter's hovering around the ranch lately and blessed us with about eight inches of wonderful, powdery snow. The only problem was that it fell today, as we prepared to move our horses to winter pasture. We began by driving the whole herd (105 making the trip today) to the pens above our runway, about seven miles. Horse drives are always exciting because horses aren't like cattle; they run most of the way. Six of us worked on the drive, two cowboys taking "point" (the lead) and the rest of us pushing (actually following) the horses along the road through the canyon and out of the valley, generally following our eight-mile-long road. It was a cloudy, calm day at the main ranch, but huge, glistening snow plumes blew like banners from the Snowy Range ten miles behind us.

We started just after dawn, and only a few deer and a couple of bighorns had imprinted the snow. The lead horses, nickering softly to each other, trotted out quickly, throwing little sprays of snow each time a hoof hit the ground. By the time they'd passed, the snow was tousled and dirty but I didn't notice that until later.

We were loping into the wind, which blasted almost thirty miles per hour, and the running horses kicked up pebbles and chunks of snow that stung any unprotected skin. It was hard to see the horses, because we were forced to ride with our heads down and eyes squeezed half shut. About every five minutes the wind paused, gathered strength, and gusted against us again. After about three miles, the horses began to tire and settled into a fast trot for the remainder of the trip. More than the horses were tired by the time we turned them into the winter pasture, a rolling area filled with golden, belly-high grass and edged with meandering streams and golden-twig willows. We'll still have to feed them each day, but there's more protection here.

At dusk we headed toward the ranch, a little caravan of pickup trucks filled with tack and cowboys, now relaxed and with that "good-kind-of-tired" ranchers talk about when we get together at this time of year. At the bridge over the North Platte, we stopped — that tired feeling suddenly dissipating. A trio of three-year-old bighorn rams blocked the bridge and stared at us, unafraid. Their horns had begun to sweep back into the majestic curl that gives bighorns their name, and they seemed to be posing for a photo, but no one had a camera. We turned off our trucks' motors and waited. The only sounds were the quiet purling of the river and a dipper singing happily. We watched the rams for about five minutes, and they watched us. Then, apparently bored, they sauntered across the bridge. Just then the sun began to slide over the horizon and their tawny-colored coats turned first a gold brown, then a rich red-brown as they leaped over the riverbank and charged down to drink at the dark river.

Two herds of deer live across the gravel road from each other, the two bucks watching each other suspiciously and eyeing their does to be sure none escape to the other side. Today I watched as a doe made a break. Without hesitating, her buck leaped after her and chased her up and down the fence line, much like a cutting horse with antlers. She tried for five minutes then gave up. He returned to his grazing, but with one eye on his doe.

We had six inches of snow yesterday, the fifteenth. It came in a beautiful, classic style, drifting slowly down in flakes that varied from tiny crystals to clumps. In six hours we got six inches. Today dawned with a perfect cerulean sky. All day the pines have been shedding slush. In fact, an hour ago the pine beside my door scored a perfect splat down my collar when I stepped outside to enjoy the scene.

This morning a misty cloud hung over the Sierra Madres, so they were seen as through a veil. By mid-morning the winds aloft had shifted, and snow began to fall. The snow was less like a flake and more like a crumb at first, then as the temperature fell it began to crystallize. In the gravel at river's edge even bits of rounded gravel form their own windshadow and they began to collect "snowdriftlets," curving gently downwind. By noon the horses that remained at the ranch were gathered in similar drifts, even with the same shape, as the herd avoided the wind by hiding behind the haystacks.

The storm slowly buried the gold-brown tufts of the grama grass and primrose and showy aster. The dead stalks, however, continued to blow in the wind for some time and created tiny cones around their bases that were the last to fill and then only when the wind began to die. In one corner of the pasture a pile of tumbleweed (Russian thistle) stacked against a fence, their wanderings ended, making their own snow collection.

Rosy finches, loner birds through most of the summer, have begun to gather in their flocks of a hundred and more. At our feeders, three flocks of varying size make regular trips each day. Their arrival is announced by the gentle fluttering of wings and urgent, soft chittering. The flock lands on the flat feeder, and each bird scrabbles frantically amid the mob of pecking beaks. Some fall off but flutter back again. Others discover the wealth being scattered on the ground and move there. This and two other flocks work the feeder, eating more than five pounds of seed each day. As one flock leaves, another arrives. A few days ago I was late putting out the seed, and they sat perched all around on the eaves of the roof, in bushes, and in the packed snow, waiting patiently and silently, with their little breaths coming in light puffs from their nostrils.

The coyotes began to sing at midday. Margie and I listened as a group of them sang from the ridge behind the corral, to be answered by another group somewhere in the horse pasture. Some people don't like the coyotes, but I admire them for their grace and ability to survive, even thrive, among so much hate. Their song is always otherworldly, and that day their voices appeared to come from nowhere yet everywhere, as they sang back and forth to each other.

To protect themselves against those coyotes — and hawks and eagles and who knows what else — the jackrabbits have donned their winter-white coats. Sometimes as I hike or ski or ride through a pasture I see one hunched with ears back and eyes open wide with fear. When I get too close, they explode into action, sometimes with such suddenness that even though I've expected it, I'm startled. Four of them are staying by our guard house now, hiding out in the shelter of the old flowers and hops vines of the deserted yard. We call them "the guard rabbits."

Our horses have settled into the winter's routine. Earlier this month they had their hooves trimmed, were dewormed and their teeth "floated" (the sharp edges filed down). As the weather turned cold in October their coats grew denser, longer, and now they look like woolly "horsey bears." Each morning they watch not-too-quietly as we load hay into a truck from the snow-covered stacks. We never have to call the horses, and they follow us in a gradually lengthening line as we put out the hay.

We bought some new horses this last month, twelve of them. They came from a guest ranch near Cody that was selling out. An exemplary bunch, appearance and personality-wise, they don't yet like it here. They have been continuously together, wandering the fence lines and creating their own sub-herd. Two days ago they were gone, and our searches were fruitless. Then a neighbor called to ask if we were missing any horses. They'd traveled about ten miles up valleys through national forest and BLM and were grazing on the sparce remnants of a snowy pasture near the highway.

Everyone else on the ranch was on vacation except Margie and me. She had to stay at the office, so I could expect no help in getting them back home. Moving horses where they don't want to go is difficult, but I figured I knew which were the boss horses and could convince the others to follow them.

At dawn I bundled up in several layers of clothes (sky clear/temperature 10 degrees/snow depth 14 inches/wind a breathy 15 mph), tucked one of our newly acquired walkie-talkies into the saddlebag next to my lunch, tied four halters and a little sack of grain onto my saddle horn, and rode out.

At the top of a ridge, even under the snow, I found the depression of an old cattle trail and followed it south. Despite the breeze I felt comfortable and warm as the sun poured over us and my horse's trotting stirred my blood. Margie had been concerned about safety so I carried the radio.

But it gave me more than an edge on safety, it helped me to share the day.

Hunting season was over, and the deer were returning to their normal patterns of behavior. As I rode over a rocky point, a dozen deer in single file trotted across a meadow a hundred feet from me. If they saw me, they weren't afraid. Other animals hadn't begun to move yet. The deer tracks in the snow were the first of any kind I'd see that day. I radioed Margie to share the picture.

Only an eighth of a mile further, I heard the clacking, grunting sound of bucks fighting. I rode over a little rise, and at the bottom of the draw, two bucks were brawling as eight does watched impassively. The bucks' horns clacked together, and they pushed and twisted, trying to knock the other down. Drops of blood spotted the snow, and still they fought on. Then the smaller buck seemed to tire. He backed away and turned to run as the bigger buck chased him over the hilltop. Of course I called Margie to report.

A mile further, a flock of rosy finches swirled over a hill and around us in a confused blur, setting my horse into a fit of mini-bucking. Another call. Then, as I followed the ridge-top, a big shadow passed over us and paused. I looked up and into the eyes of a golden eagle only thirty feet overhead. Its wings were spread out in an eight-foot span, and the bird hovered easily in the wind that skimmed the hill, like a kite on a string. Then, with a slight twist of wings, the eagle turned and soared on. Did I call "Radio Margie?"

I found the horses in a little, over-grazed meadow and rode slowly toward them then stopped, letting my horse rest. For five minutes the escapees whinnied and trotted nervously about the little meadow, but when

neither I nor my horse moved, their curiosity brought them closer until they surrounded us. With a few handfuls of grain I was able to catch the four leaders and tied the halter rope of one to the tail of the next. Soon I had a train and, holding the lead rope of the boss horse, I led them around the pasture. When the others saw we were about to leave, they decided to follow. At first they trotted and fanned out behind us, but after about two miles they began to tire and were having independent thoughts.

Several times the followers became leaders and took off on their own, going south again instead of heading home. When that happened I led my train in a slow-motion chase until I had them gathered and standing. Then I turned toward home again, walking slowly, coaxing and not herding. By late afternoon we were home, and I gave them an extra ration of grain with their hay, to let them know it was easier here than out in the windy sage. Then I radioed Margie to report.

All the critters appear to be hiding today, or working at it. Early this morning I stood at the skeet range to look down on our valley and across the empty horse meadows. The only animal I saw was a badger, head low and snuffling along the ground as it searched for something, anything, to eat.

Down by the river, gravel bars have appeared in the low, clear water, and I walked along one of them watching nervous fish darting away from my shadow at almost every step. Most of their kinds have been gone for weeks, but today I found five geese and five mallards paddling/walking in the shallows. They were funny in the way they walked, rumps rising and falling with each underwater step. The mallards took flight, but the geese all put their heads down low, almost at water level, trying to look like rocks. Even the strip of black on their heads added to the illusion of "rockness." On a hillside I saw a herd of deer. I quietly opened the door of the pickup and got out then began to stalk them for a closer look. I crouched low and slowly worked my way for a hundred yards, almost crawling from one sagebrush to the next. I'd crept to within two hundred yards and was feeling a bit like some ancient hunter stalking prey when I realized they weren't deer, they were rocks.

It snowed and blew all night. Now, sage and stream and grass and pond are covered with wind-polished white snow, trackless and smoothly undulating. Facing slightly away from the low morning sun, tiny points of pure color shine brightly in red, blue, and green. The upraised snowflakes refracting the rainbow's spectrum like bits from a shattered rainbow.

In their summer passages, critters come and go mysteriously, leaving signs visible only to those who truly look. By this evening, however, the snow will be peppered with tracks that reveal to even the most unobservant the numbers and types of animals who live here.

My favorite deer path is near a bridge on Big Creek, just above where that stream flows into the big river. Last summer I saw a pair of does, helping their spotted fawns to cross the sun-dashed riffles, dainty silhouettes against the dancing brightness. Today, as they cross, they'll be walking on the water.

The path will deepen and keep pace with the new snows as the deer and bighorns pass over it. In spring the packed trail will be the last to melt, both here and in the sagey hills. The path stays in approximately the same position from year to year. Because the same animals use it consistently, a careful observer can enjoy watching, say, the growth of fawns.

Meanwhile, I love to inspect the daily changes. Today's tracks reveal two fawns and a doe behind as they crossed (the doe's sharp hooves making heavy indentations over those of her young). A yellow splash on the white snow and a still-steaming pile of brown pellet-dung reveal they are so recent the deer are probably watching me. A few gray and waxy winter hairs cling to a branch. The tracks jump to the side a bit, the branch probably jabbed the fawn.

Bucks are larger than does, generally, and I always thought that the size of the hoofprint was the way to tell the sex of an animal from its tracks. But I've seen quite a few does as big as bucks. And how do you tell the sex of younger animals? I found the answer in a book by Tom Brown, Jr., titled *Field Guide to Nature Observation and Tracking*. It's not the size of the tracks but the spacing one should study. Females have wider hips, to make birthing easier, so they tend to show tracks where the rear feet step outside the tracks of the front feet. Bucks on the other hand, have broader chests for fighting. Their back feet step inside the front or form a line of tracks.

When a musky animal scent, like wet feathers, drifts in a secluded grove, I look closer and find a rounded depression in the snow, where the deer bedded down for the night. Around the edges of their bedroom I find a bitterbrush with several ragged-edged branches, which one of them had paused to nibble.

The trails are used by other, smaller animals, too, making use of the work done by the larger deer. Coyote tracks, clawed and deeper, show it was trotting along, perhaps on the way to its mousing grounds on one of the south-facing slopes. Winter animals appreciate these sunny hillsides, where the snow is softer and more shallow, or even melted in the strong winter sun.

A fine, granular snow begins gently. It grays and obscures the landscape, making my nature observations more difficult. In the great, expanding views of Wyoming, there's much to see, but you have to pause and look carefully. So much of it is perfectly camouflaged, almost invisible until it moves or some other creature, more sharp-eyed than we humans, sees it. I always watch for ravens and crows, the neighborhood snoops, who watch everything and everyone. Today I saw a crow clan flying toward me. When they suddenly veered left and began diving toward a sagey hill, I knew they were onto *something* they considered fun. They were about a quarter mile away, and through the binoculars I found what they were taunting, an adult bald eagle. It stood, dark-bodied and white-head-and-tailed on the carcass of something small, perhaps a jackrabbit. Ignoring the crows, the eagle was enjoying its meal; bits of white fur floated away on the light breeze as the bird plucked and ate. The crows circled and dove, cawed and challenged the bigger bird. Every once in a while he looked up at his tormentors and once raised his wing as if to ward off a too-close crow. As the eagle finished his meal, the crows became bored and flew on. Ten minutes later, the eagle hopped along the snow for three horse lengths, spread its wings and soon was a well-fed dark spot receding on the horizon.

Deer are back around the ranch buildings now, nibbling at the dead flowers along Main Street and walking in single-file lines through the chest-deep snow on the first fairway. At mid-morning, two bucks sparred in the day pasture as a group of does and yearlings stood nearby, apparently ignoring them but in reality watching closely. But the rutting season is about over, and most of the bucks are friends again or too exhausted to fight.

Several beavers moved into the big bend on the North Platte, just upstream from our bridge. Ambitious critters, they cut willows and alders and started a dam across the river and built a lodge. Before they'd progressed very far, however, the river froze on an inside curve. Now the lodge is a snow-covered island amid a sea of clear, gleaming ice that cracks and pops in the first light of morning. The beavers are snuggled safely inside though, and I imagine them nibbling aspen bark they've stored, discussing plans for their spring onslaught of the Platte.

Over Thanksgiving we had thirty friends (including children) out for a couple of days. Next morning it was warm and sunny, so we decided to take everyone out for a picnic. Margie found a pretty site at the mouth of Cottonwood Creek, and we started a fire beside the stream, just below a new beaver pond. For several weeks, it had been quite cold at night, and their pond was frozen. The children's laughter slid over the pond as they shoe-skated on the ice and climbed over the beaver's lodge. We spread out lunch atop a traditional checkered tablecloth and spent several hours enjoying being together. Under the ice, the poor rodents must have felt they were being besieged, and we never saw them. Even so they helped create a memory for all of us.

After eating, we walked along the river. It was unfrozen except for ice along the shore and encircling rocks midstream, like crystal crowns. The pathway, about fifty feet from the water, was littered with deer and coyote tracks and glittering, dinner-plate-sized chunks of ice. We paused to reflect on how the ice chunks had gotten so far from the river. Suddenly, a violent gust of wind poured down the river. It tore ice sheets from the midstream boulders and along the shore, and we ducked as they skipped around us like flat pebbles across the water. Mystery solved.

Sunday, after our guests departed, I paused at the bridge over the North Platte; there's always something new to see, or old things in new ways. Quito, the border collie, was asleep on the seat. When I stopped the truck mid-bridge, he stirred then went back to sleep. In the warmth of the afternoon, ice chunks calved off the truck, and he jumped up each time; then, finding nothing exciting, he dropped to the seat and returned to dozing.

This day there was only one other animal in sight, a lone goose wading through the shallows between ice floes. The poor thing kept honking almost continuously, as if it were calling for other geese. Was its mate dead? Was it injured so it couldn't migrate? Did it choose to stay on? At the moment I saw her, she was peering around with her head low as if seeking others. It was so quiet — no wind at all. The only sounds were the purling of the river over and around the ice, and the lonely goose calling. Then the light began to change as the watery sun slid down over a mountain. Low, scattered clouds diffused the lowering sunlight. Near me everything turned pale blue-gray. In the middle distance, the hills became salmon pink. At the horizon, the peaks were brushed with alpenglow, a pale orange-pink floating on bluish shadows that were rising slowly, dissolving the color until all that remained was the deepening gray. On the top of a wind-bared hillside, four clumps of antelope, twenty-eight in all, lay in the grass or grazed quietly, facing the setting sun. They were probably just enjoying the last warmth before morning, but again I wondered — as I have so often in the past — do animals understand and appreciate beauty? They seem to.

Lynn S. is a longtime friend. One late evening, he and I took a long walk around a "mountain park" (open grassland, usually surrounded by ponderosa pine and aspen and often with slopes climbing to the high mountains). It was late in the afternoon, and the shadows were deepening. On the horizon, low clouds tinged orange and gold threw a rich, warm light through a notch in the mountains and over the landscape.

We heard a rumbling and felt the moist ground trembling. We looked uphill. Suddenly, a cow elk burst from the trees and raced downhill toward us. A breeze in our faces and the low light behind us had prevented her from seeing us until she was about fifty feet away. When she spotted us, she swerved mid-stride and dashed into the trees below us. In a moment, we heard/felt the vibrations again, but louder/stronger, and 22 more elk raced toward us in stampede style. This time they were only twenty or thirty feet away before they saw us. The group split, and they ran around us so close we could smell their moist, cattle-like scent. They ran downhill about two football fields and gathered in a loose group, milling and watching us nervously.

Lynn and I slowly sat in the grass at the trail's edge, barely moving. We'd been like that for about five minutes when we heard the breathing, a heavy panting, behind us. I turned slowly and saw in the shadows, a bull elk in full antler, only fifty feet away. We'd startled him, but he wasn't afraid, just cautious, and he'd frozen in place while he studied us. After about five more minutes, his breathing quieted and he decided we were okay but not safe enough to be investigated closer. He lowered his head and walked into the trees. We could hear him circling around us, and he joined the cows and calves below. Almost dark now, the mountain notch was pale, multi-color-lighted against the darker peaks. The elk were dark shadows, as the bull pushed the gang down the slope and out of sight.

December

Most years we're well covered in snow by this time, but in some years the snow stays north. Whenever that happens, people get concerned and tense. It's not just the fire danger of the moment, but the potential lack of irrigation water for grass and stream water for the fish next summer. Our neighbor is one of the older residents of the valley, and when winter still hadn't arrived, he was asked whether this was the driest winter he'd seen. No, he said. Back in 1934, when he was a student at the University of Wyoming, he'd driven to Lake Marie with a date to go ice skating in January. Why was that unusual? By that time of the year the lake normally has eight to ten feet of snow over it. But the winter of 1933-1934 was the height of the dust-bowl period, and any moisture falling at any time of that year was unusual. In fact, during the spring of 1934, the small streams dried up, trout died in the low, warm water, and where green grass normally covered the June pastures, they were pale tan. Dust devils spun over the dry ground, scouring away the fine particles of good topsoil and carrying it off toward Nebraska. (Once I saw a hummock about twenty feet across and covered with dense grasses. When I asked about it I was told, "That's the height of the soil before the wind took it east.") In 1934, desperate ranchers looked at the trickling North Platte River and knew there wasn't going to be any irrigation water at all. That summer the river got down to three percent of its normal flow. Ranchers sold their cattle for two cents a pound, losing a penny per pound because it cost three cents a pound to get them to Denver; but few were hardhearted enough to just let them die.

Things haven't been that bad for a long time, but ranchers are always a bit nervous in dry spells, and of course we were all glad when the snows began.

The snow finally began bucketing down and blowing into places you wouldn't think snowdrifts could form. Snow fell at half an inch per hour all one day and part of the next. The wind piled and packed snow in front of our office door, so I had to break through two feet of it when I left at the end of the day.

Our birds always seem to know what the weather's going to do. The night before the storm they mobbed the feeders and polished off four pounds of sunflower seeds in two hours. During the storm, they were little well-fed featherballs huddled on the lower branches of the conifers outside the office. They were protected by the branches above, which acted like roofs and caught most of the snow, although the branches tossed wildly in the wind. At the edge of a little willow thicket near the office, a small buck spent the day curled up out of the wind, catnapping as the snow collected on him. Not a bad day at all.

This morning I discovered one of our spruce trees in the yard was "girdled" (the bark cut all around, which kills the tree); in the branches above, the culprit, a porcupine. It lumbered down from the tree and was beating a slow-motion retreat when we decided to catch and move it. John E. showed several of us how to nab the spiny rascal. He squatted on one knee and moved almost within swatting range. The porcupine swiped at him with its tail, and John grasped the long hairs at its tip and slipped his other hand under the base of the tail. As he slid the hand back, following the direction of the quills, he grasped the tail and lifted the porky off the ground without getting stuck — too much anyhow. We put the porcupine in the back of a pickup and freed him about a mile downstream, in some new gnawing grounds.

One snowy morning half a dozen friends joined me on a wildlife tour. We took binoculars and climbed into a Suburban for a drive upriver to see if we could spot any animals. A light snow drifted down in the still, twenty-five-degree air. Our first sightings were five or six little groups of deer, each with its own big buck and usually with an up-and-comer following at a distance. Then, way at the top of one of the hills, we spotted a bull elk with branching antlers, silhouetted against the sky. On the grassy slopes below grazed almost two dozen cows and several more antlered bulls of various sizes. A bald eagle left his soaring and settled on the "jin" (dead and bare branches at the top) of a pine tree. Then a herd of more than forty bighorn sheep with six rams and (most exciting because the survival rate has been poor) six lambs.

Tragedy.

With warm days and very cold nights, rafts of ice froze, thawed, broke into small bergs, then reclumped and backed up at curves. In a week, the Platte was covered with a layer of crumpled, soft floe-ice two miles long and two feet thick. At about noon yesterday, when it was at its softest, a three-year-old bighorn ram, with horns curled three fourths of the half circle they would eventually make, tried to cross the river. He'd picked his way about halfway across when he fell through. Although he was strong and healthy and his struggles broke the ice further back, he couldn't gain a foothold. Hypothermia set in quickly, and he lay helpless, his body encased in the packing ice and his head above.

Each day his body would have moved a bit further downstream, but the game and fish department prizes the horns as a way to figure out how healthy the animal was. Five men and one dog came when I reported the death, and they struggled for several hours to get it out. After several failed ideas, one man was stationed on the opposite bank, and the dog, with a rope attached to its collar, was called across the ice, which easily held its lighter body. After several passes, the rope was securely wrapped around the horns, and the men, pulling together, were able to free it from the softening ice.

The study revealed a healthy three-year-old ram with one broken tooth and several minor ailments. Still, he had been powerful, a ram that one day might have challenged the alpha ram for breeding rights. Accidents, too, prove to be part of the concept of survival of the fittest.

The bighorns, like those we saw upriver, are gathering in herds, preparing for those dramatic head-bashing fights between the rams. Each day they're sparring at the salt licks and at the base of hills. By next week we'll hear the clack of horns cracking together in real fights. Next June, lambs will be playing on the hillsides, hiding under their mothers' shadows when a golden eagle passes overhead.

It's snowing today and blowing across the roads

and through the trees. As the winter gains force, we've noticed a big change in the deer. For one thing, they've changed color, from the russet of summer to winter gray, so they can blend with the sagebrush. They now have thick coats under long guard hairs that create insulation so effective I often see animals walking along, their backs totally covered with a blanket of snow. All summer they grazed on the grass but, since it's under snow now, they've turned to browsing, eating this year's new growth at the tips of bushes. A thick layer of fat makes the deer look very healthy. They need that fat, because about a quarter of it will be used for winter food, and of course it makes even more insulation. When nights are commonly twenty degrees below zero, heat (energy) preservation is critical. Last summer, when it was warm, we barely saw them except at night or in the early mornings or evenings. Now they sleep in until the sun's well up, so they can take advantage of its warming rays.

Although the wind among the ranch buildings is more lazy, the snow curling gently off the roofs has created two-foot-deep drifts. At the highway, about eight miles away, the image changes. Even with our grader working to push it away, the snow is piled into eight-foot berms. Out there the wind is a workaholic — and it's headed our way.

When I put out birdseed this morning, there were eight big black-and-white magpies as well as rosy-finches and both mountain and black-capped chickadees. The magpies perched on power lines, their long tails bobbing and tipping as they worked to balance themselves. When I walked in the door of the house, I looked over my shoulder to see the big birds settling down on the feeder and scattering the little ones with a wild flurry.

The horses have created their own corral. Although their pasture is about 300 acres, the snow is so deep they prefer to stay where they've beaten it down. One horse stares across the untrampled snow for a moment then starts into the snowfield. He plows through chest-deep snow for about a hundred feet, then turns back to join the rest, where he pauses to shake himself and return to eating — enough adventure for one day.

A tiny mouse hurries across the snow, throwing a tiny, scurrying shadow as it darts about trying to avoid...everything.

Stellar jays flap/glide down from the bare cottonwoods, looking like broken shards from the sky.

Last night, at 2:58 a.m., recorded when our electric clock stopped, the power went off. The temperature was twenty degrees below zero and, with even the mercury yard lights out, it was pitch black. I first noticed the lack of electricity when I stirred in bed and saw my breath — when there's no electricity, there's no furnace, even though it's propane-powered. Groping, shivering through the house, I lit the gas stove and the two wood stoves. Thank goodness for backup heaters. It was half a day before the electricity returned, but with the heaters, our water didn't freeze, and no pipes burst.

We're entering our coldest time of the year, and the animals are nervous, eating throughout the day and night, gathering into herds that seem larger each morning. Yesterday I watched more than 200

pronghorns among the sage, the lambs of the year frolicking and the adults grazing in scattered clusters or lying in the sun. The deer are still in their harem groups, most with huge, antlered bucks that keep them herded together almost ruthlessly, but always leading them into the most lush pastures. Even the grouse, both sage and blue, seem more hungry as they pick at the buds on sage and willow or scratch in the dry, wind-blown soil around the bases of the rabbitbrush and bitterbrush. When it's minus-forty degrees, they'll need all the extra insulation they can get from the fat they've stored. As for me, I don't know if it's the promise of cold weather or just the approach of the holidays, but I have to admit, I'm "grazing" a lot more myself these days.

Yours from Wyoming, where we have an excuse for holiday overeating: We're copying the animals and building fat against the cold.

An elk researcher down in Colorado had radio-tagged a number of cow elk and was flying around listening to their transmissions, trying to discover a bit more about their migration patterns. Surprisingly, one of his transmitters was beeping way north, and he tracked it all the way to Cheyenne, Wyoming, a long way for the "old girl" to walk. He flew around in circles until he decided the signal was coming from *inside* a building. He may have thought he had the goods on a poacher. Anyhow, he landed back at Denver and drove to Cheyenne, two hours away. When he arrived, he discovered that the building was, in fact, the headquarters for the Wyoming Game and Fish Department, and the beeper track led him to the desk

of a fellow researcher in that state's deer-research lab. One of the beepers in a boxful had accidentally turned on and happened to have the same frequency as the elk transmitter the Colorado man was following. They shared a good laugh and turned off the transmitter.

The river is finally frozen completely, and the wind has blown the snow away. Whenever this happens, the river ice becomes clear as crystal and polished to a glossy sheen. Before refrigeration, it was the kind of ice people would use to cut and store for the summer. At this time of the year, I often think about one of our neighbors, now gone, and the day I helped him make ice in the old-fashioned way.

Bruce had a refrigerator and a freezer but still enjoyed the "old-timey" activity. Having it gave him some degree of connection to the old days, which he liked, not to mention at least some disconnection from the power company. When he needed help, he thought of me because of my incessant questions about the old skills. Besides, he needed a helper, and I was available. His pond had frozen in mid-November. Snow acts as an insulator, so after each snow he'd shovel it from the pond, to let that clear ice form and deepen. When I arrived, it was zero degrees, and the ice was almost two feet deep, with bits of algae frozen here and there in the ice window and cruising trout visible far below.

First, we scored the ice. Bruce had an old truck that died, but the motor still worked. He'd mounted the engine on a sledge made of angle iron. A simple pulley system with v-belts turned an unguarded three-foot saw blade in front. Slipping and sliding clumsily, we dragged the roaring, heavy sledge back and forth across the pond, creating a two-feet-by-three-feet grid of rectangles. As the blade ate its way easily along, it threw plumes of ice dust fifteen feet into the air, painting rainbows in the sunshine.

Then I used a long ice saw with two-inch teeth and a two-handed grip that lay at right angles to the blade. It, too, slid easily through the ice, and in about five minutes I'd cut fifty feet along one of the scored lines. A metal tamping bar with a flat blade at one end easily broke one chunk loose, and we used big ice tongs to pull it onto the ice. We continued pulling the chunks of ice until we had about twenty of the giant ice cubes, each weighing more than 325 pounds, laid out atop the frozen pond. The ice slide easily to pondside, where a tractor and low sledge waited. We muscled it through the snow and onto the sledge, then drove to the ice house.

The ice house was a dirt-floored cabin, about fifteen feet square with two-foot-thick walls. For insulation, the space between the walls was packed with more sawdust from a local sawmill. Beside the door, another sweet-scented pile waited. The inner walls were thin metal plates, once used on old offset printing presses. Most had rusted, but on some of them you could still read the news and even make out some of the photos. After we covered the floor with a six-inch layer of sawdust, we stacked the ice on top of it with small gaps between each block, which we also filled with sawdust so they wouldn't melt together. When the first layer of ice filled the building, we scooped another layer of sawdust atop it and returned for more ice blocks. Two hours later and five layers higher, we had a building filled with ice and scented with pine.

By the next September the house was still half full. One night Bruce and I sat on his porch talking and sipping drinks chilled with that beautiful, clear ice, a few with bright-green algae floating mid-chunk.

A "chinook" is blowing. Yesterday morning at feeding time, the temperature was minus-twenty-three degrees. This morning it was twenty degrees above and rising fast to the forty degrees it is now, at about noon. Silent patches of sunlight still race over the ground, and the melting snow runs off the roof and down the icicle channels.

What began gently is now a howling beast eating the snow (chinook is Innuit for snow-eater), melting it and carrying away its moisture. The horses knew it was coming, and those grazing at the far end of the pasture began to run with the wind as if driven by it. They stopped at the haystacks and hid behind them with their tails to the wind. Tumbleweeds rolled over the roads and pastures like giant rabbits scurrying, then stuck on barbed-wire fences like Peter Rabbit in Mr. McGregor's garden.

Jennai called from the main gate, four miles away. She was in tears because a deer had leaped in front of the car as she was coming home. Although the car was just fine, the deer was still alive but paralyzed. Could I come and help? Of course.

When Justin and I arrived, Jennai was in the ditch with the dying doe, its head cradled on her lap as she stroked it gently. The deer's eyes were wide and calm as she lay waiting. Jennai continued home, and I had the task of putting the doe "to sleep." It's never easy, and I was dismally unprepared, having only a .22 target rifle in the truck and no knife. Several shots were needed and I was grateful that Jennai wasn't with us.

I promised myself to be even more careful than ever when I'm driving. But it's said that there are two kinds of drivers in Wyoming, those who have hit deer and those who will hit deer.

It's been warm, even to the upper fifties here at the ranch, and the snow settled about a foot. The river had been frozen solid. At the curves, where it was strongest, the wind had cleared the snow and polished the ice to a satiny gray luster. Two days ago the surface was slushy and rumpled as the river broke free in several places, flowing greenish-gray over and through the remaining snow. Last evening, when I left Hubbell House, one of our guest cabins where we'd been working, I saw a movement on the golf-course edge and saw a coyote trotting along through the willows at its edge. Although the dogs began to bark, it ignored them and spent its time poking around logs, stumps, and snow drifts, looking for mice, I suppose. I had a great view and spent about ten minutes with him, watching as he hunted in the bluish light of dusk.

Yours from Wyoming, where zero has returned but the coyote has not.

A perfect winter day. The rest of the nation is in a deep freeze, but a high-pressure area keeps the cold at bay, and we're enjoying a balmy thirty-five degrees. The nights are still very cold, however, and in the morning, where the river is open, it steams into the cold air. At dawn I watched two bighorn rams butting heads as the hollow echoes of their clash bounced off the cliffs.

The moon is full tonight. What causes the blue haze of the full moon on the snow? Does it happen everywhere or only in the mountains? Does it relate to the haze one sees in the distance, making mountains far off appear bluish? Is it more pronounced in the winter in the snow, or does it only appear that way? Does it have anything to do with the fact that the light from the moon is reflected and so what we see here is re-reflected? So many questions.

I never can resist a full moon and a late-night cross-country ski along one of the two-tracks we use in the summer for putting out salt for the livestock. The skiing is especially nice when the wind is calm and I can enjoy the gentle schussing of my skis through the snow. Tonight I drove to the base of Slim's Draw (where we go for our Friday-night cookouts) and skied up one of the two-track roads toward a salt lick two miles away.

As I neared an open meadow, I heard the thudding of hooves and the swishing of heavy bodies dashing through the brush. Then I saw them, ghosts racing in the moonlight suddenly materializing into a herd of pronghorns, which disappeared again into the dusky blue light. In seconds all that was left to me was the torn snow and the scent of bruised sage.

Further up the mountain I startled a herd of elk. The lead bull held his head high and horizontal and turned to face me. But the rest of the gang (the name for a herd of elk) slipped and slid, falling in the snow with hollow clumps in their sudden panic as they

stampeded away. Then I was again left in silence with only the rumpled snow and a slight wet hair scent to tell me that they had really been there.

Returning downhill I stopped often to look around and received a final greeting. Silhouetted at the top of a little rise stood a huge buck deer with so many forks that he appeared to wear branches instead of antlers — what is called an "erratic." Beside him stood a smaller buck with three points on each side. Both watched me a moment before calmly strolling over the hilltop, bachelors out for a midnight stroll.

The next day, as I skied along through a narrow canyon above a stream, the silence broke with the rustle of snow sliding and the rattle of rocks falling. Then, the scrambling and panting of animals running as a deer and pursuing coyote leaped up from the valley and across my path. When they saw me they continued up a steep cutbank with the energy that comes from fear on fear. The coyote forgot its prey and ran up another steep cutbank. He easily scaled it, until he got to the top where a four-foot vertical wall stopped him a moment. Then, fearing for his life, he leaped at it again and grabbed at the exposed grass and roots with his forefeet and claws, his back legs dangling. He thrashed for what seemed like a long time to me and probably felt longer to him, then with an extra surge, he pulled over the top and galloped into the sagebrush. Farther down the slope, the doe performed much the same maneuver. With no claws to help, she took almost ten seconds with her back legs struggling for a hoof-hold before she gained the top.

About a half mile into the canyon, two yearling deer leaped from the embankment, now about eight feet high, and onto the road center. Without pausing, their second jump took them across and down a heavily treed hillside. When I looked over the small cliff, I expected to see a wreck, perhaps even one of them perched in the lower branches of a tree. Instead they pronked down the remainder of the hill and across the valley. In moments the only signs of their passing were the deep tracks in the snow and ice crystals drifting on the wind from where they'd brushed trees in their kamikaze dash.

Yours from Wyoming, where there are no lift lines and the others on the slopes are always interesting to watch.

Christmas was unusually warm. Although it was white, as Christmas should be (according to the song anyhow), the day itself was almost forty-five degrees and sun-filled. At night the nearly full moon cast a beautiful blue-gray light across the snow, giving the landscape a bright-dark, ethereal look. Margie and I had driven to town to visit friends and returned about 11 p.m. When I'd gone about a mile up the road, I saw a large movement to my left but couldn't make out anything specific so stopped the car. Whatever it was was moving toward us — and fast. Then pounding hoof beats and the swish of sage being brushed aside filled the air. Suddenly a herd of pronghorns materialized, and more than a hundred galloped through my headlights' glare, ignoring us. Then, just as suddenly, they dematerialized, and that noisy shadow continued upvalley. Like the ones I'd seen a few weeks ago, they left only the torn snow and pungent scent of smashed sage as a sign of their passing. If it had been Santa and his reindeer we couldn't have been more surprised.

January

Well, it's officially another year, a quarter of the way through by my strange reckoning. One of the towns decided to have some extra fun and parody the Times Square ball drop. They hauled a giant plywood trout to the top of one of the town water towers and dropped it as the seconds ticked down to midnight. It stuck partway, but "Father Time" came to the rescue and unstuck it.

Although December 30th was bitter — way, way below zero — the morning of the 31st was not. By 9 a.m. a few veil-like clouds hovered over the mountains and the temperature rose quickly. Yesterday it snowed lightly, covering the hay stacks with a soft, white frosting. When we went to feed the horses this morning, the south-facing sides of the stacks were already beginning to steam as the snow melted in the morning sun. Amid the horses, a pair of coyotes lounged in the sun, while the horses nibbled the frozen grass only a few feet away. When we began to throw out the hay, the horses came running, but the coyotes only watched us lazily, yawning occasionally.

Television plays a rather small part in our family's entertainment. Last night we played with a new Christmas gift, a board game. Justin quickly mastered it, easily beating all of us, so of course we got bored and began to look for other diversions. Justin, Jennai, and I went outside and had a snow-chunk fight. (It was too cold for balls, so we used the softly frozen layer atop the snow.) Margie joined us, and we played in the midnight snow, wrestling and laughing. In the shadows nearby, two large gray/white jackrabbits hunched forward on the snow-covered lawn, sampling the husks and seeds the birds have wasted at the feeder and ignoring our noise.

This morning, the first of the new year, the sun rose at just the right place to throw first light down the river canyon. I first noticed it when I looked out a window to the east and saw a slab of fallen sunlight on the ground between darkened peaks. During the night, the steamy vapor from the warmer river, which was still open in many places, had coated each tree with ice, and they glowed with the back-light, creating a magical, crystal forest. By 9 a.m. the trees were warming, and the crystals gradually fell from their perches. They drifted straight down in the calm air, giving the effect of a snowstorm on a clear day but only under each tree where they knifed into the snow and created a jumble of glittering crystals.

When I gave the horses their morning grain, magpies perched on their rumps then moved to rails and rocks where they sat on their feet to keep warm. They waited patiently for the extra grain they knew would fall from the mouths of the sloppy horses. Crows had been cruising the snow, and I could see a flock by another barn, squabbling over the remains of a jackrabbit left by a coyote. Was it one of those we saw dining near our house last night?

When the temperature is minus-thirty-eight, as it is now, the brittle snow squeaks loudly under my two feet and under the 480 feet of the horses as they mill slowly, trying to keep warm. Their breath freezes on their whiskers, and they look like little old horses. Moisture collects and freezes on bits of dust in the air, and the morning light dances with silvery ice motes.

Each horse has its full-length hair coat. It's calm this morning, but on windy days the hair rolls in waves like grass on a summer meadow. As each horse's body heat/moisture trickles away it begins to evaporate then forms into ice crystals on each hair. Most of the horses in the remuda carry white ice blankets across their backs and crests. A few are completely encased with frost and look like glass horses, glowing with a white aura when backlit by the rising sun.

As the sun climbs higher, some of the horses drop to the snow and begin to roll, breaking the ice crystals. Rising, they lean forward, knees bent, and shake the snow-dust free. This keeps them dry and warm. If the sun had shone on the crystals, they would have melted and trickled down to the unprotected skin, chilling even the thickest-coated horse.

We drive our ancient, high-sided hay truck — "The Streak" — in a tight circle through the shadow of the mountain, spreading the hay in a hundred or more rumpled piles, pale green against the trampled snow. Across the meadow, where the sunlight is already strong, a dozen horses stand quietly, their bodies sideways to the rising sun, soaking up heat like reptiles atop rocks. Black horses warm up quicker and watch the hay truck carefully; the white ones take longer to warm, but sooner or later their ears perk up and turn toward the sound of the feed truck. Then, a few at a time, they begin drifting toward the hay truck but staying within the light, avoiding the shadow of the mountain.

As the truck passes into the light the sun feels surprisingly warm in the cold. Even at this temperature I am perspiring from exertion. When I pull off a sweat-soaked glove, vapor rises from both hand and glove, evaporating into the super-dry air.

Clusters of horses gather round each hay mound, dividing themselves in a kind of peaceful disorder. Each knows his place, whom he can kick and who can kick him, so laid-back ears are usually the only threat

necessary. Horses have buddies. As usual, several groups of pals are eating from the same mound, like humans over coffee at the local donut shop.

We fed an extra half ton of hay today to help the horses maintain their body heat. Even at 2 a.m. they'll continue to eat. Once, on a frosty moonlit midnight, I drove by the pasture and saw the horses, blue-gray shadows in a blue-gray light. Every head was down as they still crunched hay from the morning's feeding. All, that is, except for a few at the western edge of the meadow, waiting for the sun.

It's even colder now, about forty below this morning. I obviously enjoy the old ways and using at least some of the old skills and foods. Days like this, though, I'm especially glad to live in the modern world. Not too many years ago I'd have been making daily treks to the river, hauling buckets and buckets of water for my family, probably carrying an axe to open drinking-water holes for the livestock as well.

A neighbor told me that, as a child, one of his daily chores was to keep open a drinking-water hole in the ice. If the ice was too thick, he'd build a fire on it, gradually melting a hole to the water. Sometimes, he and his father would cut the opening and then build a small snow-chunk building, like an igloo, over the hole. The snow house kept the air warmer inside, and the hole seldom froze too hard, even on mornings like this.

The dew point was zero Fahrenheit yesterday. That means the air contained so little moisture that it couldn't snow until the temperature had fallen to zero. Sure enough, as the thermometer's arrow pointed downward, past that critical point, the air began to fill with tiny flakes and continued throughout the day. Still, the air was dry and held only a trace of moisture, so by this morning we had a mere two inches of new snow. But there was a special treat, the whitest white snow possible.

It was minus-eighteen as I stepped outside, so cold my nostrils froze shut a moment when I took a breath. Leaning over a bright cluster of snow, I took a few flakes on the tip of a knife blade and held it under my pocket microscope. Perched on the glinting knife blade, under 30x magnification, the edges of each flake stood out clearly, and their crystalline structure was intact. At the edge of each was a pinprick of color in brilliant red, orange, or blue. In fact, by tilting the flakes at different angles to the light, I found most colors of the spectrum. As those same pure colors twinkled from the edge of the flakes in the snowfield around me, they blended into brilliant, pure white. By tomorrow we expect a warming trend, and those flakes will nestle more tightly together, break, melt a bit, and that brilliance will be gone. Oh, the snowfields will still be white and lovely, but it will be more subdued, the soft reflected light of white satin, instead of the flashing refractions from a palmful of diamond flakes.

I looked out the window a few minutes ago to see Quito dashing full speed across the meadow. At first I couldn't see what he was after, then a coyote leaped out of a cloud shadow into the sunlight and slowed to a leisurely lope. When Quito was about fifty feet away, the coyote turned and ran toward him. Was Quito surprised! He planted his forefeet in the snow and skidded about five feet, turning to run as he slipped,

and the chaser became the chasee. The coyote was a big male and could have done some serious damage but seemed to be enjoying his version of a game. He got close enough to make a couple of nips at Quito's tail then stopped, sat on a snowy hummock, and watched the dog as he ran to my office door. The coyote seemed to be laughing as he lifted a front paw and rubbed his nose. Seeing me, he turned up-meadow, trotted into the cloud shadow, and disappeared, leaving a thoroughly embarrassed border collie cowering by my knee.

Yours from Wyoming, where you never know what's going to appear outside your window.

It's unusual to see moose in our valley, so I was surprised today when I saw two. "Just passin' through," the young bulls weighed in at perhaps 1,200 pounds each. They fed on the tops of willow shrubs, chewing the finger-sized bare branches and doing their part to prune and strengthen the plants. Even when I got to within 200 feet of them, they showed no fear of me and, in fact, ignored me. I studied them through my binoculars, to get a really close in look, and was impressed by their antlers. Although not extremely large, they were interesting in their texture, which was a battered and polished white. Some of the tines were broken from sparring in the recent rutting season, and the antlers subtly reflected the sunlight. I watched them for a while until one raised his head and walked toward me through the knee-deep snow; I left to watch something less formidable.

It's one of those perfect mountain days. There's not a breath of wind, and the sky is flawless blue as far as

I can see (which is quite a ways, perhaps thirty miles). I haven't seen the ground since early October, and last week we had about fourteen inches of new snow atop the unmelted three feet from the last few months. We've gone through about eighty pounds of mixed birdseed so far and some five pounds of suet, but it's worth it. We have the full range of winter birds, from nuthatches and creepers to chickadees, Stellar bluejays, juncos, and flocks with dozens of gray-crowned rosy finches. The snow's so deep in our meadow that the elk haven't spent any time there this winter, but there's a lot of grass left under cover. I know the elk will return as soon as the snow starts melting, perhaps in our "January thaw," which I expect sometime in the next week or so.

One of the great pleasures of living in the mountains in the winter is the January thaw. It usually arrives in mid- to late-January, typically after a period of deep cold and heavy snow, when we're really tired of winter. Only ten days ago Laine was spending most of his days in the road grader, plowing snow. One morning was so cold that a one-ton metal piece on the grader, already weakened by continual vibrations, snapped because it was so brittle. The next day the chinook wind began. The temperature rose thirty-five degrees, and the wind howled all day and night. When I went to the river next morning, most of the river's snow cover was gone, replaced by a satiny, steel-gray ice coat that glistened in the sun. The temperature had risen to the mid forties, and in the bright light it felt even warmer. I stayed a while.

Watching the weather reports, I sometimes have to laugh. The idea of what constitutes bad or good weather surely does depend on what you do for a living and where you are at the time. Last week I visited with some neighbors, and we listened to the weather report. In downtown Denver it was going to be just *terrible*, with about six inches of new snow. Driving to work the next morning was going to be very slow. I watched my friend's face throughout the report. He was delighted. Six inches of snow meant almost three-fourths inch of moisture, and that means a better chance of irrigation water when it melts next spring. Another friend in our circle was also grinning as he thought of himself skiing through the new powder snow. Me? I have to agree with both of them — snow's wonderful most of the time.

There was a period a few years ago when, for five years, we had less snow than is required to maintain our aquifers or do summer irrigation. Ranchers were in a bad way for three years in particular. Their pasture and irrigation water, which comes from melting snowpack, were gone by mid-July instead of lasting through August. Even at a large nearby ranch, they were able to make only about 5,000 tons of hay instead of the required 6,000. Now it's turned around again. There are more than four feet of snow on the ground, and we've used our snowplow more in the past two weeks than we did all last winter. It should make the summer especially green and give our rivers and streams an extra boost while helping the spring-spawning rainbow trout. It may be blowing and white outside, but the grins on ranchers and fisherfolk are as wide as the Wyoming horizon.

Another bitter cold night, our seventh in a row, ends gradually. Snow crunches underfoot, and my fingertips are benumbed even under thick gloves as I look up at the deep, black sky. It's 5 a.m., and the horses were alarmed and noisy, so I came to check on them. All's well and I'm cold, but I stay to watch the dawn. Gradually the black changes to gray, then blue gray, and I go inside. I make some coffee and, from a warm window, watch as the sunlight spurts over the hillside and splats into pools on the mountaintops to the west then gradually expands and slides downward into the valleys. As I return to feed the horses, the sun feels warm on my face, but the shade is cold. It's warming up though. The temperature's risen to one below zero.

Ruthie R., one of the cowboy's wives, a tired-looking but poetic and observant lady, told me that she thinks of the early rays as scouts for the happy invasion of the sun. In the "attack," animals are beginning to move, starting with those that spent the night high atop the ridges, where they waited for the warmth of the sun. Then they slowly follow the sunlight down into the valleys. The first I see this morning is a golden eagle perched on the jin of an ancient ponderosa pine. It stretches, shakes, and fluffs its feathers, sending bits of sparkling ice and dust motes swirling into the cold air.

In the past few days we've had about twenty-six inches of new snow. While the deer and other grazers have a more difficult time in the deep snow, it definitely helps others. Snow forms a blanket over the earth and acts like an insulator. I remember digging to mineral soil under two feet of snow and finding the soil soft and moist, easily diggable. Mice, voles, and other little rodents live relatively safe lives in the winter as they create tunnels under the snow, invisible to owls.

I've even imagined myself, shrunk to mouse-size and wandering their trails, through "miles" of passageways lit by the sunlight filtering softly bluish through the snow. I'd often have to wade across mini-torrents of melting snow, and I'd have to be alert for the dangers of a weasel or badger on the prowl. Sometimes the trail would end where a pocket gopher was packing soil from its digging into tunnels that would create "eskers" on the ground when the snow melted. I'd peer upward through long shafts punched through the snow by the long legs of deer and breathe deeply at the refreshing air channels.

Even some of the birds make use of the snow blanket. Three blue grouse picked their way across the snow, approaching a spot where several willow bushes protruded from a drift. The birds burrowed into the snow and didn't come out. Next day they still seemed to be there as the wind howled overhead. They were safe, out of the wind, and spent most of the day napping and dining on the willow's buds. (Somehow, the birds can even determine which of the buds are female and prefer to eat them, the most nutritious, first.) While we have to shovel and drive through it, snow sometimes comes as a blessing for the smaller animals. On the other hand, our "burrow" is a warm cabin with a woodstove crackling softly, a great book, and a hot cup of coffee.

Although it has been a week since the last storm, snow hasn't settled much and still covers the sagebrush so deep that only the tops show. Rosy finches and horned larks gather along the roads and fly up in desperate flocks, returning to scrabble for seeds in the gravel. This morning was warm and sunny, and I paused as I hiked a well-trod deer trail, soaking in the warmth and beauty of the blue sky against the whiteness of the snow. Then I ducked spontaneously as a flock with several hundred gray-crowned rosy finches flew over a small rise and dodged around me as they would a rock or tree stump. For a moment the air was filled with their high chirping calls and the swishing sound of their wings in the cold air. Little puffs of swirling wind from their wings blew against my cheeks. Then they rose en masse and flew in formation, as if one were calling "All left," then "All right." I didn't move, and they ignored me as they returned to settle in a clump of juniper trees, plucking the freeze-dried purple fruits on the tree and walking about under the cover of the branches to snatch up fallen fruit. After a few frantic moments they rose again and as I watched them I realized there were five separate and equally large flocks patrolling the snow slopes in one square mile. I watched and listened for half an hour before they all disappeared, as if the formation leader called, "All, move on."

The January thaw has returned. Yesterday at 3 o'clock I sat atop a rail fence, leaned against a tall gate pole, and basked in the sunshine. My watch thermometer measured the temperature at 45 degrees. Then at 3:08 the sun went down, and by 3:20 the temperature was 27. When everything's white, it doesn't absorb much heat, and when the sunlight goes, so does the warmth.

February

In our valley a dozen abandoned threshing machines sit, surrounded by sagebrush, in what were once fertile wheat fields. Farmers here were beaten when the drought struck in the '30s and just drove away from their farms and useless machines. In one of those fun coincidences we have from time to time, I had a seat-mate on a plane going from Atlanta to Richmond, a tanned and energetic old man. We talked about Wyoming, and he became very excited when I told him where I lived. He'd grown up on what is now part of this ranch. His family had been owners of one of those abandoned threshers. They'd left at the tail end of a dust storm, when the family's third wheat crop in a row failed for lack of rain. I could tell that nostalgia had him in its grip and he laid his hand on my arm and asked softly whether I knew an old house at the base of a long hill, which he named. "Of course I do," I said, "But it's in pretty sad shape now." "Well," he said, "my dad built that house with my help, and we lived there for seven years, me and my sixteen brothers and sisters." From May through November or early December, he told me, the boys lived in a tipi by the river. When it got really cold, the whole family crammed into the house. Back in Wyoming again, I walked the dimensions of the ramshackle skeleton of a house — 800 square feet for nineteen people!

A pair of cowgirl poets came to town one snowy day. We traveled through another blizzard and gathered in the school gymnasium, with just a few more than a hundred others, for some welcome midwinter fun. The ladies were so entertaining that even the bleachers felt comfortable. Their topics included answers to questions about cowboys: Why do cowboys wear moustaches? And, what does a cowboy's head look like under that Stetson? There were stories too, about Jake and Jerome (two elderly cowboys still trying to do their jobs) and about Burt and Clyde (the Marlboro man and a bachelor from hell). The best were ones the audience could relate to or that made fun of the hard ranching life, like a description of "fetchin' parts" from old vehicles stored around a tool shed. My favorite was about the "Chicken Whisperer," who trains free-range chickens without stressing them.

This time of the year is particularly difficult for the animals. Each week the snow deepens, and the nights are well below zero. Many of the bigger grazing animals, weakened by their several months-long struggles against the cold, die. A week ago a pronghorn died beside our main road and has been teaching us an interesting lesson.

We first saw the carcass when Justin and I drove to the school bus. The female pronghorn had died in the night. In the snow around her body, tracks told the story of her passing and of the coyotes who appreciated her death. After putting Justin on the bus, I returned to the carcass to decipher what had happened.

The pronghorn's tracks wandered erratically through the sagebrush. She was alone and moved slowly, stopping often. The old girl was obviously tired and sick because there were nose prints in the snow about every ten feet. She'd nibbled a sagebrush but let the unchewed twig fall back onto the snow and moved on. As she staggered toward a hillside, she stumbled and fell to her knees, then got up and continued until, at roadside, she fell for a last time. Torn snow showed that she'd convulsed or struggled to rise. Other scrapings, these with clawed paw prints, showed where four coyotes ran in to finish her.

By morning, the coyotes had eaten the innards but little else. On the second day one of the haunches was eaten and the third day the other haunch. By the fourth the rib cage and forelegs were gnawed and the hide lay rumpled and frozen beside the body. The fifth morning a bald and a golden eagle fed a few feet apart while ravens and magpies waited. The sixth day I missed, and the seventh the carcass was gone, with only the head and part of the neck remaining. Nothing appears to have gone to waste, and the nutrients of her body supported for a time a dozen or more other animals.

We have a nice group of "ouzels" at the ranch. Ouzels, or dippers, are slate-gray birds about two-thirds the size of a robin and with a sharply pointed beak. They have a somewhat wren-like body form. They're a bit chubbier than a wren but have the same slight upturn to their tails. What makes the ouzel unique is its ability to feed and walk under the water. This morning I sat by the river, listening to the water rippling around the openings in the ice. They're usually solitary, but today — because most of the rivers are frozen over — six ouzels kept their own territories along the openings. Each was diving into the frigid water just where it slid under the edge-ice. They stayed down for four to eight seconds, then popped up, skimmed like motorized birds across the water's surface and rocketed back onto the ice like penguins returning from the sea.

Although one can't see them at work on the bottom, I'm told they actually run across the rocks on the stream bed, wings about half outspread, as they poke about the rocks, searching for mayfly and stonefly larvae. It was warm as I watched those birds, but I've seen them work when it's zero, and they even like it enough that they sing, the only winter birds that so honor us.

This morning, on that eight-mile ride to the bus, we found something that at first wasn't so wonderful, a just-killed deer carcass beside the road, lying in a fluff of pinkish snow. Steam rose gently into the air from the rumpled body, and fresh cougar tracks led to the river. We felt we were being watched and had to meet the bus, so we drove on. I returned 45 minutes later, and the deer was gone, or at least moved, hidden under the branches of a low tree where it could be eaten in privacy. I still felt like I was being watched and left quickly, so I wouldn't disturb the cougar further.

After receiving one of my letters when he returned from a frustrating trip to the U.S., one of our guests, Andrei V. from London, England, tucked his tongue in his cheek and wrote:

"Unfortunately I spent last week in New York and got caught in two snow storms, one of which sent me to Bangor, Maine, on arrival and the other delayed my departure to London by thirty-six hours. In between, the offices were more or less deserted, and as such my trip was a total write-off. While you were counting deer and bighorn on the ridge tops, I couldn't even count muggers in Central Park, as even they stayed home due to the unusually cold weather. So you'll forgive me if I'm not too lyrical about snow right now!"

I've heard that "When it rains, it pours." Not too long ago, we had a real snow drought in progress, but we just had the equivalent of that old saw in terms of snow: "When it snows, things collapse and close." None of the locals had been skiing lately, because there were so many rocks that you'd damage your skis. That's no problem now because we just had four feet of new snow. It poured down so fast that you couldn't see through it, and driving became a real hazard. The biggest problems, however, were the avalanches, hundreds in one day. They covered highways and closed the Interstate for two days, tore trees from the hillsides, and buried a few cars and hikers. For the most part, though, we and our neighbors recognized the danger and stayed home, feeding the horses and birds, reading by the fireside, appreciating the snow for what it is: springtime water.

Sunday, Quito and I went cross-country skiing (he wasn't on skis). We started up a flat trail upriver. I enjoyed watching the variety of tracks, while he spent his time sniffing at them and digging at unseen mysteries. After about three miles, I'd settled into a watch-your-feet mode and was gliding along at a good clip, when I was startled by rocks tumbling softly through the snow near me. The dog pressed against my legs nervously, and we both stared. Poised to run, up to their bellies in the snow, ten deer stared back at us from only fifty feet away. They were so close I could see the moisture around their eyes and the ice crystals on the hairs of their muzzles. When I showed no threat, they relaxed but continued up the hill, still plowing through the deep snow.

Late February

At 7 a.m., it's four below zero and dead calm. The only branch moving is from a mountain chickadee searching for anything edible. In the snow a few tracks show where a winter-white jackrabbit crossed the yard, stopping to nibble at one willow after another.

Yesterday was warm and thawing. The North Platte was gradually working itself free and flowed for a time but is now refrozen in a greenish, slushy carpet over the snow. Two black and white magpies fly along the riverbank, through the hazy morning air that is filled with tiny, glowing pinpoints of drifting ice crystals. Like the chickadee, the magpies are hungry, patrolling six to eight feet over the river in search of edibles. Their only tracks, however, are the swirling eddies of crystals in the cold air.

February is a harsh month. While January has its share of deep cold, you expect it and accept it. You know the first three weeks will try you and your house's heating system, not to mention the water pipes. But January has a soul. It often leaves you with a smile after a night of minus-forty degrees gives way to clear skies, and daytime temperatures skyrocket to the mid-fifties in that January thaw.

Then February slides across the mountains one dark, cold night. While January was convincing you that spring was near, February was preparing itself to prove that there are two or three more months of winter. Each year about this time, I'm reminded of a February a few years ago, when the weather was particularly tough.

In the first week an arctic front, which had held Alaska by the throat for several weeks, apparently got bored with the north and drifted south to pick on other states. The front lazed its way down the east side of the Rockies, presenting Denver with temperatures down to minus-twenty degrees. But while the East Slope crackled in the brittle cold, another front kept us here in the mountains warm, with highs in the teens for several days.

At the edge, where the fronts rubbed together, the western front gradually began to chill. The warmer air held more water, and as it chilled it began to lose what it did have. Tiny flakes formed and drifted downward constantly in a gossamer cloud. This continued for three days and nights.

Each day the temperature fell lower, but even when the air plunged to minus-twenty-five the snow continued, depositing almost three feet of "champagne powder" snow. Every meadow, every house, every fence carried its load. Fence posts looked taller because they wore caps of snow a foot high. Even the wind seemed too cold to move.

All night the snow gathered on the horses, creating a sort of blanket that held in the warmth and coated their whiskers with rime from their breath. In the morning, before the sun and their body heat melted the snow and soaked them, the horses shook themselves and rolled in the snow, then leaped up to buck and run around the pasture, some sliding and falling to jump up and run again.

We knew the wind would begin soon and wanted to have an extra car at the highway in case we were snowed in. Laine and I drove two cars the eight miles to the road. I drove the lead car through the untracked snow, using its right wheels to feel for the angle marking the edge of the road, or riding in the shallow ruts hidden under the snow. Approaching deeper snow I gunned the engine, and powdery snow flew over the car top as I blasted through one drift, then another, creating my own roaring, hissing snow cloud.

At the highway we have an extra electric meter and plug, just for the block heaters of cars and heavy snow-plowing equipment. We left the car and, with less drama and stress, drove home following the ruts we'd made on the trip out.

The next day, Sunday, I left for Virginia on a staff interview trip. By mid-morning the ambient temperature was minus-fifty-three degrees at the ranch, and it held there all that night. School was canceled that morning. By Tuesday the temperature had risen to minus-forty-seven, and the school could be heated, so students were told to report. It was warmer, but the wind roared along the hills at thirty mph — a wind chill of minus-ninety.

One of Margie's jobs while I was gone included driving Justin (aged twelve at the time) to the bus eight miles away. That Tuesday it was calm and cold at the ranch, but the car was warm; it had been plugged in all night. She called the bus driver to say, "Please don't leave until you have Justin with you; we're coming to meet you." She had a sleeping bag in the car, and they were both bundled well, but she wore only pajamas under her coat. We'd lived out like this for more than a quarter century, and she was prepared but not concerned.

But while the wind at the ranch headquarters was fairly calm, she couldn't know that at the highway eight miles away, it was still caterwauling. As they climbed the hill above our airstrip, a climb of twenty degrees, she switched to four-wheel high then to low. The Suburban waded through drift after drift until they came to one a hundred yards long and mired with snow halfway up the door.

The walkie-talkie was dead, and their only hope was Justin, who understood he'd have to rescue his mother. Their main hope was the bus driver, who they hoped had waited.

Forcing the door of the car slightly open, Justin

hugged his mom and said, "Don't worry." Then he waded into the wind and drifts. As his red coat disappeared into the swirling snow, she said a prayer and settled down to wait — and worry.

Because she was concerned that if she turned the motor off she couldn't start it again, she let the car run, opened the window, and pulled the emergency sleeping bag up around her. Snow blew in the window and drifted across her lap.

Meanwhile, Justin slogged toward the highway. Some of the snow was hard packed by the wind and made for good walking, but he'd unexpectedly hit a soft spot and fall. His jeans froze and rattled around his legs, becoming so stiff they broke in one fall, exposing the bare flesh above his knee.

Fortunately, his red coat was a flag, moving slowly through the snow, and the bus driver and his friends on the bus watched as he struggled toward them. An hour and a half after leaving the car, he climbed aboard the bus. Huddling by the heater, he told the driver about his mother. She radioed the bus barn and they called a neighboring ranch for assistance.

By late morning, Margie's lap was about covered with snow and she was numb, not just from the cold, but from not knowing if he'd made it safely. Then she saw a tractor pushing through the snow, and our neighbor, Ben C., waving encouragement. Relief warmed her even under her snowpile — Justin had made it and was safe. She managed to keep her composure until Ben opened the car door, then she broke into tears of thanks and about broke his neck with a hug.

Then it warmed again. As February began to wane, we had two feet of wet snow one day, and the next ended with a light rain. It was a drizzle that wet the trees and their needles thoroughly. Then, about 9:00 that night, the rain changed to snow. The big flakes gathered like cotton on the trees, and by this morning the mountains appeared covered with flocked Christmas trees. Even when one of the big, blue Stellar jays landed clumsily on a branch, most of the snow stayed in place. At 11 o'clock another front gusted by and winnowed the snow from the branches. Within another hour the branches were green-black again.

In the early morning I study a lone aspen by a lodgepole pine. The aspen's bark is silvery greenish-gray on one side, dark charcoal on the other. Tilting slightly toward the east, the tree looks as if it's leaning out to embrace the sunlight. Only four feet away, a small grove of lodgepole pines has branches that still hold dollops of snow a foot across, the last remnants of that two-footer on the forest. The meadows, however, stretch white and satiny and hard-crusted.

Two black Abert's squirrels romp at the edge of the meadow, easily running across the crusty snow. Their ear-like tufts are upright and alert, their tails bushed out and brightly lit by the low-slung light of early morning. They run toward a tree but turn and scamper on into the open, where, at this time yesterday, I'd watched a harrier hawk soaring and tilting a few feet over that snow as it searched for food. The squirrels are unwary, unconcerned (caught up in spring love?), as they chase each other on the snow then disappear around a curve in the meadow, and I don't see them again. But neither do I see the harrier.

March

The snow has begun to melt, soaking into the ground. As I rode by an abandoned homestead this morning, I could still see evidence of the family's inexperience. They must have built it in the summer, without consideration of the winter conditions, for even in this thaw, the cabin was surrounded by snow. The drifts had melted and refrozen into icy patterns — like shattered glass that, for a brief time each day, lay in sun-splashed splendor.

This house must have been abandoned about 75 years ago, judging from its state of decay. When the family built it, they evidently wanted to take advantage of the magnificent scenery. Cut into the brow of a hill, it has a wonderful 250-degree view, and it certainly is shielded from the wind. The problem for the family was that it's also in the wind shadow. I've seen it almost completely covered with snow. Although snow's a good insulator it probably made for some pretty dismal winter days, because the sun shines on the house for only a few hours each day. Just 100 yards in either direction from where it was built they'd have lost a bit of the view but been in sunshine. On the other hand, from the distance of 75 years or more, it's easy to second guess their reasons, and I hope they found happiness.

Life and the world look different through dark glasses. They lose a bit of brightness and sheen, but sometimes there's a better focus. I am wearing glasses on this day of hazy, scattered clouds and warmish winds, alternately squinting and wide-eyed. Plant shadows form and fade, sharp-edged then blurry on soggy snow and damp, gravelly soil. Old flowers still cling, pale brown husks atop ground-hugging greening rosettes — my first sign of spring, which I'd have missed without the darkened glasses.

Weather can change rather quickly here in Wyoming, as a neighbor recently moved here from New Jersey found out. Two weeks ago we had a late-season snowstorm. At first it came gently, with tiny flakes that nestled in the needles of the pines and stacked atop fence posts and added another foot to the already snow-filled meadows. Since the temperature was about 10 degrees, the snow was dry and light, just fine so long as it was calm. But then the wind started up, and the snow began curling from the pines, creating a white curtain of a blizzard that flew horizontally under a clear, blue sky. The wind continued for three days and nights. When it finally stopped, the trees and posts and meadows were swept clear of the new snow, and the old crust had been polished to a satiny sheen. Where did the new snow go? Some of it sublimated (like evaporation, but where the solid snow turned back into water vapor) and moved on to Iowa. Much of the rest had piled into huge drifts, filling little valleys and the north slopes of the hills, and into the neighbor's road. He slogged five miles on snowshoes to ask for help. His phone was out, and he'd buried his "Cat" five feet in the soft snow. It took four men with a front-end loader tractor and our highway-type snow blower all day to dig out the heavy machine. As the men finally got it cleared, one of the cowboys from another ranch, who had come to help, told the neighbor, "Now, y' see that tunnel in th' snow? By t'morra it isn't gonna be there an' if I was yu, I'd git my vehicles t' the highway now." The man did, and by next morning the wind had snow-packed the trench that had been twelve feet deep and 200 feet long. Ah, yes, spring was just around the corner, but still a few blocks away.

Now, two weeks later, spring finally seems to have drifted into our valley. Most of the snow has melted in the pastures and even on the north slopes at the neighbor's road, the snow is beginning to disappear.

This morning I woke to a squadron of Canada geese honking low over the house. When I stepped outside it was about forty degrees, and the redwing blackbirds were trilling from the willows by the river. Later, when I hiked up Mullen Creek, I saw a horned lark and a bluebird at their shared (sort of) perch. The lark would stand atop a rock point, preen a moment then fluff out his feathers, puff out his breast, and sing. After a few bars, the bluebird would dive down on him until the lark flew off and let the bluebird perch, preen, fluff, puff and sing. After a few choruses by the bluebird the lark would dive, take over, and repeat the process. I watched them in this rotation seven times while I was there and they were still at it when I left. At least they were being civil about what must have been a good stage, or perhaps it was a pulpit as each was preaching about his own greatness.

What a beautiful month we are having. While to the south of us Denver experienced one of the driest Februaries on record, we had about four feet of new snow. Now, it's beginning to warm and the river has new leads melting back, getting longer each day. Last week there was only one lead, dark and oily looking against the white snow. A dozen dipper birds squabbled and chirred along its edge, fighting over the right to dive into the frigid water for food. Now they've spread out along a half mile of so, each with its own fishing section (sort of like our summer fly fishermen). Yesterday we had about eight inches of new powdery snow. The last flakes fell as the sky was clearing, and as I looked toward the sun, the air sparkled and danced, like sunlight on water.

Seven white-rumped bighorn sheep graze across a hillside, cautious about me but not frightened. Friends from the Game and Fish Department told me they'd seen seventeen sheep with eight lambs from last year, an excellent birth and survival rate.

As usual the bighorns were on the sunny south-facing slopes, making use of the open ground and napping in the warmth, or nibbling at the tough but high-proteined twigs of a bitterbrush. (One time I tried nibbling a young and tender twig but quickly spat it out. It's an appropriate name.) When I want to animal watch in the winter, these south facing slopes are the best. The snow isn't as deep as on the north, and the wind eddies more quietly, so I often settle onto a rock and enjoy a passing parade of animals.

Today all I saw were the bighorn, grazing quietly as dark cloud shadows raced across their hillside. One minute the sunlight created a snow sheen varying from velvet to polished silver, a reflected light so bright I had to squint through my dark glasses. The next minute I peered through cloud shade.

Earlier in the day it snowed, falling in flakes that were really clumps of snow, about two inches across. Now it's cooled a bit more and the falling snowflakes are normal sized, but dropping straight down in the windless air. So far today, we've had about nine inches

71

of new snow. Out here, without traffic noise or overflying planes. You can *hear* the snow fall. Scientists have recorded the sound of crystal crashing onto crystal at about ten decibels — half the sound of a human whisper — and creating a soft, murmuring hiss. Even the birds are quiet, waiting for the storm to end. They won't be too hungry though because last night, just before the storm, they mobbed the feeders, as if they knew it was coming. Our aspen are covered with such a layer of snow that they are bent like huge, white bows, almost touching the ground. They appear to be damaged and will even stay bent over if you shake off the snow. They're mountain trees though and have evolved for just this kind of day. Over the next thirty hours or so they'll rise again.

Yours from Wyoming, where our spring morning began with the soft crashing of snow.

Spring continues to drift into our valley on bird wings. The Canada geese have been here for a while, flying in honking squadrons low over the river. Now they're settling down to homemaking, and their nests are full of huge, warm eggs. A pair of great horned owls has been nesting for some time now, and we expect to see owlets soon. I stepped outside about 6 a.m. a few days ago and it was already forty degrees. Down by the river the redwing blackbirds trilled and in the marsh up Mullen Creek a snipe "winnowed" (making a whooo-whooo-whooo sound with its wings) as it dove and swooped low over the marsh, declaring its territory. Redwing blackbirds were trilling from the willows by the river. At meadow's edge, a half dozen bluebirds flashed from one fence

post to another, setting up pairs and territories. Below them, in the short, tan stubbles of grass, two killdeer hurried about with their high-pitched whistling calls and fluttered away from me with a broken wing display when I got too close to their nest. They needn't have worried, though, because I couldn't find the nest even when watching from a distance.

But it's springtime in the mountains, and that was yesterday. Today all those birds are huddled in trees, or beside our barns, or like the geese in their nests, gradually covering with snow. Wonderful! More water for the river. Fishing's going to be great!

I was blowing the snow off the golf-course greens today. It's one of those special chores we have to do to protect them from snow mold. Even under the deepest snow there's a tiny series of caverns close to the ground, where the warmth of the earth has melted the snow above it for an inch or less. In this sunny, warm, and moist environment snow mold gets ready to grow, spreading its spores and preparing to attack the very roots of the grass over which it is spread. We remove the snow, let the sun evaporate any moisture on the grass, and treat it with special, nontoxic chemicals.

The dog, Quito, was with me, as usual, and wasn't much interested in the proceedings until I started the snow blower. As the snow arced up and out, he became very excited and began to leap and snap at it. I could hear his whimpering and the clack of his jaws even above the machine. He jumped and bit the snow, performing graceful mid-air pirouettes as he chased the snow plume. If he landed in a soft patch of snow he sank to his chest then climbed back out to continue his fun, and did it for three hours. Thinking of the movie, *Dances with Wolves*, I nicknamed him "Dances with Blizzards." As I write this in the evening, his black hairs are shiny, his white almost dazzling, and he's fast asleep at my feet.

Dawn came bright and filled with thin clouds that sifted through the aspen, through sunlight so thin it couldn't throw a shadow. I was off for an early-morning hike, and at a little meadow alongside Mullen Creek, I paused to rest and watch. About a hundred feet away, a yellow twig willow trembled slightly, and a beautiful red fox walked out into the sagebrush. It was a large male, about eighteen inches high at the shoulder, alert and unafraid. Two inches of new, fluffy snow lay atop two feet of old, crusted snow, and his delicate tracks lay clear in his back path. In the diffused light, his rusty red coat glistened, and his tail almost dragged on the snow, so full it was about half the thickness and as long as his body. Although I moved behind a willow, he knew I was there but ignored me as he hunted. The fox walked slowly across the snow, tipping his head from time to time as he listened for mice. Three times he pounced on the snow, but the crust held, and the little rodents were safe in their sunlit snow caverns. Frustrated, the fox paused, lay down on the snow and looked at me as if to say, "Hmm, what now?" Then he got up, stretched, and loped into a grove of aspen, where the snow was deep and soft. It made harder going, but easier hunting. In only about ten minutes he'd caught and eaten a mouse

and a vole before wading back onto the packed snow and trotting away.

Our snow, which had been thigh deep for a month, has settled to mid calf. The snow sags gently, like an inflatable mattress with a slow leak. In the meadows, the snow looks like soaked cotton, softly rumpled and gently conforming to the land's curves and dips. When you walk across the snow, it makes a hiss-splash sound, and a car driving through throws the slush aside. In minutes the ruts fill with running water, brown yet blue as it reflects our spring sky.

Sage and bitterbrush and buckbrush have been covered for more than a month, with only a few tips showing. Now they thrust their dusty green leaves or driftwood gray branches over the snow, capturing the sun's warmth and creating grassy patches that grow and blend with others. On these sunny days the leaves of the evergreen sage begin to photosynthesize amid the rising scent of damp, warm earth. The old leaves from last year are still attached and working, but the new leaves are beginning to push out. In another month the tired, old leaves will fall, and the new ones will be ready to create food for the sage.

Yesterday I stood at the edge of the North Platte and watched as the ice began to break up into slabs six feet long that floated downriver until they hit a rock or solid ice. Then, the river water, which was a copper brown, began to flow out over the top of the ice and to melt it further. That was at 11 o'clock in the morning, and we thought spring had come. By 1 o'clock the temperature had fallen almost forty degrees, and it was snowing. Today, it's melting

again, but the river is solid, filled with tumbled and broken icebergs.

It's time for spring skiing at the big ski resorts. As a stunt, some people actually ski in bikinis and shorts. Here at the ranch we enjoy our cross-country skiing, because of the wonderful natural things we see, but I haven't yet given in to skiing in shorts. I've lived too long in the mountains with their fickle climate to put myself at risk, but on short ski trips I often wear no jacket, just a short-sleeved shirt. You do have to wear sun screen, or you get burned even "under" your chin because the sun reflects up from the snow. Animals are beginning to stir from their hibernations. Their tracks crisscross the streamside and through the cabin area. I surprised a glossy-coated skunk as he dozed under a bush along Mullen Creek. When I skied by he stood up, stretched, and slowly turned his upraised bottle brush tail toward me. Cautiously, I went on my way, and he curled back up to continue his nap.

Spring's not yet sprung, but it certainly is "cocked." The first calves of the season rest in the sunshine atop scraps of hay. The snow has a different character now, crusty enough to support me as I walk across it in the morning and sodden, grainy by noon. Our hillsides are becoming islands of snow instead of islands of sage. All winter the land has borne the weight of snow. Now it heaves gently, as if taking a deep breath. Everything's in movement, and rocks tumble down the mountains and onto the road. It's a time to watch the hills as well as the road.

This morning was clear and warm, and "mud season" has arrived with sloppy wetness. Our snow continues to melt with a quiet fury, as if it's tired of the mountains and anxious to move on to the ocean. On roads and paths that are on the shaded north sides of about anything, the snow packed and stacked all winter. Now it's gradually trickling into the thawing soil, but there's ice only a few inches down, waterproofing the subsoil. Muddy ruts form on the roads that trap the cars; even those with four-wheel-drive, can't climb out.

It's the Vernal Equinox, the first day of spring, and although it doesn't look springlike, it surely does feel it. Two days ago we had twenty-eight inches of snow (how's that for a not so warm welcome?). Because it was falling at an inch and a half an hour, we scooped it several times that day, to avoid being snowed in. Now the sun's back out and the melting has begun. Every path we shoveled is bare, surrounded by shimmering white so bright that sunglasses barely help. The storm was unusual too in that, after the last flake settled, the air was calm. Normally it would be followed by howling wind that arrives to blast the snow from the trees and make blizzards and dangerous driving. All day yesterday, the sun poured over the pine and spruce trees and heated the dark needles. By noon the branch tips oozed meltwater, which formed thousands of bright icicles that, by 4 o'clock shimmered in the lowering sun. Today the dripping and icicle building continues, but most of it is invisible as the snow sags, settles, and soaks into the meadows, the best kind of moisture for the grasses and the flower seeds we and nature planted.

Next morning: The sun has, of course, been rising earlier, but dawn's still very cold at 7,500 feet above sea level. As I looked to the east, whole forests were frosted, silhouettes with silver edging. One can't look at the big picture too long before they begin to see details, and I found myself enjoying a few this morning. A shower of ice crystals made me turn my attention upward as a flash of bright blue, a Stellar jay flew into an aspen and began probing for cold bugs on the sunny side of a branch. Then a coyote trotted up the meadow and paused to rear up and punch holes in the crusty snow as it hunted for mice. He'd barely disappeared into an aspen grove at the upper end of the meadow when a herd of more than seventy elk loped across it, sinking to their chests as they ran, grunting and squealing. All in all it was a near-perfect morning.

Next day. The spring snows continue, alternating with bright and sunny warm days that give us hope spring really will come. About 2 o'clock there were several loud "booms." Everyone working that day rushed to the bridge over the North Platte to witness the spectacle of the ice breakup. For an hour the river's pea green water surged higher and higher. Two ton chunks of ice climbed onto the river banks with a crackling like giant bonfires as they crushed willows along the shoreline. Then, an ice dam formed that raised the river's level almost ten feet, pushing the ice further onto the flattening bushes. Floe ice chunks as big as Suburbans thumped and piled against the bridge abutments, shaking the whole structure. Then, just as it seemed like the bridge might collapse, the ice dam broke and the center of the river flowed faster as the ice lake drained. In another half hour the river had returned to its banks, leaving walls of ice eight feet high along the shores and filling the willows. Next morning the river was still covered shore to shore with ice slurry and chunks up to six feet across. Branches and tree trunks floated amid the gray porridge. By afternoon the river was open and lapping against the shore ice walls that were still eight feet tall.

Those who have to commute to work and often think of weather as an enemy were praising the beauty of the week we'd had and talking of an early spring. This morning, on a visit to a neighbor, Charlie D., we sipped coffee in his office and looked out at the warming day, wishing it would get cold again. He tipped back in his office chair and laid a scuffed cowboy boot at the edge of his desk and reminded me that May 1 is a good day to start spring. Sunrise and sunset will be far enough apart and the days warm enough that the grass can begin to grow. Melting snow will drip-feed the moisture and give the cattle and horse food a good burst of growth.

But, if the march of spring is too early, all the meltwater will be gone too soon, and with it the irrigation water. So, he fretted a little on this pretty day as we sipped our coffee and watched the clouds on the horizon to the west.

On the other hand, as I said before, it's March, and that was this morning. At about 1 o'clock, a blast of wind rattles the willows and changes the picture. The temperature stumbles downward a few degrees at a time, down thirty-five degrees in an hour. Charlie got his wish.

Birds that have ignored our seed-filled feeders for days, flock back. As the wind increases, they seek shelter under the eaves of buildings and in the edges of willow thickets. Poor things. It was only a few days ago that the redwings and geese had returned.

Two days ago, a bluebird scrabbled for hidden

bugs at the edge of rotting snowdrifts, and we wondered how he could find enough to eat. But nature provides for her children. In the night we saw them, clouds of tiny insects (mayflies?) in the barn lights. They were probably the same ones we saw at the river earlier that day, emerging from the water around every rock we moved.

Occasional blocks of ice calved off from the shore and continued to float down the brown river, stacking up on the outsides of river bends. There's a broad and shallow sweep in the river, just before the canyon narrows. It caught the ice, forming a dam, and the caramelly water flowed atop the ice, softening the ice further before it poured back into the main river again.

I returned to the river in the early evening. The openings were still there, but the water once again dove under the piles of caramel-colored ice. Even in the spring, the river's ice cap was thickening.

As I walked back to the ranch house, it began to snow again, a typical spring type, more slush than crystal, barely whitening the ground but adding .025 inches of valuable moisture to the pastures. The old snow acted like a sponge and soaked up the new snow, holding it to freeze hard as the temperatures fell.

Although, in the shadows, about thirty inches of snow lies on the ground, spring is definitely nearby. Yesterday a single, open stretch of water flowed under the bridge, twenty feet wide. Today it opened to about eighty feet. Four Canada geese floated in an eddy, dipping their long necks into the cold water to feed on the only grass around, where the river flowed up a low bank. They garbled to each other conversationally,

contentedly, as if glad to be back in Wyoming. Some of the south-facing hillsides are already almost bare of snow, and a cluster of twenty deer grazed on the wet grass. Bucks are losing their antlers now, and one grazed in a sage field, carrying a single antler, and it was about to fall. It hung down one side, swinging slowly as he walked and banging against his neck each time he leaned over to nip at a bush.

Animals have been less visible for a while, as they spread out to the opening grasslands. Last week they came back. Our first group was more than 200 antelope, trotting in skeins through the wet snow of the sagebrush flats. Now deer are beginning to return to the open hillsides, and this morning a gang of elk paraded down a short, steep hill to gather, a squealing puffing gang, in a small aspen grove. It's antler-shedding season for them, too, and like the deer I saw a few days ago, one spike elk was a unicorn, with its remaining antler swaying loosely but still upright, like a loose tooth of an eight-year-old child. At river's edge four white male mergansers waded in the shallows and watched me nervously then took off and flew upstream just above the water, their wings almost touching their reflections.

On the mountains, the clouds lift and fall, creating a soft, shadowless light and spritzing raindrops over already soaked pastures. Even now, rain here means snow on the peaks to the northeast and water saved in the snow(bank) for summer.

I involuntarily breathe deeply. Scents pressed into the soil by days on days of high air pressure and the weight of snow are being released as the low moves by. They trickle upward and drift among the matted and tousled grasses. I walk through rising perfumes and wet grasses and musky scents of old, composting manure, moist earth, spring rain, soggy wood and wet horses.

Now the raindrops increase in size and frequency. They are the percussion section of the spring symphony, the sound they create as different in their falling place as a cymbal is from a snare drum. They hiss on the grass, plop-plop in deep puddles, barely blip as a grain of salt diving into a still pool and creating an almost imperceptible ripple. A high, tinny rattle comes from a metal roof and a bass thumping from wood shingles.

Yours from Wyoming, where the animals are out of hiding and the air not only feels and smells good, it sounds good.

We have yet another bright and sunny day, the tenth in a row. It feels (dare I say it?) like spring. A horse-breath-warm breeze started to blow last night. For several hours it moaned around the house, rattling everything that was loose and some things that weren't. Today it's eddying and gusting but still warm.

The river looks nothing like it does in summer. All around us the hills are weeping in the warm sunlight. Snow melts and drips into the silt and gravel and ground-up rock, carrying it to rivulets, then to streams, and, finally, into the river itself, dyeing it the color of thrice-boiled coffee, beginning its journey to the Gulf of Mexico.

Jackrabbits, white all winter, are making their summer change back to gray-brown. Their coats are mottled brown and white the color of plants against the snow, so even in the change they are still invisible.

The hills and the greater part of our valley are tempting and close, but I won't be visiting them today. After almost a week of warmth, the snow has changed to slushy granules. It's still knee deep, but too weak to support even long cross-country skis.

Still, a picnic seems in order, so I slog to a soggy embankment on Mullen Creek. Perched on a flat, cold rock, I munch a ham sandwich and enjoy the purling of the newly opened stream. Its water is coppery silver and already higher on its banks than the last time I saw it in December.

Last night it finally froze enough to firm the snow, and this morning I went for a cross-country ski, or at least started on one. The snow's still deep along the valley floors, about hip level and topped with a thick crust, the result of the cold night before. Quito went with me. Unfortunately, because the wind still blew last night, the crust wasn't consistently thick, and it alternated between soft and hard. I'd be moving along at a fast clip, and suddenly the snow would break, burying my ski tips and pitching me nose first into the snow. Getting up was an interesting challenge. But the one who had it hardest was the dog. At first he ran along the snow top, chasing rabbits and having a marvelous time. Then the warm air began to soften the snow. He discovered it as he was racing after a bunny when the snow fell through, and he literally disappeared. In a moment or two he poked his head out of the snow with his ears down and an embarrassed (really) look on his face. He tried walking on the snow again and fell through again. After that he stayed in my ski tracks, and we both watched the rabbits dancing on the snow.

Our day has been cold and clear but windy. Now, as the sun slips behind Bighorn Ridge, it throws its light among long, pale gray cloud shadows. When the snow blows into the shadows it becomes invisible, but a gust traveling from shadow to light carries "electric snow," it seems, for each flake catches the sunlight and flashes off-on-off-shade-light-shade, as if flickering.

The Platte is dark, muddy green and meandering through the ice as if it were flowing through an ancient valley floor. It gradually spreads over the surface of the entire river and further softens it. Bits of slush float on the fast current, then gather with a pair of Canada geese and four mergansers in an eddy. Scattered across the river, ice shards poke four feet and more into the air, thin blades that tilt slightly downstream and twist slowly in the fast current. All winter the river hid silently. Now it gurgles and rejoices in its freedom, running here and there, like a child just released for spring vacation. Those mergansers have left the eddy now and are floating downstream, blackwater rafting.

At the edge of the river, tree branches wave like thousands of arms in a warm wind. Snowmelt drips from branches and rocks. In the daily freezing and thawing cycle, the soil becomes damp and friable. Fissures in the cliff gradually open, and one rock breaks loose, rolling with a great explosive clatter over rocks and through trees, shattering a twenty-inch-thick giant before it splashes into the river.

The road, too, is seeing sunlight again, and the water from melting snow leaves it greasy and rutty. Trucks slide down the ruts like kids' cars at an amusement park, except that mud splashes forward and to the side. Today the sky and ground are the same color, and it's hard to see where they meet. On some of the south-facing hills, melting snow reveals rocks and grass, which draw a skyline. In sage meadows the deer gather in bands of five to twenty, generally in like-age groups. The yearlings are skittish as they graze. In the sunlight they appear grateful to walk without punching holes through the snow. At night the snow refreezes into a thick crust that breaks easily and jabs their legs, scraping from hoof to thigh with each step.

But that crust is a morning problem. By mid-morning, tufts of grass and half-buried sage wave in a warm breeze, and sunlight envelopes me. But change is coming. Here it's rather quiet, but across the valley the bright white of the snow is dissolving in a pale shadow as it sweeps over the hillside. I pull out my binoculars and watch its progress. Judging from its sweep over fence posts, sixteen feet apart, it's moving at about twenty-five miles per hour.

A golden eagle dives along the edge of the shadow, its wings folded back in a delta shape. It almost brushes the sage tops as it spreads its wings and brakes to land atop the carcass of a steer. What amazing vision. All I saw through my binoculars was a low mound. From farther away, the eagle recognized it as food. Now another eagle splashes down in the snow, and several ravens arrive to squabble over the prize. The eagles are four times the size of the ravens but the black scavengers aren't intimidated. They even leap in to snatch the food bits right from the eagles' beaks.

Each night it freezes again, and the moistened

topsoil begins to refreeze into "night flowers." The rounded clumps of ice crystals grow slowly, sucking moisture from the soil around them and pushing soil upward, even tearing out roots and lifting plants from the soil. Sometimes they form cracks, and frozen seeds drop into the cracks where they'll continue to be mixed and moistened until that series of nights when the temperature stays warm enough for them to sprout. Another one of nature's planting processes.

Late March

All winter, whenever we start to load the hay truck, the horses began to nicker and prance with anticipation. Now, as the snow melts and the grass thickens, the horses almost ignore us when we come to feed them. As another layer of heavy, wet snow builds over the grass, however, the horses are very interested in the hay truck. They hear it start up and, from half a mile away, come running, just like in winter. We throw the hay out a little at a time, and you can almost see their anxious mouths watering at the thought of that "juicy" hay as they trot along behind the truck. The boss horses generally stop to eat first. Those at the end of the kick line always have to trot along the half mile or more that it takes to put out the ton and a half of hay. Each morning the same horses, the ones at the lower end of the kick line, are forced to trot along to the end of the hay windrows before others will let them eat. We save the best bales for them. In about twenty minutes everyone's eating, and if the wind is right you can hear the soft crunching for another half mile.

To see, really see, animals in the wild, one must practice and be patient. Humans are noisy as we clump our way through the woods or along the streams, and an invisible stampede takes place as the animals dive for cover. If you're patient and sit quietly for half an hour or more, not moving, then things begin to return to normal. Practice is necessary because you first must know what to look for — a flip of a tail, a light spot on a dark hillside, movement that's different from the kind created by the wind. When a bird lands on a branch, the leaves flick in a way that's very different from the riffling motion of a branch in the wind. As the bird pokes under the leaves in search of insects, it shakes the tree further and in a very characteristic way. Viewing the animals doesn't require super eyesight, either. I have astigmatism, but because I know what I'm searching for, I can spot a deer or two on a hillside a half mile away. And that's what I'm doing today, practicing wildlife watching and patience.

April

A few years ago, Justin and I went for a late-night cross-country ski. It was about five below zero, but the moon was almost full and very bright, so we couldn't resist. The day before had been warm, and the snow refroze with a four-inch crust, making it easy to glide atop the snow. As we headed toward the river, we saw a small cloud over it and decided to investigate. It turned out to be a small lead, where the water had opened up and begun to flow over the river snow. Being warmer than the air, it created a pocket of fog that slowly drifted down-river. It was well past midnight when we returned home.

In our sunny horse meadow the snow is gone, and early this morning, for the first time this year, I walked it on grass. All winter, northern pocket gophers busied themselves digging snow tunnels and packing them with soil from their earth tunnels. The snowdrifts have melted now, and eskers, or "gopher garlands," of solid soil lay like two-inch hawser ropes, meandering several yards atop the greening grass. New mounds of rumpled, soft soil, almost like potting soil, were dumped at tunnel ends. Discreet soil plugs hid the true entrances.

Then, at one of the mounds about thirty feet away, I saw a movement and swung my binoculars to focus on it just as a pale brown pocket gopher peeked cautiously out. Their lips meet behind the huge incisors, so they can carry dirt and rocks without getting them in their mouths, and it looked all yellow-orange, bucked tooth. Because its life is spent mostly underground its eyes are tiny, myopic-looking spots, its ears so tiny it appears earless. Not seeing me, and

feeling safe, it rustled its way into the grass, poking seeds and dried blossoms into its hair-lined cheek pouches and getting more "jowly." When the cheeks were so full it looked like they would burst, it turned back to the hole, snatching a bedraggled bistort on its way. Just as it slid into the hole, I was distracted by the "screeing" of a red-tailed hawk, and when I looked back at the hole it was plugged again. I've seen the marks of pocket gophers on the landscape for twenty years, but this was my first actual sighting.
(Late afternoon of the same day)

It's snowing again, huge soggy flakes falling through air barely below freezing. The snow-clumps fall on dark gravel roads, melt, and puddle into glistening brown pools. They fall on wet grass and press it down and onto brittle, brown husks of thistle heads, creating white berets that stick, even in the light breeze, which blows the snow at a twenty-degree angle.

An hour ago it was drizzling, and now the half-melted, or half-frozen, snow gathers around pines and spruce, leaving dark ovals of bare ground near the trunk. Chickadees and juncos perch in this dry haven, fluffed and hunched to keep warm. The air is hazy as I walk quietly through the forest, and snow gathers on my hair and shoulders then quickly melts to bright water droplets on my wool coat.

Earlier I threw out some popcorn and bread left from last night, and within minutes a noisy band of crows gathered to clean it up. Not far from them a robin lifted its wet tail feathers above the snow and ran from one bare batch to another, then tipped and stabbed and tugged at worms.

This morning I looked out my office window and

was watching a miniature rabbit, a type called a Nuttall's cottontail. It was quietly nibbling the greening grass on our lawn then suddenly tensed and leaned forward to stare in that wide-eyed look of its kind. Two robins were disputing a territory that included a big grove of blue spruce that was filled with possible nest sites. I've seen robins fighting before but this was a first-class brawl. Red breasts flashed in the morning sun, and their black heads reminded me of helmeted bird gladiators. Time after time, they flew into the air a foot or two, spinning and twisting, heads back defensively and "bapping" each other with their wing feathers. They were mostly silent, but one or the other did squeak occasionally as a downy feather was torn out and floated to the grass. Thirty seconds, forty-five seconds, a minute, and they still fought. Suddenly, one stopped and turned slightly away, his beak open as he panted. Then, he walked quickly away. Mr. winner pursued him at a run until the loser took off then flew to what was, for this moment anyhow, his tree. The rabbit had watched the fight too and now looked at me as if to say, "Whoa. Wasn't that a fight now?" Then he hopped into the tall grass, pausing to look both ways on a trail before crossing, and disappeared.

The river has been ice-free but still low in its banks. Now, as the mountain snows melt and fill the streams, the river rises in the first flush of spring runoff. It turns the color of coffee with just a tad of cream. It's already flowing over rocks normally four inches above water, creating brownish whitecaps. In the canyon there's a hissing roar, like the sound of a distant jet. As the soil on the riverbanks softens, a stream-side boulder collapses from its perch and splash-thocks into the water.

Both banks of the river wear bright-gold sashes, courtesy of the yellow-twig willows, which must be juicy, judging from the bighorns and troupes of deer I've seen browsing on the tender tips. Tender they may be, but I tasted one, and they're as bitter as lemon rind. Ah, well, as Aesop said, "One man's meat is another man's poison."

The hillsides are open now, with only a few deep ravines and shaded areas holding dirt and pine-needle-covered snow mounds. Bighorns are down in our meadows. Although many of the hills show big patches of green, where the new grass has begun to sprout, the bighorns seem to be malnourished. They graze in the fertile meadows, wolfing down the greening grass. Last week we put out new mineral and salt blocks. The mineral is already one-third gone, and they've spent the last three days lounging near them, getting up several times during the day to gnaw at the pinkish blocks, then returning to loaf or revisit the meadow.

Several four-year-old rams are with the group, and two black-and-white magpies perch on the rumps of the grazing bighorns, pecking lightly at parasites hidden under the scruffy coats of the sheep. Each ram lies on his own rock, above the ewes, the dominant fellow on the highest rock.

Small towns have some great ways to raise money,

and, with so few people to participate (we only have about 1,000 in our area), the funds-seekers have to be creative, even in some of the more mundane kinds of events. Our town has a casino night each year, generally put on by the local chamber of commerce, whose members put up the prizes. Most of the events are standard — card games, ring tosses, dart and balloon boards, etc. But the most popular lately has been the "Chicken S**t." (Actually, the name was recently changed to Chicken Bingo, to give it better acceptance.). Chickens, as you may or may not know, poop a lot. Two or three chickens are put into a small cage and set beside a board with numbers and squares painted on it. Around the circumference of the square is a low chicken wire fence. You place your bet on a certain number and, when all the squares are filled, one of the chickens is set onto the board. If the bird poops on your square, you're the winner. It's uproarious fun.

For the past week it was a return to winter. Even three days ago it was snowing and the temperature hung at minus-one! And it's April! Unfair, I'd say.

Late one afternoon, Margie was driving to get Justin at the bus stop, when a golden eagle swooped onto a huge jackrabbit that was crossing the gravel road. The impact killed the rabbit immediately, but because it was so large, the eagle couldn't get into the air fully. Only two feet above the ground, the eagle struggled to rise, and the dead rabbit bounced along, putting a little cloud of dust up the road for a hundred yards, until the bird looked over its wing and saw the car. Startled, it dropped the carcass, banked sharply, and flew to a tree where it perched and glared at the car. When Margie and Justin returned twenty minutes later, the eagle and rabbit were both in the tree, and fur drifted on the breeze as the eagle plucked then fed.

We have a number of Navajo rugs here at the ranch. Some of them date back to the early 1900s. A part of our heritage, they have lain on the floor of our community room for the past sixty years. After having them cleaned and restored, we hung them for display and to protect them.

I was frankly surprised when people began noticing them more, not less. Like the guests, I find myself contemplating them more. In some ways it's almost a mystical experience. One often feels surrounded by the personalities of the Navajo who wove them. Each rug is different, an expression of its weaver. I began to imagine them as filled with smiles.

First there is the weaver at work among her sheep, tending them, trimming the wool, cleaning, carding, and spinning it into yarn. She smiles to herself as she recognizes the wool, colored differently from one or the other of her favorite sheep.

Then she is at the loom, sitting cross-legged on a sheepskin-cushioned rug. Children play around her, running, teasing each other, distracting her. More than one smile goes into the rug from their antics. She settles down into the rhythm of the weaving, tapping the yarn down, selecting the yarn she colored from various desert plants, slowly developing the patterns on the rug that are already alive in her imagination.

Finally, she removes the rug from the loom, shakes

it, runs her hand over the oily prickliness of the raw wool, lets the sunshine play over the rich colors, and she smiles with satisfaction.

I wonder who she was. What was she like? She's gone now, but a piece of her remains, a part of our tradition.

Two Canada geese were at the river this morning. A pair, they were playing with the river. I heard them honking and watched as they flew upriver, just above the water and around a bend. A while later I saw them again, floating with the current and "brown-water" rafting downstream. Their calls were different, almost like laughter, as they enjoyed their run toward the bridge half a mile downstream, then took wing to fly upstream and float down again. I don't know how long they did it, but I watched them make six trips this afternoon.

Every day there are more springtime firsts. This morning we awoke at 3 o'clock to a racket of bird song as each species tried to outdo the others in singing their territorial boundaries. The kestrels are back and over short-grass meadows, searching for mice. The geese, instead of swimming and flying up and down the river, have become serious and are building nests, laying eggs. At the river's edge the soft clay is covered with holes, punched by the sharp hooves of does and yearling fawns. Our first marmot of the season sprawled at the Howdy Gate, dozing on a sun-soaked rock. After napping almost six months without eating, his grizzled brown coat flapped like the ears of a

spaniel when he saw us and ran for cover. It was foggy last night, and the pussy willows emitted a spring scent, or was it that the dew — collected on the pussies — had drifted all day over damp soil and through moist sage, gathering their scent? Whatever, it means that summer can't be too far behind.

It's snowing again, a wonderful, heavy spring storm that's laying down a zillion flakes at a time and piling up at about an inch an hour. Outside it seems calm, but looking across the open meadows, the snow is falling at a 45-degree angle, and forests 100 yards away have disappeared. Two blue spruce trees, each well over sixty feet tall, are collecting hundreds of pounds of snow on their branches, slowing the wind, and protecting a mixed flock of Oregon and dark-eyed juncos. As they hop about in the snow, they seem quite nervous, almost frantic, in their search for seed. They're continually chasing each other from the feeder, and three levels of activity have developed. Junco featherballs, on the branches, fluff and hunch over miserably, watching the eaters below. At the feeder itself, four or five juncos each work their own areas. There's a good supply of white millet on the trough, but it's buried two inches down. To get to it the birds hop forward with both feet; then, as they hit the snow, they leap back, scratching trenches that eventually reach seed. If another bird tries to hop in, the digger chases it away. Meanwhile, on the ground, a dozen have gathered to pick up any seeds that splatter over the side of the feeder. They seem to be doing equally well with less effort.

A mountain springtime is:

Snow atop green grass in damp pastures.

Tiny snowflakes drifting gently down one minute and huge, wet flakes blowing horizontally the next, silvering the hillsides and flocking the sage and spruce.

Golden twigs on the willows and swelling bud-tips turning to soft, velvety pussies.

Clear, sunburn days followed by cloudy, freezing and wind-burning days.

Rain and snows that arrive to slicken the roads whenever we drive out in the hay truck, creating deepening ruts in the bentonite clay.

Birds creating and defending territories against intruders, real and imagined. Some see enemies everywhere. Like the robins that fly at windows and hubcaps, fighting their reflection because they think it's an intruder in their territory. Or the Harris hawk that flies into a picture window, attacking its own attacking image, and sits on the lawn, dazed, for half an hour before flying off to challenge another reflection.

Birds that sing in the sun and shiver and sing in the snow, occasionally shaking the gathering snow-mantle from their bodies and fluffing against the cold.

Shaded lavender and yellow pasque flowers wearing hairy coats against the cold as they rise in shadowy spruce groves and at the feet of oozing snowdrifts.

Deer and horses and antelope and bighorn sheep, losing their winter coats in untidy mats that catch on rabbitbrush or drift on the breezes until birds gather the bits for their nests.

The weather made a dramatic change today, and it came suddenly. At mid-morning the sky was clear and branches hung unmoving in the still air, but it just *felt* different. Six deer grazed nervously in the sagebrush near Overlook Trail. They normally ignore us or watch without concern. When they saw me today, however, they leaped away and "pronked" uphill, thumping over the sage into a juniper grove. About noon the horses bunched together in nervous groups, and the leaders began prancing about the meadow, their heads and tails held high. In minutes all 100-plus were running and bucking through the new grass, not in fear but, it seemed, in celebration. I watched the mountains behind the ranch disappear in a fast-moving cloud bank that poured over the tops of the hills and into our valley. With the clouds came the wind that tossed the dry grasses, and a short-winged hawk that hunted through the fog, so low its wings almost brushed the sage. Within minutes the sky was clear again, the branches hung unmoving, and the horses returned to grazing quietly. It's springtime in the Rockies.

Hummingbirds arrived today, wing-trilling overhead. Later, as I worked with a young colt at the corral, one flew in to check out my red bandanna, thinking it was a flower. Now I'm already thinking about summer and the special joys the hummers bring.

Already the little birds dart and dash through the forest edges, dancing in the pools of sun. In that light, their colors are bright neon; in the shadows, muddy. This afternoon, a hummer bathed in a little puddle less than a pencil thickness deep. I've never seen it but I've been told they sometimes even use the water on a rain-soaked leaf.

It won't be long before these broadtailed hummers will perform their mating rituals, the male making his dramatic vertical climbs of 100 feet and more then power-diving toward the perching female. Normally the wing beats are about seventy-five per second, but in one forty- to fifty-foot dive they can reach 200. A special notched primary at the tips of his wings makes a whistling "syrrr" as he flies. Sometimes he flies up and down several times then buzzes close to the female. If she likes him, she'll fly up to join him, and they perform several joint flight maneuvers, like jets in precision flying up and down. Most birds have power only on the downstroke. Hummers power up *and* down. That's part of the reason they can fly as they do, even upside down.

It's a good thing that they're so mobile. Each day they must eat almost half their body weight in sugars and tiny insects. That's right, insects. They spend most of their day darting from flower to flower and insect swarm to insect swarm. Right now they have only the bugs; there are few flowers yet. When it comes time to nest, she (the male doesn't help with the nesting or rearing at all) will hide her tiny nest on a branch and camouflage it with a second, leafy branch for shade. The eggs are the size of a pea. When they hatch, they are *hungry*, and she'll have to feed them as many as three times each hour. Right now she's enjoying her freedom.

Margie and I were in St. Louis this past weekend. But what a shock! Their lilacs were blooming; ours won't begin to bloom until the middle of June. The wheat fields across Kansas are bright green and ripply in the wind; our grass just got buried under another snow-and-wind storm. I'm not complaining though; we need the moisture. Trees actually had leaves on them back east; our cottonwoods will get their leaves the last part of May or perhaps even early June. There are benefits to late springs though. While our midwestern friends are sweltering in ninety percent humidity and ninety-degree heat this summer, we'll enjoy twenty percent humidity, and temperatures in the upper seventies.

May

May Day. People really think of spring on this day, and of May poles, May baskets, and flower garlands. Wonderful, pagan rituals.

But here in Wyoming the cowboys are turning on the irrigation ditches despite the fact that mud season is still with us. Our roads are rutted to about twelve inches deep. If the road is sloped to the side, the ruts give you a sense of security and keep you out of the borrow ditch as you bounce from side to side, up or down the road. As the ruts deepen though, and you get more concerned about getting high centered, you try to stay out of the ruts, straddling them.

It's pairing-off time. Ravens and crows, dark shadows, cut low over the tan, snow-matted grass. Geese are still on their nests, which are scattered more or less equidistant, along the edges of the river. Yellow-twig willows are bright, but still leafless, by a pond where two pairs of wood ducks take sudden flight. I wonder if the "woodies" will stay this year or just pass through again. (They didn't stay.)

In the wetlands, the air is filled with the sweet willow scent, movement, and the sounds of birds. Each species joins the performance but creates its own music, singing without consulting the others. It's as if the violins played one song, the horns another, and the flutes and drums followed their own plan. Yet the cacophony of bird song, to me, presents a wonderful symphonic presence. Each morning it's the same, yet different, as new singers join and others drop off.

As I rode out today, to open our irrigation system for the summer, I spent some time at one of the local beaver ponds. When I stopped and tied my horse to a bush, all was silent; but I continued toward the stream and sat by the dam, not moving. As I waited for the animals to accept me, I considered the pond.

The water pouring into the pond was tea-brown, heavy with organic matter flushed from the hillsides. Bits of tan organic foam drifted into the center of the pond, circling gently. Some of the foam surrounded tufts of grass at the dam's top, and some gathered below the dam, as the water poured through willows and rocks. Then it was whipped into more bubble clumps, which gradually broke apart and flowed in a dozen tapering lines from each spillway. The lines slowly flowed downstream until they were broken apart on the rocks.

After about half an hour, I began to be accepted. A brown marmot crept cautiously to the pond's edge for a quick drink before it darted back into the rocks. A blue heron settled down and fished, posed like a gray statue at the edge of the dam. He only moved in a slight flinch when a little kestrel flew low over him and into a break in the willows. Yellow warblers began to twitter in the willows, and a pair of golden-mantled ground squirrels chased each other through the damp, rotting aspen leaves. The beavers stayed inside their lodge. I had to continue upstream, to open the irrigation ditch. Coffee break over.

We're blessed to have a major river and four major streams flowing across the ranch. Stream-side, riparian, land is rare here and important. These lands make up less than three percent of Wyoming but support the majority of our wildlife and domestic animals. Even most towns are found along the streams. The ranch, too, is in one of these riparian zones, at the bottom of a broad, open valley, on the Mullen Creek/Nash Fork Shear Zone to be exact. Some of our neighbors' wells are three hundred feet deep, but since we're at the low end of the valley, our three wells are twenty-nine, fifty-two, and thirty-two feet deep respectively.

Willow and alder thickets provide shelter and food for

animals (deer, yellow warblers, and snipes, to name a few). They slow the water and let it soak into the ground, raising the water table so it can trickle out later, when the stream level drops, assuring water all summer.

We have several irrigated pastures with some water rights to the 1870s. Water rights were given out beginning back then, and an irrigation ditch has a specific date attached to it. If the water is scarce, an 1870 water-right-holder can continue to soak his pastures while an 1871 right-holder must turn off his ditch.

Like our neighbors, we raise cattle. Cattle are part of the West, but they do create problems. They like to spend their days near the stream, where grass is greenest and the shaded glades keep them from getting too hot.

Ten years ago, our stream looked like this:

Deep hoof prints from cattle are impressed all round the streams and ponds. What they don't eat they often damage as they lie in the sunshine, or crush as they walk the meadows. They poop on fishing trails and trample banks, breaking them down and destroying fish hiding places. The manure falls, or is washed into the still water of ponds and the fast water of the stream, feeding the spirogyra and other algae that, by midsummer, thicken the water. It does make good habitat for black diving beetles and water striders and fresh water shrimp, but it's just too much of a semi-good thing.

At one pond a diving beetle perched atop an alga island, with the spent body of a mayfly in its jaws, and fed on it until my shadow passed over. Then the beetle startled and ran, abandoning the mayfly. A cluster of eight blue darners drifted on another small, bubbly island of pond scum. One flew off to investigate a moth, struggling upside down on a third island of greenish slime. Then a garter snake poked its head onto the surface. It dove when it spotted me but

appeared again several feet away. It surfaced and swam atop the water with the same motion it would use on land, disappearing in a rush mat.

As the cattle prowled along the riparian zone, their hooves stirred the silt into the stream and pressed down the banks. The stream bed gradually widened and got more shallow as it filled with mud. Vegetation along stream banks grew old because the new growth was eaten by the cattle. After several decades, the willows no longer overhung the stream to provide shade or protection for the fish. A few stalks of yellow-flowered mullein — lovers of trammeled soil — remained standing on their woolly stalks beside others, torn and beaten by the cattle. Wild roses clung to the banks, but neither they nor the mullein gave shade for the fish.

Worse, the water table had dropped, and plants that once grew a hundred feet from the stream now clustered only fifty feet from it, as the sagebrush pressed toward the water. The few rains that came flowed across the bare ground, heated the water before it poured into the stream. Mid-July water temperatures rose close to the deadly seventy-three degrees at which trout would die. Even at seventy degrees, the water held less oxygen, and algae bloomed.

We wanted to repair the damage, but first we needed to know the fish population. The Wyoming Game and Fish Department sent out a crew to do a fish census. It revealed that a typical section held five fish, ten inches long — but there should have been dozens. Most of the fish were "stockers," farm-raised fish, that don't take care of themselves well; some don't even know what to eat except trout pellets.

So the fish population was low, and there was little spawning. The fish lived as in suburbs, single-fish dwellings

— no room for more. We needed to make the habitat more agreeable, protect the banks, and build trout "condos."

Of course, the Army Corps of Engineers had to review our plan and give their approval. That plan included making the work as natural as possible, to use rocks instead of wire or concrete and, where machinery was necessary, to use a special backhoe with wide tracks. The tracks would spread the weight of the machine out, so it wouldn't damage the stream or meadows. After months of paperwork, they approved, and we began.

The first thing we did was to fence off the entire stream. Electric fences carrying 1,200 volts of solar power kept the cattle from the stream. Then we put in rock dams that created riffles and plunge pools, where the trout could hide.

To keep them from moving in the current, the boulders for the dams weighed one to two tons and were placed in the creek in upstream sweeping V's. The keystone rocks locked the dam more tightly when the stream flowed high, created quiet pools above and bubble-covered plunge pools four to five feet deep below, where the fish could hide and watch for floating food. The dams weren't barriers, so the fish could migrate upstream in their spawning travels and downstream when the water level dropped in the fall.

Next, we opened up an oxbow, an abandoned stream bed, so we could flood new wetlands. Beavers moved into the oxbow and created ponds that raised the water table and helped create more wetland. Soon fifteen acres were flooded from one to three feet deep. Where only the year before there had been only a couple of dozen waterfowl, now hundreds began to stop on their migrations. Scores of pairs stayed on to raise their young, and soon the ponds were busy. Two and three green-headed mallard males at a time courted each brown female; Canada geese laid out huge nests atop hummocks; delicate green-wing teal cruised the shallows;

long-legged avocets probed the mud with their long, up-curved bills; and phalaropes swam in tight circles, creating vortexes that floated food to the surface where the birds could stab it with their needle-like bills. All these stayed on to raise their young. Each morning the air was filled with calls and the whistle of bird wings.

Without the cattle eating them, the willows began to regenerate and spread as the water level rose and soaked back into the soil, raising the water table. The stream banks, now protected by the willow roots, created little caves for the fish to hide in. Even the stream bed changed. It narrowed and deepened as the silt was carried downstream and no more arrived. Soon the clean rocks were covered with little dark spots, the millions of caddis, mayflies, and stoneflies that would provide food for the fish. Each year we began to see more fingerlings and fry as both rainbows and browns began to spawn. Families of mink began to move in to raise their young and entrance the fisherfolk.

Finally, after five years of work, there was a follow-up fish census. Where there had been five fish there were 97. The trout condos were sold out, and they were in good neighborhoods.

This past week I spent three days walking along Big Creek and the North Platte River. Although there was a serious purpose (we're producing a fishing map of the two waterways) it turned out to be as much a relaxed day as it was work. Wildlife of various types delighted me every few hundred feet, and a four-mile walk took about five hours. The beavers have created several nice ponds, and I found a youngster working in the daylight. It ignored me for about ten minutes, then when it saw me, it dove with a loud, cracking tail-whap. Wild cats are quite rare, and one seldom sees them; but on this day I found the clawless prints of both a cougar and a bobcat. Most of the deer and elk have shed their antlers, and I found several nice racks, polished white at the tips and as yet unchewed by mice. I left them so they could be gnawed on, giving the small animals a good source of their minerals.

A horse trader from Cody, Wyoming, had brought about 150 "dude horses" to town. Cody — as a center for the guest ranch industry — was a good market, and he expected a good crowd. The trader played it big, renting and closing off the street beside the Irma, Buffalo Bill's old hotel. We went to buy some horses.

Sale day was not springlike. By dawn, snow began to fall straight down, almost like rain in still air. The flakes (really clumps of flakes) were so huge they soaked our hat brims and melted to drip down the backs of the crowded buyers. The horses stood in porta-pens, in growing puddles rimmed with brown snow, their heads down, quivering. Most paid no attention to the crowd; they were in their own zone of misery.

There was tack, too, but the crowd was there to buy cheap horses, not halters and saddles, and the auctioneer struggled. Helpers prowled the crowd as the man held up one piece after another, selling it for pennies on the dollar.

Buyers in yellow slickers moved among the pens — squinting at the stock, stomping their feet to keep warm — and talked together about the merits of each horse. Occasionally, one would take a horse by the lip and open its mouth looking intently at its teeth to determine its age. One man in a greasy Stetson paced, unconcerned with the horses' temperaments, looking only at their weight. "The Killer" bought horses for dog

food or the European market, and his price this day would be low.

As each horse was taken to the auctioneer, he was saddled and bridled, the trader told about the guarantee he would give, the particular horse's special merits. Then he jumped on to show off the horse and its training. We tensed as the first horse we planned to buy entered the circle. It was a nice bay with four perfect white socks. We were ready to bid when the trader started to bridle it, or rather tried to. The horse reared back, almost falling into the crowd. It spun and pulled the man slightly off the ground. In the end he took it back to its pen with no bids except from the man with the greasy Stetson.

The auction droned on as cowboys moved to the porch of the hotel, away from the snow and closer to the cups of free coffee. A few feet away, cars and trucks passed by, their tires hissing through the water on the wet pavement.

As the day progressed, the owner continued to show horses in the little pen. He had gathered a nice group of horses, but the prices were low, and he grew more grim as the day went on. We bought a pretty fourteen-year-old mare for $150 and named her Irma, for the hotel where we'd bought her. The next day was bright and sunny. Who can figure?

It's May 9, and we're snowed into the ranch. Yesterday the storm began as the wind picked up. At bedtime we had a foot of snow on the ground, and by noon today we had two. Because the snow was so heavy, power lines and trees collapsed, and we lost electricity at ten in the morning (and finally got it back at about 6 in the evening). Now the wind has picked up, and drifts are forming. It looks like February.

I'd expected both a contractor to arrive. A couple from the ranch, had gone to Denver to pick up the wife's mother for a visit, to see their new granddaughter. They were late, and about 3 o'clock I started for the gate to check on them. The going was hard, but as usual the Suburban waded through easily. About six miles from the ranch, and still two from the highway, I began to climb in elevation. The snow began in earnest; the drifts increased in depth and compaction. Still I continued because I couldn't see anything beyond an eighth of a mile and was concerned they might be stuck somewhere out there in the fogginess. As I approached the last curve before starting downhill to the highway, I felt the car turning more sluggish and gunned it. Suddenly an "iceberg" leaped up, curling from the front of the car where it had been pushed, and as it rose to six feet, the car stalled.

No gear was of any use. The wet snow was polished by the spinning tires, and when I tried to get out of the car the door wouldn't open. Rolling down the window I discovered the reason; I was mired in about two feet of snow and well packed in place. So I crawled out the window. Even though I was less than a half mile from the highway and should have been able to see something, I could only make out gray shadows in the snow-filled air. None of them looked like cars or people, so I decided to walk the 3.5 miles to the gatehouse, where there's a phone, and to call the main ranch for help.

I wore a cap, but because of the blowing snow I needed more protection, so used a rug from the floor to wrap my head and neck and keep the snow from filling my coat collar. When I started walking, I discovered it really wasn't too cold, just windy, and although the walk was slippery and difficult in the drifts, I found myself enjoying it. A few hundred yards from the gate house, Laine and two ranch hands picked me up and we drove his chained-up pickup to retrieve the Suburban. Even with the winch it took us half an hour.

On the way back, we stopped at the gate house to call the ranch and were told that a similar drama had been playing on the other side of the ridge, only a few hundred yards away from where we'd dug the car out yet totally invisible to us. The contractor had a cellular phone that worked and he'd called to report that he and our friends from the ranch were all stuck. We got the road grader and started back to help dig them out. By 7:30 that night we were all headed home, exhausted by our wintry spring ordeal, when we saw something that made the day worthwhile.

A hundred yards from us, at the base of a long, tapering cliff by the river, a close-packed gang of 65 elk were starting up the steep hill. They had pushed themselves together like a crowd of humans leaving a football stadium and looked like one living organism. They had to move as a group. The leaders watched us only a moment and started up the sixty-degree slope, almost pulling the others along, a brown river flowing uphill. Three stragglers, probably older or weaker, couldn't make it and turned back toward us. One tried to jump a wire fence and for a moment was tangled. We watched, transfixed and horrified, as it struggled and clumps of hair gathered on the snow. Finally it broke free and, obviously cut, struggled up a more gradual slope. When the other two stragglers joined her, they made graceful and successful leaps over the fence but were still obviously decrepit individuals. In moments all were gone as they continued to higher and more windswept slopes.

Summer visitors are beginning to return to Wyoming, now that winter's about gone. Most of them are wonderful and fun to have share our valley; but some cause problems through their thoughtlessness. One of our neighbors recently bought an old house that had been abandoned for some twenty years. It's mostly intact, but vandals were a continual problem, as they poked around the old place they considered abandoned and walked away with a few souvenirs. My friend put up a no-trespassing sign, which was ignored. The final straw came when someone not only ignored the sign but crawled through a window and made off with a fancy cap from the old bannister, which he'd planned to restore. This week my friend solved his problem.

I drove by the house late one afternoon and saw a person on the porch, settled into a chair with a gun on his lap. Hmm, I thought. That might work, but it seems a bit extreme. When I drove by later in the day, he was still there, and that night and a couple of days later. This morning I ran into my friend in town and asked him, "Are you *sleeping* on the porch?" Practically doubled over with laughter he finally gasped, "It's a dummy! A dummy with arms that flap in the wind and with an old broom laid across its lap." Since it's been on duty, there have been no trespassers.

It won't be long before our chef, Kent, will be here, and we can enjoy his wonderful cooking. Before he arrives, however, about a dozen of us eat at our house, taking turns cooking. We all look forward to his arrival and being able to have a meal prepared by someone else, especially as our muscles are still getting used to flexing after the long winter. One night after dinner, we were looking at a book that is filled with frontier recipes. There was coon pie, with no meat, but flour and water and coon oil rolled into fritters and fried in coon fat. And steak pudding, which is flour and fine-shredded tallow mixed with water and rolled into a paste, filled with seasoned mutton or beef and perhaps a chopped onion. After spooning the paste into a cloth bag, it was put into an iron pot, boiled three hours and served hot.

If coffee was running low, the frontier folk made a good(?) substitute with bran and molasses: four quarts bran and one-half tablespoon molasses mixed thoroughly, then browned in a slow oven and stirred every three minutes until dark and rich like real coffee.

A lovely spring day. It's sixty-seven degrees, and the blue sky is filled with scattered puff-clouds. Tan organic foam floats lightly in river eddies, like sailing vessels adrift at full sail. On low sand bars the thin branches of red-twig dogwood jab above the water, and the mini forest catches debris that will later settle, both feeding the willows and growing the sand bar.

A goose steps from the bar into the dark water, dips and fills her beak, then tips her head back to let the water flow down her throat. Twice more, then she wades into the fast water and paddles around to face the shore. Her gander appears and, without drinking, joins her in the water. They paddle-float gently downstream to another, older bar, and the gander waddles out to begin picking at the grass. The goose pauses at the shore, almost chest deep in the water, then turns toward the river to call with a series of "hah-hinks" that echo across the river for ten minutes.

Crows caw, a hermit thrush trills its wonderful, echoing song, robins declare their territory with a medley of songs, a yellow warbler rustles and chitters in a nearby willow bush, and a ruby-crowned kinglet flashes its red crest momentarily then flits out of sight into a spruce. On a rock nearby, a masked marmot pokes its head up, sees me, and ducks with a piping whistle of warning. Droning around my head a red-tailed bumblebee decides I'm not a good source of pollen and moves on. Above them all is the gentle, foaming river sound. A perfect, noisy day.

Winter is hard on deer, but spring can be their undoing. Sometimes a deer will make it through the frozen time but be unable to digest the rapidly greening grass. A gaunt doe nibbles around the base of a sagebrush, where new, green, and tender shoots push up through the pale, stiff stubble. She's pregnant and old and a little sick but steady on her hooves. I can't help but think as I watch her that perhaps she's enjoying her last pregnancy, grazing through her last springtime.

The pasque flowers, with their hairy stems and tender purple flowers, are in full bloom. They're called pasques because they normally bloom around Easter. This year they're blooming a bit later, although the rest of spring seems to be progressing normally. Even so they blanket (or rather, kerchief) the hillsides under Douglas firs in a smoky purple and appear to revel in the moisture and warmth.

On a small stock-watering pond, water and shore birds poke about the silvery surface or hunt its dark, muddy edge. A bronze ibis wades the shallows and probes with its curved beak as a killdeer pokes diligently on the shore. It startles a western meadowlark, which flies away singing its warbling call.

Every day looks more like summer. Although the trees don't have their leaves yet, and won't for another three weeks at least, the grass is beginning to green. It's the time of year to drag the meadows, which spreads out the horse manure to benefit more of the grasses. I was on a tractor, pulling the drag and spewing clouds of dust into the air, when a young female coyote trotted along the edge of one of the irrigation ditches. When she saw me at work, she sat on her haunches to watch. I stopped the tractor and turned off the motor, and her ears relaxed. In fact, she had the appearance of a dog that wants to get acquainted but feels some danger. One of the ranch dogs, a lab/retriever cross, was with me and had been chasing the Wyoming ground squirrels. When he saw her, he immediately ran at her. The coyote wasn't perturbed. She waited until the dog was about ten feet away, then leaped up and dashed away from him in a straight line. When the dog was about to bite her tail, she dodged at a ninety-degree angle. The dog kept going straight. She did this two more times before he gave up and trotted back to me. Quito would have appreciated the humor. The coyote followed him for a few minutes, then draped herself across one of the irrigation ditches, paws hanging over the levee, wearing that same curious, ear-down expression. I continued my work and she "supervised" for a while, then trotted along the ditch in the direction from which she'd come.

Justin was hiking along a trail by Mullen Creek today when he heard a high-pitched squealing nearby. He'd barely stopped when two weasels rolled down a little slope in what looked like a fight to the death — a squabbling, bloodied, rolling furball only six feet away. They continued to tousle, totally oblivious of him, for some time, perhaps a minute. Then one of them saw him and squealed, and they both ran into the tall grass. They probably weren't fighting though, just mating. It's good not to be a weasel.

Mid-May

May and June are frenzied times for birds. Each morning is filled with calling, flitting, chasing, and squabbling. The mornings' choruses are wonderful but I often wonder, "How can even the birds know who's talking?"

It's warming nicely now, and the hairs from bighorns, deer, and horses cling to barb wire fences and sage as they begin their molt. Each morning the birds are at the fences, gathering the long hairs and flying with them to their nests.

Today we saw the first bighorn ewe heading for the lambing grounds. She was grazing very slowly and, it seemed, heavily, along a near-vertical slope. By this time next week she should be overseeing the antics of her new lamb. They're wonderfully agile little creatures that spend most of their day bounding along the slope or napping in their mother's shadow. I particularly enjoy watching them in the early evening, when the two of them are lying close together on the grass, catching the last warming rays before sunset.

Snow — four inches of wet, clinging heaviness — presses the willows and grass into the mud. Rooftops and aspen drip, and by 7 a.m. rivulets are already trickling down sage-covered hills. It's thirty-three degrees now and calm, but only 150 miles to the south and east, by Denver, there's a 10,000-acre forest fire. It exploded from one tiny campfire to a ten-square-mile char-hole in less than six hours. It was breezy here yesterday, but down there forty-five-mile-an-hour winds created that havoc. At noon our snow is gone, and it's drizzling lightly. But then it is still Mud Season. Will it ever end?**

At breakfast this morning Casey W., one of our fish guides, was excited. He told me this story:

Last evening after work, he went fishing (what else would a fishing guide do in his free time, even if the stream's are muddy?). After a couple of hours he was "skunked" and decided to call it a night. As he put his rod back into its rack on his car, a gang of elk ran down a steep hill and became confused when they saw him. In a few seconds they'd melded into a shaggy group and splashed

across the stream, where they calmed and stood staring at him staring at them. After ten minutes they continued on their way, and Casey was about to get into his car when he heard more but quieter sounds behind him. He turned to see a cow moose and twin calves strolling single-file toward him from the still unleafed willows. Slowly he crouched by his car and she walked by so close he could smell her musky odor. Casey was nervous, having heard about the dangers of moose with their calves, but she ignored him and led the calves across the stream, where they browsed their way into another clump of willows.

Yesterday was warm and a great day to watch the big hunting and scavenging birds. Turkey vultures on the ground are ugly, but in the air can glide for hours on the slightest updraft, barely moving their wingtips. I watched one this morning. It first appeared as a speck in the distance but quickly grew until it rocketed by me at more than sixty miles an hour, riding a tailwind. Half an hour later, it — or another — returned and struggled to land into the wind on a fence post, but the wind kept blowing it away. After several tries, when it finally was perched on the fence, it faced the wind, smoothed its feathers, and used its streamlined body to stay in place. Meanwhile, a golden eagle hunted the hillsides just out of the wind, so low that its wingtip almost touched its shadow. On the same hill a kestrel (sparrow hawk) fought the wind to hover over a little vole, diving onto it then staying on the ground to eat.

Late May

Other animals are on the move, too, and taking care of

their young. Yesterday I saw a fox trotting along with a mouthful of Wyoming ground squirrel, headed for its burrow and litter of kits. The fox was fairly large and, I think, a male. Although its fur was thick, it was getting blotchy and irregular, so I knew he was beginning to shed into his thinner, but still gray, summer coat. I tried to follow him, but he was understandably cautious. When he disappeared in a willow thicket I lost sight of him, although he probably hadn't lost sight of me.

This is the hardest time of the year for humans who live in the high country. It's been spring for some time in the lowlands, but here we're still frozen at night, and the trees don't have leaves.

It's been alternately warm and cold this month. Actually, it's been alternately warm and cold today. At 7 a.m. the grass and tree branches were frosted. By 9 it was in the mid-sixties and sunny. By 10 it was almost eighty. By 10:30 the clouds were back, and it was forty. Mid-afternoon brought snowflakes that filled the air but didn't stick, and by 5 it was warm again.

Some of the new ranch hands, college students from southeastern universities, weren't used to the sudden changes, and as it warmed up they left their jackets in the trucks. When the temperature fell they practically ran back to get them.

The aspen, however, aren't fooled. I've been watching them, and they're cautious. By early May their buds had swelled slightly, and there was a tiny spot of green at the tip of each. Then they waited. By last week the buds had swollen to three or four times their winter size. The bud scales slid back easily to permit them to grow without breaking. Catkins are emerging from the buds and have been dangling their tiny flowers in the breezes for several days now, waiting for pollen grains to drift in.

When the leaves emerge, at first they are tiny, wrinkled versions of the summer leaf. Gradually, the trees pump them full of moisture. The leaves grow, and the wrinkles disappear as in a collapsed balloon that is refilled.

From even short distances the trees look as if pale green mists have settled on them. At first the hills in the background are still visible, but each day they are more obscured as the leaves expand and turn from pale to dark green.

All our birds-of-the-summer are here now and singing out their territories. Yesterday I awoke at 3:30 a.m. It was cool but not cold as I stepped out the door to listen. The eastern horizon was dark, but a hint of light rimmed the top of Savage Ridge. Even at this hour, the birds were on the job, and the air was filled with a cacophony of bird song as they tuned their instruments for the day.

About three years ago, on a May morning, a boulder the size of a dining room table, weighing perhaps a thousand pounds, crashed down the mountain. It leaped a road and struck a pair of trees, each of which was about thirty inches in diameter, breaking them in four, then splashed into the river. Next morning the devastation was impressive, and a dark passageway showed through the trees. We were busy preparing for the guest season, but I promised myself I'd follow that path. Today I finally did.

Actually, from the litter at the cliff base and along through the existing forest, this cliff has been calving off pieces, like a glacier into the sea, for centuries, perhaps centuries of centuries. It's part of a rock mass that shows on geological maps as about 1.7 billion years old, a brittle quartzite that contains thousands of vertical cracks. These collect debris like leaves, falling pebbles, blowing dust, and snow. The freezing and thawing gradually push the cracks apart, and on some spring morning the final .0001 inch is spread. The rocks separate and crash downward.

I decided to see if, after three years, I could track the rock's fall and started up the "tunnel" through the trees. It took me through a mixed forest, with Douglas fir, ponderosa pine, western juniper, and smaller shrubs, from shrubby cinquefoil to holly grape. Since it's on a north-facing slope, undergrowth here is thicker than in most of the forest. Snow lands here in October. Because the winter days are short and cold, and because the sunlight almost never penetrates, the snow often stays until early May. As the moisture gradually trickles into the soil, the warm air has already stimulated the trees and shrubs, which grow faster and thicker, which protects them from drying winds, which makes for a thicker forest, which gathers more snow, which...

I continued upward, past one squarish, lichen- and moss-encrusted boulder, about nine feet on a side, laying at the base of a Douglas fir. The fir's diameter was almost three and a half feet, perhaps more than five hundred years old at this altitude. Judging from the lichen and moss, they'd lain together for a couple of hundred years, and the fir still looked like it was trying to rise after being tackled by the boulder. Another boulder, only four feet across, rested against the shattered, gray hulk of a stump, the remnant of a broken tree that stopped the boulder's fall. Smaller, rounded rocks and boulders of varying sizes were scattered through the forest.

Still following the path, I startled a mallard 170 feet above the river; it fluttered off into the trees, crashing into dead branches in her fright. Mallards often put their nests a long way from water, but I'd never expected one here. The nest contained nine pale greenish eggs and was barely visible under the protecting branches of a ground juniper. Before they cooled, and to give the mother as much time as possible to recover from her panic, I hurried on. I thought to myself that those ducklings, when they hatch, will have a very long waddle to the river.

As I approached the cliff, I could see a clear path of dead trees and bushes; overhead hung a huge, tilting outcrop of quartzite. As foreboding as this appeared, it wasn't the source of the boulder. It was still covered with a gray, orange, and black layer of lichen so hadn't shed any rocks in several decades at least.

Then I saw it, up a little chute between the cliff and a pile of shattered rock — the pale tan, bare edges of the parent rock. I sat below the scar in the rock and looked down at the river 1,140 feet below, contemplating that morning. On the way up I followed the grosser destruction. Now I'd go down and look for details to recreate that morning. Here's the story of what happened that morning three years ago:

The expanding ice finally wedges itself the critical micromillimeter, and the rock breaks from the cliff. It free falls three feet onto a relative that followed the same path years before and drops nine more feet onto a slanted surface already covered with shattered debris from other rocks' passages, some hundreds of years old. Next, it leaps twenty feet and lands atop a juniper and what had been a huge cinquefoil. The shrub is crushed, and the juniper is shredded, its branches broken and partially stripped, its roots twisted from the soil as the rock turns on its way. Another leap, only ten feet this time. It bounces off a semi-buried flat rock and starts to roll, tearing up more bushes and grass and bluebells and currants. Some boulders it merely brushes, leaving white scars on the rock. Then it crushes a 300-year-old juniper and begins to roll faster, tearing the soil and throwing pieces of itself into the air, leaving a foot-deep depression in the snow-softened soil. At

99

a second drop-off it leaps twenty feet out then down, hitting a bigger boulder that deflects it a full forty degrees to the right, into an open meadow. No trees larger than a human thumb grow here, and the reason is clear as the newest destroyer flattens a dozen — and dozens of boulders have rolled here. The rock turns into the edge of the meadow and hits the base of a two-foot-thick ponderosa pine, snapping it like a pencil and throwing the tree aside as it rolls on and into another big ponderosa. It approaches a road and has fallen 975 feet by this time. It leaps the road-cut, landing on another ponderosa, forty feet tall and with two trunks of thirty inches each, breaking them like twigs. One trunk falls across the road as if cut with a chain saw. The other trunk is thrown ten feet down the slope and splashes into the river alongside the boulder, which has ended its hot race in the cold, brown waters of spring runoff.

Yesterday morning, Margie and I took a hike up the Eagle Rock Trail. It's one of our favorites because you can get up high quickly and the views are spectacular in all directions. This day's walk, however, was even more eventful than usual. First, we discovered a yearling deer. The poor little thing was draped across the top wire of a fence with its fore-hooves barely touching the ground, wide-eyed with fear. I was gently lifting it off when it gave a loud *baaa* (just like a lamb), pushed against my legs, and pulled itself backward over the fence. It landed with a thump and lay still for a moment. Then it shook its head, leaped up and trotted away with only a slight limp. Some of the ranch horses were in a nearby pasture and, curious, came over for a few pats. Next we saw a herd of deer, probably the bunch the yearling had been with, slowly wading through the sagebrush. As we reached the ridge top, 11 bighorn ewes in two slightly separated groups spread out on

a steep hillside across the valley from us. Half of them grazed in the open, hill meadow. A hundred yards uphill, the others lay in the sunshine on the greening grass. They were quietly chewing their cuds, looking outward from a rough circle, seemingly relaxed but alert and watching for dangers. They watched us watching them for some time, then an eagle gave its *scree* call and they all looked up. Margie and I did the same and joined the bighorns in watching the eagle until it rose out of sight. The sheep watched it far longer than we could see without the binoculars.

A bald eagle pair continues to build their nest near the top of an old, half-dead ponderosa. Last year was the first time they used the nest. Although big by nest standards, it was small compared to the way it's grown now. A month ago the pair began to remodel the nest. She seemed to be in charge for he would bring a branch for her inspection. Sometimes she seemed to approve, and he'd add it to the growing platform. Other times she'd refuse it, and he'd drop the reject then fly off for another. By the time they finished, the two-year-old nest probably weighed five to six hundred pounds.

Now the eggs have hatched. There were three eggs at first, and all hatched. The first hatchling, however, took the food from the second, which took food from the first. At the end of a week there was only one young eagle alive. We assumed it was the oldest, but it was probably just the strongest, part of nature's automatic selection process.

All summer we'll get to watch the adults as they perch in trees along the river, watching for surface-cruising trout. For the next two months, the adults will be busy trying to feed themselves, and one very hungry eaglet. By the time it finally leaves the nest, it will be almost as large as its parents.

June

A wonderful scene just *blazed* past my office window. All the horses have been together for a month now, grazing in our spring pasture, and the wranglers just brought them to the corral. All 130 of them streamed down the meadow toward the corral. There are so many horses in so many colors — blacks, grays, sorrels, palominos, red roans, frosty roans, blue roans, appaloosas — all of them are so slick and shiny in the morning light that they looked like a tumbling rainbow, complete with thunder.

With so many horses, we buy, sell, or trade about twenty every year to keep the herd strong and safe. We normally buy the new ones through the winter, but we just bought five more, and it's going to shake up the herd. Because horse society is so well organized, we have to consider that when buying. They have a definite "kick order." There is, for example, one horse that can push any others aside, kick or bite them, etc., and they can't do more than sidle away. At the other end of the line, there's one poor horse that everyone can pick on. They're usually the ones that have tucked themselves into a corner of the corral and, with their head down, try not to be seen. It seems unfair, but the kick order does keep the herd from fighting continually. Everyone knows their place; body language (laid back ears, wringing a tail, head down, etc.) can convey a message or a warning. In the wild, an injury could put them at risk of being killed by a predator, so fighting is engaged only as a last resort. Horses have buddies that are usually together, whether in the corral or meadow, even in the same places each day. In fact, when our wranglers go out to catch the horses each morning, they have a corral schematic. It shows the groups of friends and their most likely place in the corral.

They'll maintain those friendships for years, but as with people, things can change. One trio (Dutchess, Cherry, and Boots) were friends for more than twenty years. But on the day that Dutchess died, the others separated and were never together again.

More of our summer staff members are beginning to arrive, and the ranch is buzzing with activity as we get ready to open. Although the trees still don't have their leaves yet, the buds are growing fast, and we'll have fully leafed trees in a few days. Even so, the students from the southeast, where wisteria and rhododendron have been blooming, look at the bare trees with a "What have I gotten myself into?" kind of expression.

We're painting our river bridge now. It's a steel-girded framework with steel and wood flooring; even hay trucks and lines of horseback riders barely make it tremble. The original wasn't so strong or stable, in fact even a walker or heavy wind caused it to sway because it was a suspension bridge. It's been gone for some years now, but I often hear stories of the original.

When the river was low, big trucks would simply ford the river. If it was high, the trucks parked at one end of the bridge, and other, smaller trucks from the ranch, half a mile away, would ferry the goods across. Even the guests in their cars were often nervous.

Margaret M. from "Chicagoland" recalled that every year when they arrived, she and her two boys would get out of the car, cross the bridge on foot, and then her husband, Bud, would drive slowly across. I asked her, "Was that so if there was a problem you could go for help?" She grinned mischievously and said, "Maybe, but if the bridge did fall into the river, we'd be on the side of the river with all the fun."

After eight months of planning, our guest season has begun. There are people all round the ranch now, riding, fishing, shooting skeet and trap, and just plain loafing. The hammocks have been especially busy so far. I heard that Denver had a high of 99 degrees yesterday — here it was 83. Runoff is about over now, and the water is clear again, the stream level is falling, and fish are rising. While on a nature walk this morning, we discovered — pressed into the mud of a deer path — the inch-long footprints of a fawn. The does are busy having their babies.

On the way to our first breakfast ride of the season, a group of guests found a newborn fawn right beside the horse trail. The spotted baby was new, struggling to get up for the first time, still draped with its birth sac. The mother had been startled by the riders and stood a hundred yards off, watching anxiously, so the riders trotted off quickly and, from a distance, watched as she returned to the fawn.

One morning we almost didn't do the breakfast ride, because the weather looked so bad. At dawn our breath came out in little pale puffs, and a spectacular purple-pink cloud covered the sky, but deep blue peered around its edges. As we left the corral the clouds lowered and darkened, dragging curtains of "virga" (where the rain starts to fall but evaporates before it hits the ground). I'd have canceled the ride, but the temperature was rising, and there was that blue sky beyond. By the time I slipped a pan of hot biscuits from the Dutch oven, the clouds were breaking to reveal three mountain ranges, the sunlight flooded the sky, and the wind became a horse-breath-warm breeze. We slathered soft honey butter on the biscuits,

nestled them beside eggs and bacon, poured hot cowboy coffee, and settled down to enjoy another Wyoming morning as viewed from the top of Bighorn Ridge.

Meanwhile, down at the riverside, one of the local bighorn ewes caused a bit of excitement. Several carloads of fisher folk were on their way back from the stream, eager for breakfast in the dining room. Just as they approached the west side of the bridge over the North Platte, a bighorn ewe and her two-week-old lamb approached the east side. I guess the ewe thought the right of way was hers. Instead of turning and running away, she sauntered across the bridge. She paused to gaze down into the river flowing below, probably glad she wasn't having to wade in that cold water, then walked right past the parked cars filled with wide-eyed humans. The lamb hopped beside her, on spring-feet as lambs do, and barely looked up at the people snapping photos from only a few feet away. Finally, the bighorns crossed the bridge and began to graze beside the river.

On another later June breakfast ride, my helpers and I arrived a bit earlier than usual. We unloaded the food truck, and I set my sooty Dutch oven onto a clump of crested wheatgrass atop Bighorn Ridge then paused to enjoy the views, both the one rolling 360 degrees in all directions and the scented and colored one at our feet. Driving there had been a special treat. The bitterbrush, also called "antelope bush," was in bloom, covered with hundreds of tiny yellow flowers that packed a wallop of sweet-scented perfume you could smell even in the Wyoming wind. Scattered between the sage and bitterbrush were big yellow balsam root and fluorescent orange Indian paintbrush and fluorescent pink scarlet gilia and blue flax and pink phlox and white and purple loco. But the one that caught my eye was a rounded pink

pod-like flower not yet opened, *Lewisia rediviva* — bitterroot.

Up in Montana it covers whole valleys, and they've named mountains for it. Although we have it here in southern Wyoming, it's more rare. We do have the rocky soil it likes, but perhaps it isn't as much appreciated here as it was in the north, where the Flatheads and other tribes gathered the tiny roots to eat. The name bitterroot fits. Even after it's dried then crumbled and boiled, it keeps its bitterness, although the boiling tames it somewhat.

Meriwether Lewis collected it back in 1804, when he passed through with his partner, William Clark. They must have come through in the spring, because, once it blooms, the leaves wither, and when the flower dies the plant seems to disappear. This isn't to say they're weak plants though. When Lewis collected his samples, he dried them in a plant press. Returning to Washington, his collection went to botanists at the Smithsonian for study. Imagine their surprise when they later found one of the bitterroots had sprouted. The scientist planted the bitterroot, and not only did it survive, it bloomed. They named the plant for Lewis, who first reported it to the botanical community (although the Native Americans had used it for centuries) — *Lewisia*. Because it was so tough, they named it *rediviva* — to live again.

An hour later, as the guests departed, now filled with biscuits, eggs, and cowboy coffee, I looked for the bitterroot flower pods. They were gone, opened now into dozens of pink flowers two inches across and so low they almost brushed the ground as they turned toward the rising sun. It's good to be in Wyoming, where the bitterroots are living again.

Most of our mule deer have twins each year, but generally only one of each pair will survive. One of our local does, however, a notch-eared old lady, usually raises both, because she has a different approach. Does it show forethought? I'm not sure, but she's done it for four years now.

In mid-May, as the river begins to rise from the snowmelt, she swims to an island in the river near the corral. She lives there until she has her fawns in early June. When they are about a week old, she begins the twice daily swim to shore, leaving the fawns on the island. They're safe on the little woodland, and probably no coyote even suspects their presence. Even if it did, a coyote probably wouldn't dare make the treacherous swim. In late June, as the river's level drops, the doe carefully brings them across to the mainland one at a time, placing her body below theirs so the swift current doesn't sweep them away. For another couple of weeks they stay in the willows close to the main ranch, coming out in the early morning and evening to graze and let us enjoy the scene. Then, at about six weeks of age, when they can outrun coyotes, she takes them further afield, starting at our flower beds.

One of our staff and I sat at breakfast, talking. She'd arrived only the day before and was full of enthusiasm for adventures she hoped to have and for the beauty of the mountains. As we sipped our coffee and downed big plates of pancakes and eggs, she told me about her first adventure. Last night she'd gone on a hike up the Sheeps' Trail, a narrow and steep path worn by our local bighorns and overlooking the river 800 feet below. As she neared the top, she had a close view of a kestrel hovering. Thinking that was probably her "wildlife adventure" for the night, she sat on a grassy hummock, enjoying the mountain view, when she noticed a few bighorn ewes and yearlings. She watched them through her binoculars a while and was about to move on when several more appeared on the ridge above her. Through her binoculars again, she watched them approaching her until they were too close for the glasses to focus. They finally passed by only twenty feet away, continuing downhill and across the bridge where they shared a salt lick with several deer. Then two pairs of western tanagers flashed by, showing off their bright scarlet heads atop yellow bodies carried through the pines on black wings where they called their pik-a-tik as they announced their territories. She's hiking another trail tonight.

I spent the late morning and most of the afternoon prowling around an alpine bog, just to see what there was to learn. Of course there was thick, green moss covering everything, including dozens of old stumps. Intermixed sedges and rushes grew over pools of water and made a soft but shaky carpet that oozed bubbles of swamp gas with each step. Where the pools were exposed, mosquito wrigglers, graceful leaches, diving beetles, and water skippers abounded. Mosquitoes buzzed around my ears, and a Hereford range bull bawled at me from the edge of the forest. I watched and listened and itched for several hours, then realized it was time to go home.

Leaving the little valley, I was strolling across the firm sagebrush soil when I came upon a russet-colored buck deer with velvet-covered antlers. I paused to watch him and realized there were two more, lying down and with their heads poking slightly above the sage. Two of the three had four antler points on one side (eight per head — out West we count the side, not the total), and one had short, two-pronged forks. At first I thought they

might be afraid of me, but, when the first one I'd seen also lay down and started to chew his cud, I knew they were at ease. I sat in the sage, too, and when I left half an hour later they were still lounging in their sage beds, enjoying the sunshine.

We took a group of young friends to a pretty hillside to watch the sunset. After tying the horses head to tail so they couldn't wander, each found a different grassy area near to but separate from the others. No one spoke as the sun began to fall. I'm always amazed at how much faster the sun moves as it approaches the horizon and, from the soft murmurs and pointing of the watchers, several of them were too. The fading sunlight covered the nearby mountains, which glowed a soft peachy color above the dark shadow rising from the valley. Our horses snorted occasionally or stomped, but otherwise it was silent.

At first the group fidgeted as they found comfortable positions on the brittle grass and tried to avoid sitting on a cluster of flowers, or a mountain ball cactus. After about twenty minutes we settled into stillness, and the animals began to move. First, a garnet-eyed killdeer, with a bib of two dark lines, scurried through the low grass with its whistling call. Then a battering sound of feathers against wood announced a sharp-shinned hawk flying into a bush then out again and into another bush only twenty feet away. He was so well camouflaged that, even with binoculars, I could barely see him. The bird sat on its perch for about ten minutes, giving several people a wonderful chance to study a hunting hawk, then it leaned forward, spread its wings, and quietly flew down-valley.

Then, as the stars blinked on in the clear sky, we remounted and rode silently back to the ranch. At the corral the quiet changed to excitement as each told what they'd seen and experienced, and they were all different.

On the high ridges, we often hear night hawks or see them darting like the little brown bats in the dusk, their white wing bars from front to back of mid-wing flashing palely in the low light. Males make sounds that confuse those who haven't heard them before, a high-pitched "peent" call at fairly long intervals. Sometimes they swoop low in a fast dive, then check, making a deep "whoom" sound as the wind rushes through the primary feathers at wingtips. It's like a miniature bull bellowing, and their flight is so bat-like that the locals call them "bull bats."

Some years ago a group of dudes slept on a high point and late at night heard the sound. It was unearthly and, to them, machine-like. So they laid awake all night, expecting to be attacked by some alien beast.

But the birds eat insects only. Their dipping and darting flights are their quests for dinner. Sometimes we see them perched on a branch, perfectly camouflaged and sitting parallel to the branch instead of crosswise like other birds.

This morning I found the nest of a night hawk, right in the bare soil of a little-used trail. The eggs and bird were almost the color of the ground, and I only discovered them when the parent swooped up and away from my feet almost as if she'd appeared from the ground. Hurrying to some nearby trees, I stopped and watched through my binoculars. In a few moments the bird returned and settled on the nest. Before settling on the nest it gently turned the eggs, to warm and moisten both sides and keep the floating embryo from sticking to the shell. She saw me but knew her priorities and stayed with the nest, tensing only slightly as I rose to continue.

About midday, Margie and I hiked to a promontory to get some exercise and enjoy the views. At 7,700 feet several clumps of stunted juniper grew between the calving-away parts of a granite boulder. Because it's been so long since we had any moisture, their new growth from this year is wilted and brown. The ground was covered with live but dry and dead-looking plants that were holding themselves back in hopes of rain. Some flowers were already drying out, their leaves browning at the edges and curling as their roots strove downward for moisture that wasn't there. Yellow stonecrop had its beautiful, starlike flowers, but their stems, which at this time of the year should be swollen with moisture, were shriveled. Below me about 400 feet and a quarter mile away, the river purled quietly at a level more like it might fall to in late August. Its water was already clear, and vast underwater meadows of green water weeds fanned out along the bottom, like irrigated alfalfa fields seen from an airplane.

We paused at a little grove of old, stunted trees. The oldest was a long-dead Douglas fir, twisted into spirals and carved into soft, gray curves by the wind and the grit it carries. Orange and yellow lichen grew on the bare limbs and encrusted the roots, which grew next to chunks of granite with the same colors and textures. Lichen takes 200 or more years to grow like that, and I began to wonder about the age of the skeletal tree. Assuming it was at least 300 years old when it died, perhaps it sucked its first bit of moisture about the time that the Aztecs were preparing to meet the Spaniards, who were invading their world.

When I lightly tweaked a stiff splinter, an almost

metallic, hollow sound resounded from the branch. Another splinter vibrated with a different tone. Was this perhaps one of the accidents that might have given humans the idea for some musical instrument millennia ago? Now an orb spider uses it to anchor her web, which contains bits of plant fluff and drying midges. In the slow breeze, light danced up and down the strands like a wire-walker, but I never saw the little artist who made the web.

Suddenly a red-shafted flicker began its territorial call, unseen as it perched in a limber pine. After thirty or forty declarations it flew, its red underwings flashing, to the tree I'd been studying and began to sing its territory again. Each time it called, its head dipped down and it hopped around the branch watching first in one direction and then in another. Another flicker responded but flew to the top of the tree under which Margie sat reading. Two mourning doves flashed by like fighter planes on a mission, and a chickadee "chinked" in the lower branches above her head.

Still the first flicker called above me. After about five minutes he hopped to another branch on the jin and hopped around to the trunk where he perched, in proper woodpecker fashion, and stared at me boldly. When an insect crawled into its view it tipped its head to see if was edible, quickly swallowed it, then returned to calling. All this took place only about thirty feet from me. I was so engrossed in his antics that, when a golden eagle flew about seventy-five feet overhead, I almost missed it, spotting first the huge shadow racing toward me, then looking up. As the eagle continued drifting across the ridge and through the trees, the flicker took wing in the opposite direction.

A magpie called from a distant caragana thicket. Another perched on a thin branch, using its long, bobbing tail to balance and changing colors as it moved in the light. Sometimes it's a black and white bird; others, deep, glistening blue and white; still others, glossy, deep green and white — all depending on its angle to the sunlight. In the winter they're the first to find a carcass or to chase other birds away from our feeders or to dive-bomb the ranch cat when it goes out for a daytime stroll. Some of the neighbors don't like magpies. I do.

One thing I miss when we don't have rain is rainbows. Everyone loves rainbows. Sometimes we have a small thunderstorm just before sunset, and by the time the sun drops the clouds will be fracturing. The low sun flies through the openings and splashes onto the western hilltops with a wonderful yellow light that gradually creeps upward as the sun dips lower. A rainbow begins to form, at first faint and incomplete, then the colors deepen as the sky darkens. Soon a full rainbow arches from one side of the North Platte and across our valley, touching down somewhere around the skeet range. Then a second appears above the first, a reflection of the first and with its colors reversed, green on the inside ring of the original, and on the outside ring of the copy. Each moment, the light becomes more richly golden. If it's dinner time, everyone leaves the dining room, to snap a picture or two, to soak in the beauty, and to talk together about the wonders of Wyoming. Like most things truly wonderful, the light and rainbow last only a moment in reality, but will be carried far and wide and may last years in memories as golden as that light.

Yesterday, Justin, was leading a group of riders out

for an early-morning breakfast ride. We put out special salt blocks for the wildlife, and as they passed by one of them a young bighorn ewe was licking it eagerly. When Quito began walking toward it curiously, Justin told him to lie down. From that position the dog seemed to pose no threat and, the ewe herself got curious. As Quito's ears pricked forward and his head cocked to the side, watching, she approached to within three feet. They looked at each other for a few moments, almost touching noses, but were startled when a camera's shutter clicked. Each bolted and ran, in opposite directions. Then from about 100 feet away they stopped to see what the other was doing. Justin put the dog on the down command again and the ewe returned. Finally the riders continued, this time with the dog leading the troupe and the ewe following for about a quarter mile before she turned uphill to graze among the rocks.

Two guests were hiking up the trail to Slim's Draw to enjoy a little solitude and the expansive view. When they stopped to rest, a sage grouse, which we've come to call the "Slim's Draw Grouse" or "Crazy Chicken," came out of the shrubs and strutted right up to them. Sage grouse are rather large birds, up to thirty inches long and weighing four to five pounds. One of the hikers leaned over and put out her hand. The bird pecked at it, hard, and without fear. They couldn't chase it away, so they continued up the trail. The bird followed them for several hundred yards, clucking and scratching at the soil, then stopped. As the hikers walked on, it flew up and glided back to where they first met it. This is the third year that she's been there, protecting her domain and giving us delightful stories.

Here's the story of our first encounter with her:

One of the ranch hands was driving to Slim's Draw, to rake and prepare it for the Friday cookout. A steep, winding two-track climbs about two miles to a little copse of evergreens, where you can see for sixty miles in every direction. It was a hot day, and the old truck vapor-locked about half way up. As the ranch hand sat in truck, wondering what to do, a sage grouse flew into the window and landed on the seat next to him. It began to peck his arm, and he fled the truck. After a while the bird, too, left the truck, at which point the ranch hand climbed back in, rolled up the windows, and watched the angry bird circling the truck. In ten minutes he was able to start the car and drove away, leaving the angry bird strutting in the road.

The next week the same ranch hand was driving the same truck and stopped, this time on purpose, to see what would happen. He'd taken a good bit of razzing throughout the week and wanted to show his lack of fear. As he sat on the hood of the truck the bird appeared, flew up to him and attacked. Laughing now at the little thing chasing a giant, he climbed back into the truck and left. The ranch hand told Justin (aged 11 then) about it. He drove his four-wheeler to the place and parked. When the bird attacked him, Justin caught it and wrapped it in his jacket to take back to the ranch to show his friends. As he approached the ranch, the bird wriggled loose and got away, leaving most of its rear-end feathers behind. The next week she was back in her territory, somewhat bald but still feisty.

For several summers Dr. Oakleigh Thorne, II (Oak) has come to the ranch to lead nature hikes and to mist net and band birds. A mist net is a long and very fine, almost invisible, net stretched across bird highways in the air. As they fly into the loose net, it forms a pocket that gently holds them until the researcher can remove them. Sometimes the bird is so interlaced in the net that it can take five or ten minutes to free it, so great patience is required. Then it's classified, recorded, and a numbered band is attached to its leg. There can be quite a few caught in a summer's netting. One season, for instance, Oak captured, banded, and freed 174 birds of 19 species. One of those bands, a cliff swallow, turned up in Argentina.

Cliff swallows are the most conspicuous, and the ones we captured most often. Of the 174, 63 were cliff swallows. But surprisingly, the next most common species, with 36 of the total, were the inconspicuous and tiny pine siskins.

The capture of a hummingbird is a special delight for the children. Oak, caught two today, a male and a female. He held the tiny animals gently, turning them slowly in the sunlight to show the gathered children the flashing red color across the throat of the male; Oak enjoyed their ooohs and aaahs as the bright red patch flashed. On the female he gently brushed the feathers at the base of her breast, revealing the featherless "brood patch." Her body temperature, he told the children, is about 104 degrees, the ideal temperature for incubating her eggs. The finale was a demonstration of hypnosis. Hummingbirds are especially good subjects for this, but you don't wave a watch in front of them and mutter, "Sleep, sleep." Laying the bird on its back, he used a fingertip to gently massage its sternum, the pointy chest bone. Gradually the bird relaxed, and when Oak opened his hand, it lay on his palm as if asleep. It stayed there for a minute, then

another, until, at Oak's instruction, one of the children snapped his fingers and the hummer flew away as if sprung from a trap.

For the past ten years a family (or succession of families) of great horned owls have nested in the cottonwood grove near Anderson House. This year they have five owlets that are just beginning to wander from the nest. Only big, gray feather balls at this point, their wing feathers are developed enough for emergency flights. One of them likes to scratch around on the roof of Anderson House, flapping its wings and leaning into the shingles as it climbs up and down, exercising and exploring. This morning, unfortunately for the owlet and the guests on the second floor, the crows discovered it. The crows enjoy "mobbing" (harassing) the owls and began their noise about dawn, diving and pecking at the young bird. One or two of the other owlets were in spruce trees nearby and remained absolutely still, their heads pulled down on their necks, peering through half-opened eyes, hoping not to be discovered. I guess turnabout's fair play though. By the end of the summer the owls will be on the other side chasing them, especially as the crows try to sleep at night.

I took a nature walk with about eight guests. We strolled on toward Anderson House to see if we could glimpse the family of great horned owls living there. No luck, but we did hear several dozen bees bumbling around the caragana bushes and watched them sipping on the yellow, pealike flowers. At first a couple of the guests were nervous, but when they realized that the bees wouldn't attack them, they began to enjoy being "pathway superintendents," as the pollen-gathering continued.

Continuing uphill and into the sagebrush, we discovered fairy trumpet (*scarlet gilia*), purple penstemon, and buckwheat and walked through air scented sweetly by the bitterbrush. The top of the hill by the skeet range offers an interesting community of plants, and we had just turned toward it when we saw a feather. Christian H. (10) is interested in all sorts of nature and was watching carefully for others when he spotted a down feather blowing lightly against a bush and picked it up too. They were owl feathers, covered with a soft velvet that enables them to fly silently, and we were studying them when Tom G. spotted the owl. It wasn't flying or even perched but lay on the ground, dead.

Its right foot still clutched a dead robin, a sharp talon piercing the red breast. One of the owl's big, yellow eyes was open a bit, and I had the feeling it might get up, shake itself, and fly off. It had been dead only a short time, perhaps early dawn. The robin was probably on the newly watered golf course, searching for worms, and was snatched up in mid-hunt by another hunter. As the owl recovered from his strike he must have hit the guy wire holding a power pole in place. There was no sign of a struggle, and he, too, must have died immediately.

Death is a natural part of nature, but at times like this it can be especially sad. This was the male of the pair that was raising the owlets. The female probably won't be able to keep up with feeding so many young beaks in addition to her own, so one or more of the young might die, too. On the other hand, they're about three months old and about ready to fly.

We tried to obtain a permit to have the birds stuffed for our museum but couldn't, since both are protected species. In the end we gave the birds, the robin still in the owl's claw, to the museum of an outdoor lab school.

For extra exercise and fun, Margie likes to ride a bicycle. Today she had ridden her mountain bike out toward the main gate and was returning to the ranch at a pretty fast clip. Because the road was bumpy, she was concentrating on her balance and wasn't paying much attention to what was going on around her. Neither, apparently, was a jackrabbit that was running through the sagebrush. The jack was almost at Margie's front wheel before she realized it was there. Shocked, the rabbit leapt into the air about four feet, staring right into Margie's also-startled eyes. She almost crashed as the jack did a flip in midair and ran back in the direction from which it had come. I imagine that the rabbit hid itself, then paused to calm down. Margie didn't hide herself, but she did lay the bike down and sit beside it for a few minutes, calming down but also laughing.

Late June

It's early morning. A yellow warbler hunts in a willow by my window. He's a lively, sun-splashed golden spot as he hop-flies from branch to branch, probing for cold and stiff insects among the dewy leaves. Capturing one, he pauses to sing, bug in beak, and flies off to feed his brood.

In the sage, arrowleaf balsamroot has carried its pretty yellow flowers atop crowns of green leaves for about a month, but now the flowers have lost their petals, and the leaves are sagging limply onto the ground, like soggy linen on some clothesline. They'll be replaced by mule's ears, their look-alike cousins. Along the streams, the almost-new leaves of the alder shine brightly, washed by the latest afternoon shower. Those rains began last week and have encouraged the spruce, whose "candles" (the new growth at the tips of the branches) are eight inches long, twice as long as normal.

When the deer graze now, they move slowly, picking at the bright-green grass and moving gratefully through the shimmering heat waves rising from the warm ground. Two-week-old fawns hide in the thickets most of the time, but each day they gain confidence and follow their mothers and yearling siblings farther into the edges of the meadows. Our deer are "muleys," mule deer with rope-like tails and huge mule-like ears. As they swivel them continually, listening for danger, the ears on the younger deer seem especially large, as they haven't yet grown into them.

It's a lazy, busy time of the year. Our North Platte River is great for fishing, but it's also superb for tubing. Yesterday one of our guests took her protesting children to the river. She had wanted her children (aged two and four) to go tubing, so she, a sitter, and the two children were taken to the river for a two-mile float to the ranch. They were dropped off at a spot we normally don't use, to shorten the trip, and had to slog through some boggy areas carrying the big tubes and the children. The kids were whining and crying at first, saying, "Mommy, I don't want to drown." After a few minutes on the river, they were splashing and laughing as they drifted past blue herons fishing and Canada geese with their goslings. By the end of the float, the two-year-old was asleep on the sitter's lap, lulled by the murmur of the river and the warm sunshine.

What a beautiful morning. I drove some guests to the air strip at 6 a.m. and felt I was driving through a zoo. The low sun threw deep shadows in the lower cliff areas by the river, but the tops of the cottonwoods glowed with a warm amber-green light. Slow driving through the narrow part of the canyon is requisite, because one often surprises deer. This was one of those times, as a doe and twin fawns trotted across the road. The doe watched unconcerned, but ours was probably one of the first cars the fawns had seen because they panicked and tried to scurry up a slope. One scrambled and fell backward two times before its rubbery little hooves caught hold and it dashed on to its sibling. In an open area just above the Howdy Gate stood a huge buck antelope, head up and regal, its body sideways to the light, letting the sun warm its black antlers. His majesty totally ignored us though we were only fifty yards away.

Margie led a hike today. About a dozen friends drove to Green Mountain Falls. The four-mile hike was up a wide path winding through white-barked aspen groves with pale green leaves and underlain with tall grasses that were sprinkled with opening flowers. About a quarter mile from their goal they came upon a bridge over a stream. On one side the path was clear; on the other snow piled six feet deep. They hesitated only briefly and then, clambering onto the hard snow, continued. It was worth the effort. A quarter of a mile over the crusted snow led them to the top of a rock outcrop, where glistening greenish waterfalls split the stream into a half dozen channels. They poured through miniature canyons of snow with a soft purling, like dozens of fountains, as they cascaded from one tier of multicolored rock to the next.

Each day the streams are a bit lower. As they recede, they leave a thin layer of scum along the edge, like a bathtub ring, but this scum is a food bank of leaf bits and twigs and drowned insects. Dippers hunt the shores, bobbing and picking up the free food.

Each day the brook continues to sing the same melody but at slowly dropping octaves. Only two days ago I stood beside it and felt like I was standing next to the speakers at a rock concert. My body tensed to the beat of rocks thumping each other, and the water raced and roared like an electric guitarist jamming. At 5 o'clock this afternoon it played "Prelude to Afternoon of a Faun," with ever-changing, gently flowing melodies. The water tones have hushed, and so has my response. As I lay sprawled on the grass beside the stream, the tension flowed out the soles of my feet, the small of my back, and the points of my shoulders. It ran down the grassy bank and into the cold water, where it was carried away amid a hatch of rising silvery-winged mayflies.

It's not always idyllic in the mountains, and no matter our activity we have to watch the weather. Friday is normally the steak fry at Slim's Draw, and afternoon rains can spoil our plans. Still, the evening is a favorite.

This week we have a business group here, and they had a Slim's picnic scheduled.

It was a busy day but all went smoothly. At about 4:30 I drove the food truck and a crew up to prepare. A hard rain fell about noon, but the sun came out and the road was dust-free, still showing the truck tracks from the ranch hands who had come a few hours earlier to prepare the site.

Cloud banks spread out through the sky; one was particularly ominous. Lightning and thunder flash-boomed dramatically, but it was obviously moving away from us, and the scattered clouds overhead seemed benign.

We took photos, started fires, and began to cook as the guests arrived. Only a slight breeze blew out of the south. There were no annoyances such as forgotten utensils. By this time, about sixty guests had joined us on horseback. The horses were tied around an ancient, gnarled pine atop a little rock outcrop. The horses were unperturbed, but the guests eyed the flashing cloud and asked me nervously, "What do you think, Bob?"

When a plane flew over, I radioed the office and asked them to contact the plane via our uni-com radio. The pilot reported that the cloud was, indeed, moving away from us.

Other riders arrived, laughing, enjoying the evening. They headed for the bar and sat down in their chairs to watch the splendor of the storm. Suddenly, the cloud split open. Golden sunlight showered through the hole and onto the wranglers and horses, a sharp contrast to the blackness behind them.

Then, as I watched northwest, a thin vapor began to form, so we were between the thunderhead and the forming cloud. It thickened, and lightning began flashing from within it.

Other cars were just arriving, but I reloaded them to start down with women and children. We set the food back into the trucks and warned everyone to stay away from metal and lone trees. There was no fear or panic — I don't think people realized the danger — and the first carloads headed down. I radioed to the ranch and told them to hold the rest of the riders and radioed for the riders on their way to head back to the ranch. Paul M. the head wrangler, and I decided to drive the horses back to the ranch, so he and his two helpers began removing bridles and turning the horses free.

Now the two clouds were racing together, surrounding us. Only about twenty men were still at the top plus a few staff members with the food truck. I gave instructions to the staff, left my radio with the bartender, and mounted a horse to help the wranglers.

The herd began a run toward the ranch, but before we'd gone even a quarter mile, a high wind and driving rain forced the horses to turn and run downhill. Trotting into a little canyon with the single-mindedness of fear, they ignored the humans who were shouting at them. I finally was able to grab the halter of the leader and pull him to a stop. The others stopped, tail to the storm, and we sat hunched over our saddles as the storm threw its fury on us, and on the ridge we'd just left.

We hunched over atop our horses and on the edge of the canyon. I had no coat or rain gear and rain trickled down my pants as if they were rain gutters, filling my boots.

But no one really thought about the cold. The lightning strobed all around us, and we were more concerned about survival than warmth. We moved away from the barbed wire fence and hoped the people on the ridge top were safe. As it turned out, the bartender had moved them well off the dangerous ridge and passed around a bottle of Yukon Jack. The men were in good, though wet, spirits.

Margie returned with a Suburban to try and get to the men but couldn't get up that long hill. A two-foot-deep stream was roaring down the road, pushing the car with it. When a bolt of lightning struck only a few rods from the car, she radioed to the bartender to load the men onto the food truck and come down.

As the storm's violence abated slightly, the men climbed into the back of the truck. Wet bentonite has all the traction of grease, so they fishtailed and slid slowly down the two miles. Gullies were filled with three feet of muddy, foaming water that almost reached the bed of the truck. At the main road, Suburbans met the wet adventurers and drove them to the ranch for hot showers.

Meanwhile, our "boss horse" and several others were under control, so Paul and I led them uphill, into the rain, which had abated somewhat. The other horses followed us until they went through a gate. As they crowded through the opening, they burst into a full gallop and headed on toward the ranch. I kept the wranglers out of the bunch, afraid that so many bodies might attract the lightning, or that someone's horse would fall.

One wrangler, Anneke H., kept slightly ahead of the herd, guiding them toward the ranch. The rest of us loped behind, splashing through muddy puddles and working to control our own horses on the slippery road. Above the ranch, Anneke opened a five-foot-wide horse gate and tried to ease the horses through, but the herd fought to go through the small opening. As the last of the herd dashed through, one horse hobbled on three legs. Its fourth swung in a circle, broken.

Four of the horses had continued past the gate, so Paul and Alex T. went after them. I unsaddled the horse with the broken leg, a pretty bay, and left it. (Paul returned later to put it down.) Since I was still a mile or so from the ranch and since I was concerned for Anneke, who was at the lead, I continued down. I'd gone a quarter mile down the hill when I heard a horse running. I turned and saw a single animal in a panicked gallop, headed toward me on the one-horse trail, its saddle's stirrups flapping wildly. She never slowed and I barely had time to raise my leg as she brushed past, knocking my horse to her buttocks and almost throwing us from the trail. As my horse stood and shook herself, the appaloosa continued around a bend below us. The next time I saw her she was running down Devil's Slide and splashing through the river.

Three other wranglers, meanwhile, were "holed up" in a little aspen grove about a mile away. They'd started up to help, via a shortcut, when the storm hit. They tied their horses and removed their boots, crouching on them. We'd been back about forty-five minutes when they rode in, safe but pale with cold and fear.

Dinner was only an hour late though, and the guests — who had gathered in the Round Room to recount their stories — had great ones to tell. This night goes down in our history as "The Slim's from Hell."

Barbara S., one of our guests, left a few days ago and sent me this note the day after she got home:

"We arrived home late Sunday night (2:30 a.m.), and as I was putting Matty [her five-year-old] to bed, he asked me to find his tape recorder. I didn't know where it was and suggested that he didn't need his music tonight since he hadn't had it all week at the ranch. His eyes were about to shut, but he looked at me and said, 'But Mommy, at the ranch the birds were my music.'"

July

One year it was wet and cold in May and cold until June. In fact, it was June 14 before the cottonwoods had leaves. Inconvenient then, yes, but it produced an unusual and very colorful July. Mushrooms were everywhere; hiding in the moist sagebrush, thrusting up through last year's leaves in the aspen groves, and even amid beaver-chewed branches alongside streams. White giant puffballs, like small pillows, bulge in the sagebrush. In the aspen groves, remnants of delicious brown morels (normally spring sprouters) and hamburger-bun-like boletus grow near deadly scarlet and white amanitas, "death angels." Early June was so cold that the flowers held back until late in the month, yet the July flowers came on schedule and stayed longer. In July their mixed scents drifted on the breezes, and they bloomed side by side — faded purple fringes of June and bright-orange paintbrushes and white field daisies of July. On a nature horseback ride with several guests, we passed through one of the horse meadows that was particularly lush. Grasses taller than a four-year-old child tossed and rippled in the breeze, and little red elephant flowers grew in scattered clusters among the rushes and wire grass of the soggy irrigated bottomlands.

July is the month of flowers.

The summer was off to a good start, then I had one of those days.

Yesterday at 7:30 I began work with a short meeting, as usual. No problems. At 7:40, when the meeting was over, things began to unravel a bit. First, the gardener came to me with a somewhat stricken look on her face. She'd hurt her foot and the doctor reported it was an injured tendon. She'd have to go home to let it rest. Carpet layers were scheduled that morning, to replace the flooring of one cabin where a skunk settled in and used *potpourri de skunk*. A wrangler came in to tell me that one of the horses was colicking. They were treating it, but it looked bad for the horse. The irrigation pump at our greeting house broke down, and it could be a week before replacement parts would arrive, during which time the grass would turn brown. Then I discovered that the gardener really had *left* a couple of days ago, and a thousand dollars in shrubs and perennials were dead by the garden shed because she hadn't watered them. Three staff members have stopped by to ask for a chance to "talk," and the chef has told me one of his cooks can't stand the heat in the kitchen. There were so many problems that at first I felt overwhelmed. Then I realized the absurdity of the last hour and that the only thing I could do for the moment was to laugh. Margie and I talked about the start of the day and joked about it. How in the world could so many things happen at once? Anyhow, by 9 o'clock I'd had about a dozen problems, and I'd begun working on them — resolving, adjusting, educating, etc. The gardener left the ranch, a couple of the foreman's children volunteered to water the plants, the horse recovered, I found a person from town who wanted to garden and cook, so we could do job-sharing, and so on down the list.

That evening one of the older horses twisted his gut, and despite our efforts, it had to be put down. The second morning began similarly but without as much serious work, so by noon Margie and I decided to escape for a few hours. When you work continuously from May 10 until October 5, even an hour or two rejuvenates the spirit.

We'd recently bought a Jeep Wrangler and decided to put the top down and go for an "explore." Even after 15 years here, we're still discovering roads and paths we haven't been on before. But when Margie turned the key, silence. We'd loaned the car to some friends, and they'd left the key in the on position for several days, draining the battery. The jumper cables weren't in their usual place, and it took twenty minutes to find some, then we were on our way.

Road construction and a slow pilot car held us up for a while, but at least it was just the two of us and Quito, and if problems came up someone else would have to solve them, or at least they'd be postponed until our return.

Hay meadows were filled with tossing grass two and a half feet high. In the sunlight there were dozens of shades of green and brassy gold; seed heads of russet or rusty brown and accents of yellow unknown flowers; and in the over-irrigated areas, little red elephants. Our mornings vary in temperature. This morning began at thirty degrees, unusually low for July 1 even in the deep valleys of Wyoming, but the temperature by midday had risen to eighty. The warm grass rolled in the wind and surrounded us with a gentle rustling/swishing.

Mule deer cautiously picked their way through the hay meadows, looking strangely steady amid the violent tossing. With surprising accuracy they grazed on the dancing seed heads. One spotted fawn followed its mother, but we caught only glimpses of it and then only when the wind momentarily flattened the grass, which was taller than the little one.

The best hay meadows are in the riparian areas along the streams. In addition to the high-protein mountain-grass hay, alders and yellow-twig willows, and red-twig dogwood, and narrow-leaf cottonwood (our state tree) create meandering windbreaks. They help keep the meadows from drying out too quickly, but they use a lot of water themselves. (A mature cottonwood uses up to 300 gallons of water a day, and in our grove at the ranch we have 264 of these wonderful trees that have diameters of one to four feet.)

A few neighbors had begun to cut their hay. Most have switched to large round bales, which are created by rolling the dried grass into cylinders weighing a ton and a half. One large wagon carries five. Some ranchers continue to gather loose hay and stack it in log structures. They look like rough cabins without roofs. Elk love to gather at haystacks in winter, but the stacks are safe because the elk can't reach over the high log walls of the structures.

Already several of these frames were packed with hay and stacked ten more feet above the walls. From a distance they looked like thatch-roofed houses. A couple of years ago one fellow experimented with snow fencing. He tied the fencing together in a circle, filled it with hay and packed it down carefully. Then he untied the fence and tied it higher up, filling and packing again. He repeated this until the stack was a cylinder fifteen feet tall. Then he retied the snow fence at the bottom, two layers high for elk protection. In a few days the wind came up and blew the caps over slightly, sculpting figures that looked like prairie-dog heads. Repeated on each stack, the meadow looked like it was filled with giant prairie dogs poking their heads from their burrows and staring at something in the distance. Some eventually toppled over, and the elk ruined the hay, so he didn't repeat the experiment. But for about four months, it was an interesting nature sculpture.

Turning down a new road we saw a lemonade stand and stopped. One of our "rules" is that you always stop to buy whatever kids are selling on card tables beside the road. We hadn't met them before and in a few minutes the parents came out to visit and get acquainted, too. We had our choice of yellow or pink lemonade, seventy-five cents per glass was the price, with two choices of glass size and free refills. A white plastic bench had a hand-printed sign on it, "Use this bench to sip your lemonade, so you don't have to sit in your car." A second plank-and-sawhorse table held outgrown toys in good condition. The girl displayed bracelets and necklaces she'd made from the wood beads of an old car-seat cover. We sipped our lemonade and got acquainted with these neighbors whose names we'd heard but whom we had never met, although they were only fifteen miles away (close out here). After half an hour we'd finished our lemonade and made four new friends — even inviting them to our July 4th celebration. What difference do four more people make when you expect 400?

By the time we returned from our four-hour day off we were completely refreshed, had seen some new country, and made some new friends. What more could one ask?

A few summers ago we put up a new addition to the children's program, a full-sized (twenty feet high) Sioux Tipi. Today, it's still set close to the river and upstream of the corral, in a pretty stand of willows. Visible from the dining room, it shows white in the sunset, blue-gray in twilight, and pale gray-orange when the children and counselors have a campfire in it. We often hear the laughter drifting across to the dining room as they tell each other stories. A cozy fire pit sits outside the tipi, and last evening a doe deer and her twin fawns nibbled grass where only an hour before a troupe of children had practiced the ancient and honorable art of marshmallow roasting. The fawns appeared to especially appreciate the bits of melted marshmallow on the grass.

I've mentioned Quito rather often in these stories, and perhaps I should tell you a bit about him and about border collies. They're quite popular around here for working the cattle and sheep. They also make great house pets, but only if they have room to roam because they're the "type A's" of the dog world. But it's their intelligence (sometimes I think it's more than mine) and desire to work that sets them apart.

Quito came to live with us when he was eight weeks old. By the age of twelve weeks he already was herding humans. Staring intently at us, he crouched low and loved to play a game where we dodged back and forth, pretending to try to get by him. By the age of six months, he'd follow the horses in and got pretty good at helping the wranglers take them to the corral. Then one day he was hit by a truck, and his left foreleg was broken in two places. A specialist set his leg and inserted two pins to hold it together. The cast forced the leg up and forward, but he moved along surprisingly fast on three legs. In fact, we had to keep him tied, or he'd be off to herd the horses.

One day I'd gone to move some cattle away from one of our gates and took the bored dog with me. The cattle like to hang out around these potential openings, perhaps waiting for some unwary person to leave it open too long, so they can escape. Some of our guests are uncomfortable with the huge animals. Cattle stare at you and with their high curiosity factor they move closer and closer to a hiker or rider, giving the impression to some that they're ready to attack.

Anyhow, I tried to move the bunch, but as I was afoot, they weren't too intimidated by me. Cattle seem to know where you want them to go and automatically go the other way. I've often heard it said that the way to get them to go somewhere is to convince them you *don't* want them to go to that place. On that day, no amount of hollering, swinging my rope, or throwing stones did much good. As I'd turn to go back to the truck, they'd follow me back to the gate.

Meanwhile, in the truck, Quito pressed his nose against the window, whimpering, and hopping from one side of the cab to the other — he could do the job so much better than this human, who obviously wasn't doing very well.

When I gave up and started to climb back into the cab he leaped past me and started after the cattle. He held his injured leg high in front of him, but the rest of his body stretched out in a full run. He circled the herd, nipping at the heels of any critters that dared to stand up to him. Suddenly, they broke and loped away from the gate. He drove them for another quarter of a mile, trotting behind and hassling any of them that even considered returning to the gate. Then he stopped and sat on a little rise of ground to watch them as they continued to trot away. He turned to look at me then hopped back for his reward, an enthusiastic "Great job, Quito." As we drove past the cattle, he studied them carefully, then laid his head on my leg and went to sleep.

At dinner there was a celebration for one of the guest's birthday, complete with table decorations and a grand entry by a couple wearing Bill and Hillary Clinton masks (not the birthday boy's favorite people). Hilarity ruled, greased with a number of cocktails and an hour of relaxed conversation and singing beforehand. Even the guests who weren't immediately involved enjoyed the prank, had good laughs, and felt included.

Today I'm leading a mountain hike up Medicine Bow Peak, the highest mountain in this area, about 12,300 feet. While not particularly tall compared to the 14,000-footers of Colorado, it's just as dramatic.

As usual, morning sunlight blankets meadows filled with wildflowers; but, also as usual, they are tossed by a cool wind. All twelve of us wore layers of clothing. On mountain climbs we always leave early in the morning, so we can be headed down before the clouds begin to form or thunderstorms threaten us with lightning.

Today is our first climb of the year, and snow banks fill the edges of, and often cross, the trail. Yellow dogtooth violets (glacier lilies) grow profusely in the frigid, wet soil at the bases of the dirty snowbanks. The rocky trail winds past two glacial lakes, "tarns," below white, sparkling quartzite cliffs that rise 900 feet and cast their reflections in the clear, green water.

On our trek, we'll pass through an elfin forest of miniature trees. We'll climb on past islands of krummholz trees, generally alpine spruce whose windward branches have been frozen off on one side so the trees look like tattered flags. Because of the dryness, cold, and short growing season, some of the trees are ancient but only a few feet tall, or even grow prostrate, spreading for a dozen feet or more along the ground. A six-foot-tall tree with a three-inch trunk might be three hundred years old. We'll have to pick our way through the islands, because the lower branches grow so densely that only small birds and mammals can find their way through. (Years ago I did manage to crawl under one, when I was caught above timberline as a thunderstorm raged around me. I stayed fairly dry and definitely out of the wind but was only marginally safer from the lightning.)

Of this group today, several have hiked with me before, and two, who are marathoners, want to race ahead. It's a clear trail, and we can see each other for a long way, so there's no problem. If it were otherwise, we'd stay together. As we meet at the top, they're on their way down.

Spreading lunch on the boulders, we gorge on sandwiches, water, oranges, candy bars, and the view. But in the clear, blue sky, a cloud is forming quickly, floating toward us. It begins as a pale mist, then thickens and darkens as we watch, so we pack up the lunch and scurry carefully down the rock trail. I don't want to even imagine how we could all crawl under a krummholz, so we hurry as fast as is safe. Just as we

reach the car, the mountaintop disappears in the now-black cloud, and thunder growls from it. We climb in just as the first raindrops splatter on the roof. Another perfect day.

Like many of the old-time cattle ranches, we have bells throughout the day — but especially to announce meals. This morning Lee D., a seven-year-old from Atlanta, gave us a new description of what the bells mean. The first bell is "Time to get up." The second bell is "Hurry up." The third bell is "Your food's getting cold."

Cowboys love good horses, friends around a campfire, cattle grazing on a starry night, pretty women, and fancy boots. Boots that are often covered with special carvings or built from exotic leathers — ostrich, water buffalo, retanned elk, etc. Our guests often admire the boots and want some of their own. Perhaps the most unusual were some that Angelo E. just had made for himself. He told me the story of the leather, which was very old. On December 10, 1786, the ship *Metta Catharina* was bound for the Mediterranean, returning to England from Russia. Among other things, it carried a load of Siberian reindeer hides, tanned and rolled tightly, then stacked in the hold. The little ship ran into a storm in Plymouth Sound, England, and sunk. Everyone aboard got to shore safely, but the cargo was lost. Until 1973 that is, when it was discovered by scuba divers. They were surprised to find that the hides were intact, especially the ones that lay encased in silty mud. All the hides had been tanned in the traditional Russian manner, using willow bark and curried with birch oil, which was popular at the time because it made the leather more resistant to water and repellent to insects. The birch oil gave the leather a distinctive aroma, which clings even today. Brought to the surface, the hides were carefully dried and oiled again, so they wouldn't crack. When the soft, chocolate-brown hides went on sale, Angelo bought two and sent one to a custom bootmaker in Texas. The new/old boots arrived and are not only beautifully made, but carry the patina of history as well as of age.

The ranch is a wildlife sanctuary, so we get to see many different kinds of animals, doing things that they normally keep secret from other humans. Two of our guests (newlyweds in their seventies) told me about a rabbit they'd seen. The two were on a horseback ride with one of the wranglers, when they saw a huge jackrabbit in the low grass. It ignored them as they rode to within ten feet of it, in fact it continued to eat grass. Then it ambled into a soft spot in the road and began to roll in the sand, giving itself a thorough bath and sending little puffs of dust drifting on the breeze. After a few moments it stood up, shook itself, and almost strolled into the bushes. Talk about a great honeymoon photo.

We drive up into the Snowy Range — Margie, Justin, and I. At almost 10,000 feet elevation, we pull into a logging road and park the car beside a meadow filled with wildflowers and rock-hard remnants of snow fields. A dead tree across a stream creates a good bridge, and we balance our way over the flowing water and a wet area filled with fading white marsh marigolds. As we hike further into the forest, a gray jay calls and swoops down to a nearby tree, hoping we'll be litterbugs. Rotting logs are scattered where they fell. Some have lain so long that their only remnant is an elongated pile of brown, crumbling wood that tapers into the ground. White bistort and yellow dogtooth violet grow in the mulch, taking advantage of the free fertilizer. Most of the remaining snow is hard enough that Justin and the dog not only walk over it but jump and play without falling through. The snow is dirty on top, covered with a sprinkling of soil, brown pine needles and red snow mold. At the edges of the snow banks, the glistening black mud forms oily puddles and trickles that join the main stream headed for the Gulf of Mexico. It may be July but it's springtime here at 10,000 feet.

This morning I was putting fly spray onto a horse and traveled back to childhood. It's interesting how a scent or a taste can bring back a memory so clearly. The fly repellent was mainly oil of citronella, which was once our only guard against mosquitoes. My mother kept a small bottle on the back porch all summer. When we wanted to go out to play, she'd shake some onto a cloth and douse us with it before we could go into the yard. Today, as I poured the fly repellent onto a cloth and began to rub it onto my horse, the warm, citrussy scent filled the air, and in my memory I was back on that screened porch. Of course I was squirming and complaining because I wanted to get out to play ball with my buddies. They were snickering because of my mother's attention (despite the fact theirs had done the same to them only a short while before). There were surprising details. Right there in the corral I shut my eyes, and saw the white painted porch with its beaded ceiling wainscot. There was the old steel screen with the two holes about an inch across, which I'd accidentally shot with my little bow and arrow. And the patch Mom created, sewing them with black thread, to keep the porch bug tight. And, of course, my mother saying, semi-patiently, "Stand still. You can go out in a minute, or do you want to be eaten alive?"

This morning I went to Big Creek to have a look at some of the riparian protection work we've done. To protect the edges from cattle damage, we've fenced it off entirely and allow the cows to drink only at specific places. I didn't have waders, so I wore hip boots and kept to the shallows along the edges. The copper-colored water swirled around my legs and continually threatened to topple me.

I'm curious about the larvae in the stream and continually picked up rocks slippery with diatoms. These single-celled plants interlock and catch debris floating downstream. The little rock-packed cases of caddisflies clung to the diatoms and bottoms of each rock, and flat-bodied mayfly nymphs slid over the surface. One rock had a stiff, jelly-like egg mass with dozens of pin-tip-sized snail eggs. As I tried to look closer, it fell into the water and sank, disappearing in the fast current.

Nearby was a tapering beach, where the cattle used to drink several times a day. Two years ago it was smelly mud punctured by dozens of cloven hooves. Today it's covered with horsetail and Rocky Mountain rush, and the rock gaps and plants are collecting more soil. Some of the soil is already anchored with spreading green pillows of moss.

Now banks undercut and create little underwater caves, where two years ago shallow beaches gave no shelter to fish. A trout or two flashed out as I probed a hollow with my walking staff. One gooseberry bush tilted wildly toward the water, and a berry-filled branch bounced up and down in the current. I picked a few of the almost-ripe berries and popped them into my mouth. They were refreshingly tart and sweet even though they left a little quid of fibers and seed bits in my mouth.

Two years ago the willows were trampled and eaten by the cattle, but now the soil is covered with tall grass already seeding out. Liberally sprinkled through the grass, wildflowers in blue, yellow, and fluorescent pink stood out against the green grass.

So far, so good.

I passed an old cottonwood tree filled with rotted-out cavities where birds might find homes. Pausing to watch I saw a movement at one hole, and a flash of salmon color darted out, a red-shafted flicker leaving the house.

It was a hot day for Wyoming, probably in the upper 80s, and the flickers' nest cavity must have been well over 100 degrees. Two unfledged flicker babies struggled to be at the opening, but one, more dominant, kept pecking at the other and pressing it down in the heat. Occasionally the bigger one would tire and they would lie together in the opening, one body atop the other and beaks open as they gasped for cooler air. Flies and gnats buzzed in and out of the hot opening and some settled around the young birds' eyes, looking for moisture. Meanwhile, the parents were getting food for them at an anthill, using their sticky tongues to lap up hundreds in a sitting.

The babies squawked in an un-flicker-like fashion, even at humans passing by, hoping that they might be fed. (Young birds in a nest are normally silent until their parents return with food, and then they beg loudly. If they called all the time, predators could find the nest more easily.) Over a period of a week those squawks changed pitch until they became the full-fledged call of a flicker.

Their feathers changed rapidly, and each day we waited anxiously for the first flight. I passed by the tree late one afternoon, in time to watch one fledgling as it dove/flew from the nest cavity, and by evening they were both gone, out into the cool night air.

About twenty years ago, several families built a wooden cross and climbed one of the hills overlooking the ranch. Holding a simple service, they dedicated the cross. It became a popular site for hikes, a beautiful walk of forty-five minutes. The cross perched atop a high rock formation overlooking miles of valleys, mountains, and the snaking, glittering North Platte River. In 1985, two of the fathers from the original families that built it were killed in a plane crash. Friends carved their names on the cross. Now it commemorates all those who loved the ranch and who have moved on.

But after many years the cross began to fall apart, and Justin built a new one. Then he and Lynn E. carried it to the top of the hill and reset it, so the tradition could continue. Like the other it seems to lean into the wind slightly, pointing up-valley. At its base, low juniper bushes with green, hard, gin-scented berries whistle slightly in the wind. On the rocks below, bitterbrush bushes contain a juice so bitter that the slightest touch to your tongue fills your mouth with astringent bitterness. The bighorns love to come here in the fall, to eat the new growth and, perhaps, to enjoy the view. Eight hundred feet below, the valley spreads out in green pastures with undulating, glistening irrigation ditches and happily grazing horses. It's fitting place for a remembrance of friends.

Animals must find humans quite noisy, what with our cars and planes and mountain bikes and who knows what. Tonight I realized that, even when I'm trying to be quiet, I usually don't succeed. I was off on a run (really a jog-walk-jog-walk), trying to move quietly along the path. As I rounded a bend, two marmots were on the trail, already on the alert. Did they feel the vibrations of my feet on the path, or the clumping clumsiness? Or maybe they heard my panting and puffing. Anyhow, one was on his hind legs staring at me, and the other just behind it on all four, ready to run. When they saw the monster that was making all that racket, one "hit the sod." It literally dove into a hole with a chirping whistle, but the other stayed upright on its haunches, nibbling a buckwheat flower as I continued up the trail. Actually, I think he was giving the animal version of a laugh.

Two weeks ago Christian H. and his family returned to the ranch. He's that young teen who has a particularly strong love for nature, especially birds. As his family rode along the river, they saw a few dark feathers on the ground. Christian dismounted to find out what left them and noticed there were more, scattered over a few hundred feet of riverbank. He showed me one he'd brought back for identification, and I incorrectly identified it as a golden-eagle feather.

Since then, though, something has bothered me about the occurrence. I couldn't figure what might have happened to an eagle that would account for that kind of feather distribution without a body. Yesterday, something else occurred that brought it into focus. Another guest was riding in the same area and found yet another feather waving flag-like from a sagebrush. He thought I'd be interested and brought it to me for identification. This time the light in the room was directly on the feather, and I noticed that it had a light, blue-gray cast to it — a great blue heron! Of course. Now I can imagine the drama as it may have played out:

A big heron fishes along the shallows of the North Platte, stepping slowly and carefully along the shallows. He tips his head slightly, focusing on a brown trout as it rests in an eddy out of the main stream. The heron's long legs give him an elevated look at the stream, so he can peer into the water at just the right angle to see the fish. Slowly the bird's long neck

pulls back into a slight "S" as he coils to aim his sharp-pointed bill slightly to the side of the fish, allowing for the refraction of light, knowing exactly where the fish really lies.

He is concentrating on the fish and has not seen the eagle above. The golden spotted the heron from half a mile above. At more than eighty miles an hour, he begins his dive on the unsuspecting heron, folds his wings into a delta shape, and his air speed increases to maximum, just as he hits the heron with a splatter of feathers.

Surprised and mortally hurt, the heron tries to fight his attacker. But the eagle's talons have already stabbed eight holes deep into his body and continue to squeeze. Feathers flutter to earth as the eagle carries the heron upstream. It flies low, because the heron is about the same size as the eagle itself. With a final sobbing gasp, the heron dies and hangs limply below the eagle as one more flight feather drifts to the ground lighting in the twisted branches of a sagebrush.

Stretched out on a lawn I am enjoying the flying skills of a flock of cliff swallows. They are flap-gliding and darting through a flurry of cottony "snow" from the molting cottonwood trees, attacking a cloud of hatching mayflies. Tiny shadows on the grass mimic their movements as they twist and dart like a squadron of warplanes in a dogfight above the cottonwoods. Our local town council authorizes mosquito spraying each summer. In fact, every Monday through Thursday night from 7 to 9 p.m., when the mosquitoes are most active, the city crews spray. Our swallows aren't quite as effective but each one gobbles down about 1,000 a night without any toxic waste.

Most of our swallows are the cliff variety, which spend their summers here then depart in early to mid-August, headed for Argentina. Their graceful nests have a nubbled texture because they are made from tiny beakfuls of mud, which they stick one by one onto the eaves of the barns and a few cabins. The jug-shaped nests cluster in colonies of two or three nests to several dozen. At first glance it seems like a nice little community, but it turns out it's more like something from a soap opera.

Here's what I mean. Bird couples A and B are next door to each other. Female A lays an egg in her nest and female B in her nest. Then the next day, female A goes off to hunt bugs, and female B enters A's nest. She pushes out the egg and lays her own before flying off to hunt. Female A returns and goes to B's nest, pushes out the egg and lays her own. This happens all around the colony. Perhaps the male A is mating with female B and B male with A female. Anyhow, everyone's genes are being mixed and one way or another passed on. The nestlings may or may not be the offspring of the couple raising them, but at least the genes from those birds in that couple are probably being passed on somewhere in the colony. If a nest should fall, which they often do, and the babies are killed, at least the genes from every bird in the colony will continue.

I love the play of light on the cottonwood leaves. Two days ago we had a series of downpours. They came several times throughout the day and until late at night, producing more than two inches of rain. Although the streams quickly muddied, they're clear now, and the only reminders we have are a slightly higher humidity and those glittering leaves. The last shower blessed us about two weeks ago when the land was bone dry, and everything was coated with dust. Except, that is, for the leaves on the cottonwood trees. Even before this new rain the leaves shone, so that from a distance the trees looked like half their leaves were silver, glittering in the breeze as if dotted with sequins. Yesterday the trees began to live up to their name and to spill out their billions of seeds, each with its own cottony fluff. In the heat of early afternoon, the air was filled with little puffs almost like a summer snowstorm. Millions on millions of the seed fluffs piled, like snowdrifts, against fences and bushes. In a few weeks thousands will sprout, but by end of summer most will be dried and dead.

I was reminded today of how folks who aren't accustomed to the country often view wildlife differently from those of us here on the ranch. Margie told me about a hike she took last week. She and five or six others were driving along the road on the way to Douglas Creek. Suddenly, on the other side of the river a dark spot began to move and took form into a bear, loping away and into the woods. It didn't want anything to do with people. This, however, made the guests feel nervous — no one commented on how great it was to see a real, wild bear. About half an hour later, as they strolled on the Douglas trail, she noticed the track of a deer, going in the same direction they were hiking. Then, a mountain lion's spoor joined the trail, its tracks covering the deer's and moving in the same direction. That was too much "nature." Every one of the guests was ready to go back to the ranch.

It's not an uncommon reaction. Some are even fearful of the cattle, and I don't mean the snorting, pawing bulls that make me nervous, too. If you haven't been around cows, they *can* make you nervous. After all, they do weigh more than 1,000 pounds and are usually very curious about the people. It's common for the whole herd to follow a hiker, giving the impression that they are about to attack.

I'm sitting now beside a shallow stretch of Mullen Creek, in a little open valley filled with tall grasses and the meandering, clear stream. The lively water flows through a little marsh in an orderly, but quick and guided, manner — like pedestrians on a crowded city sidewalk. Most water dashes past obstacles then slows but pushes on to its ultimate destination. Other waters pause like shoppers peering in windows or visiting friends, eddying in little circles.

The channel is sandy, and at the inside corner of each bend there are tiny bars with gravel on the upstream side and blue-gray flies scurrying over the sand. My impression is that the soil is deep here; I'm sitting in an ancient beaver pond.

Stepping to the edge of the stream, my foot presses water from the soil, and it flows into the stream carrying with it flecks of mica, sparkling fool's gold. Filamentous brown algae, the color of dirty cotton, wave gracefully on the bottom; but when I pull out a strand, it hangs like an old, torn flag in a drizzle. I search for fish edibles in the strands but find none.

I wade into the water, hiking shorts on and socks off, to enjoy a little stroll downstream. Ice cubes wouldn't melt in the water. It numbs my feet quickly, but I continue. Trout evolved for this, reveling in the frigidity. They do poorly in the shallow streams near ranches, where the water has been heated by the solar collector soil, as it was used for irrigation before returning to the stream. If the water gets much over seventy degrees, they'll die from the heat.

Now I find the fish edibles. Stonefly and mayfly larvae cling to the rocks. At the edge of the water a single small mayfly (naiad), with its three-forked tail and abdomen gills, waggles its body and gradually moves upstream to the next clump of algae. Right behind him six brook trout, from tiny to almost catchable, swim lazily until they catch sight of me. Then they panic and dart from one side of the stream to another until the current catches them and they, one by one, are washed over a little waterfall and downstream.

Dark circles drift along the bottom, shadows from invisible bubbles floating downstream. One minute there is sunlight and shade and upside-down sky reflecting from the stream; the next, pale shadows only, as the clouds hide the sun. It's late afternoon and the white bistorts along the edge of the stream cast their dainty shadows from atop two-foot-tall, leafless and threadlike stalks.

Continuing, now in a little meadow, I come upon a little patch of nettles. They're the ones that give a sting that leaves red marks and itching and burning skin, but these are young and promise to be delicious. Fortunately, I have some gloves and foraging sack with me, so I pick a bunch for dinner.

If you haven't eaten a nettle, you have a surprise

waiting for you. Back at the kitchen we start dinner. As the other foods cook, wearing rubber gloves this time. I rinse the plants and stuff them into boiling water. Twenty minutes later we settle in to a dinner of steak, baked potatoes and spinach-like, bright-green nettles with butter.

The monsoons have visited. Beginning last week wave after wave of clouds washed over us, spilling millions of gallons of water that they've been collecting since the Gulf of Mexico, an "upslope condition." Unlike the normal storms, which bring little moisture and come from the northwest, these are wet and from the southeast. Drizzling continued throughout a day and night. Last evening the front slipped by in the darkness, and this morning our valley was filled with clusters of evaporation clouds, rising into a cloudless blue sky.

By afternoon the clouds returned in a typical mountain pattern: clear mornings and cloudy afternoons that give way to clear evenings. Today one bank of clouds, as it departed, threw a skyhook onto the next bank and dragged it in to hide the stars. But although the humidity is high (35 percent), the clouds hold their moisture.

No matter how comfortable and able to compete a person is in their home environment, they feel more vulnerable and make silly mistakes in a new one. Sometimes it takes something simple to help you get accepted, or laughed at. When I first came to Wyoming after I'd stopped teaching school and

moved to a ranch, I was still looked on as a "city feller." The next spring, as I helped a friend with branding, I was given a typical beginner's job, to vaccinate the calves. One "hand" on horseback roped a calf and dragged it to two other men, who wrestled it down and held it as a fourth branded and a fifth castrated the males. Then I'd move in and inject a vaccine under the skin. My big moment came when a particularly large calf wriggled loose and bucked around the corral, dragging the lariat. I got caught in the rope and was flipped into the air and landed on my back but kept the syringe held high and out of the dust. Several of the cowboys commented, "Did you see that? He kept the needle out o' the muck." It seems simple, but after that I was accepted as one of them and quickly moved to the pros' jobs of throwing and castrating the calves. Such luck.

I was reminded of that today, as I was riding with a ranch guest to check out the horses in a rather distant pasture. A Wall Street type, he was trying to exude confidence and telling me he always felt in control. He "made observations easily" and applied them to whatever situation he was in. From my standpoint, he did seem at ease and probably could be a "good hand" wherever he was working. That is until we went through a gate, and he closed it again — with himself on the wrong side. I wanted to laugh, but I'd been there myself so pretended not to see as he opened it again, stepped through, closed it again, and remounted.

Cowboys often seem to have an off-the-barn-wall sense of humor. Perhaps it is because every one of them I know loves few things more than a joke. They love it whether played on a dude or one of their own, or on themselves. Later, as I gently teased my friend about being on the wrong side of the gate, I was reminded about a joke played on me this last winter.

Several of the cowboys had plans to spend the day shooting badgers. The believed that the cattle, in their blundering, would fall into the foot-across holes and be lost, or at least break their legs. Although I'd prefer they leave these interesting and useful critters alone, since they were shooting them I asked them to save me one if it was particularly big and in good condition. I've created a small museum at the ranch to explain about the history of the place and to give information about the area. The museum could use a mounted specimen to tell about badgers and how they fit into the environment, so people would learn not to shoot them.

Well, they shot one early in the morning and decided to have some fun with me. They propped it up on some sacks in the truck bed, posing it with the clawed legs outstretched. To add realism and shock value, they propped the mouth open in a gaping attack mode and used a rubber band to pull the upper lips back into a vicious snarl. It rode like that all day in the minus-ten-degree air and froze into a badger ice block. Stars were turning on in the dusky sky when they returned and were delighted to see that I'd gone to town for the evening. They left it for me, propped beside my door, where I wouldn't see it until I was only a few feet away.

I returned about midnight and strolled right up to the door before I saw it by my leg. Although I can't verify it, Justin claims I jumped about ten feet. When it didn't move or make its badger growl, I crept closer and realized they'd gotten me good. My buddies probably laughed themselves to sleep.

Our work, especially in the summer, keeps us going from very early morning until almost midnight. Since I haven't had any real time free for a while, I decided to sleep in today. That was unusual for me because, not only did I feel like I wanted to sleep in — but I actually did. I slept until 9:45. A normal sleep-in for me is 6 a.m. Still feeling at ease, later in the morning I decided to take a walk and see what kind of critters I could discover and started along the cattle trail on the river's edge.

There was a light breeze, and the air was filled with the sound of running water from the river and from an overflow irrigation ditch. Yellow warblers chittered in the trees, and in the distance a single raven called. As I began to climb a small, rocky cliff, I heard another bird calling, this time the plaintive, whining call of a young hawk. I couldn't see the bird but could tell that it was up on an overhanging outcrop not far away and decided to investigate. One of the parents took off and flew toward the river, beginning a series of circles over the pines on the other side. It was a prairie falcon with its typical long, tapering wings. The young bird's calls became louder as I neared then stopped. When I was about thirty feet away, I had my first view. The young bird, perched on a little ledge, stared at me, unafraid and curious. I was about to move closer when I heard a whistling from feathers that grew higher-toned and felt the draft as one of the parent birds blasted by me about five feet away. Then, from the other side, the larger female came even closer. Deciding that I'd better move before they got really mad, I backed down the rock.

When I continued my walk along the cliff, I surprised three hawks perched on rocks and was trying to discover if it was one parent and two young or the same young and two parents when first one, then the other of the parents took off with their challenging *wsheee* call. Again I climbed toward the young bird and was about twenty feet away when my foot slipped on a loose rock. I looked down to secure my footing, and when I looked back again the bird was gone.

I continued to climb up the rocks and startled the adults two more times. Finally I climbed a pinnacle of rock and sat astraddle it about two or three hundred feet above the water. From where I sat there was only a light breeze, but down on the river the trees tossed wildly, and the river was rumpled by the passing wind. At this height I could even see the holes in the river, with big trout lounging in them, and the shallow riffles, where the sunlight reflected from both the water's top and the sandy/stony bottom. I couldn't get close to the falcons, but I had a sense of what they could see every day.

The rides to meals are more than picnics. They are shared experiences and togetherness outdoors and in a relaxed setting. At lunch and dinner, the only two with small children, it's a fun and safe place for them to explore a bit and, at the Wednesday Big Creek cookout, a chance to wade and get wet. By midweek, parents are relaxed and more willing to let the kids experiment. One father laughed when his six-year-old fell into the stream and waddled over, arms outstretched, sneakers sloshing. We hung his wet tee shirt on the edge of the grill to dry and enjoyed the boy's antics. If it had happened a couple of days earlier, the father confessed, the boy would have been in trouble.

Our Friday dinner atop a small mountain has the added allure of grand views and sunsets exploding with vibrant color to the west, softer colors to the east. Even the children pause to look.

After dinner and singing around the campfire, the guests who rode horses up will ride back. By the time they get to the top of the ridge above the ranch it's generally pretty dark, and some guests get nervous. But horses are made to graze and to walk dark trails in moonlight and even starlight.

A horse generally sleeps very little, some think only about four hours a day. They continue to graze throughout the darkest nights, and their eyesight has to give them enough information so that they don't eat something poisonous. How do they do it?

Like most animals that hunt or eat at night, they have a membrane called a *tapetum lucidum*. When you look at a horse in low light, you can see a slightly bluish tint to the eyes, the tapetum. It's a mirror-like membrane that sits behind the retina. When the light goes through the eye, it bounces off the back of the eyelid and back to the tapetum, then back to the optic nerve. In essence, animals blessed with this membrane can see at least twice as well as humans in low light. A trail that shows to us humans as merely black shadows probably is like the brightest moonlight-on-snow evening to the horses. So going down a trail in the moonlight, I relax and enjoy the ride.

It's dry again. The clouds and virga have teased us as they swept past. Most cloud bases are high, thin. Yesterday they strobed with sheet lightning and growled with thunder but, despite their promise, gave no rain. Our river's lowering and warmer, more August-like than July. The fish have been gathering in the deeper pools, fighting for the floating morsels. In the quiet frenzy, even the wise, old fish have become careless. Most of our fisherfolk are catch-and-release enthusiasts though. They catch them, admire their size and spirit, then gently free the fish, often without removing it from the water.

At 4 p.m. a storm flashes and crashes and rumbles promisingly through the valley. For ten minutes the wind tosses trees and shrubs; roofs and gutters overflow, then they drip as virga again pass overhead. We had .2 inches of rain, and now the valley is filled with welcome dampness. The leaves shine brightly, and even though we know it will evaporate too quickly, we feel like the land, filled and refreshed, and the fisherfolk are returning to the rivers.

This morning our gatekeeper told me this story: He'd been rocking on the front porch of his cabin, near a grove of yellow-twig willow bushes. Thirty feet away, a young cottontail was nibbling on the mowed lawn, when a yearling mule deer stepped cautiously out of the willows. The deer shook its big ears and walked toward the rabbit, which stood up on its haunches and waited for the deer to come closer, as if waiting to greet a friend. Touching noses, the two reminded him of Bambi and Thumper. Almost as one, the two animals sprang apart and began to run about, bucking and jumping in an animal game of tag. Then, as suddenly as they'd begun, they stopped and touched noses again. Then the deer melted into the willows and the rabbit returned to grazing on the new-mown grass.

The past week has been a resort operator's dream: beautiful, clear days and crystalline nights. And the three rain storms we did have came at the most convenient, for us humans, times. One poured at lunch, two drizzled at dinner, all three when we were inside and could enjoy them, and they didn't spoil anyone's plans. The grass continues to grow so fast we have to cut it twice a week; we're going to have a wonderful hay crop. Each morning there are two jackrabbits (about ten pounds each) by the pool and nibbling on the golf-course fairway. Normally their ears would be cocked and moving constantly, listening for danger. They must feel pretty confident though because their ears hang free, like lop-eared bunnies. Even when the guests hurry past on their way to breakfast, the rabbits barely look up.

Our guests know how much I enjoy watching nature and teaching them how to observe, so every once in a while one of my "students" tells me a story. This morning one of the fishermen returned with a big grin on his face. "Caught a lot of fish did you?" I asked. "Yeah, I did, but this was even better." He told me what he'd seen as he returned to the ranch after fishing on Big Creek. When he climbed into his car, a marmot whistled about twenty feet away and scurried onto some big rocks to pose and let my friend take a few pictures. About a hundred yards down the road, a tawny doe crossed the road and then at a bend another doe was nursing her fawn right beside the two-track. He turned off his car to enjoy the scene, when he heard a soft chuckle and looked down at a blue grouse right beside his car. As he watched the grouse, movement in the sage behind her revealed two powder puffs of grouse chicks. They stepped onto the road and began picking around for seeds and insects. He told me he felt like he was in an episode of "Wild Kingdom," and he was.

We're in the midst of our warmest season. But while most of the nation is in an oven, we're at least simmering on the edges of the stove. In that softer warmth our wildflowers have begun their seasonal progression. Only a couple of weeks ago the edges of the horse meadows were covered with yellow mustard flowers. Now the same meadow is white from daisies, creating the illusion of a snowdrift blown lazily over the green grass. Even a walk through the sagebrush is a special treat because of its scent and because there are sudden bright splashes of color. The blue or purple of penstemon, the yellow of stonecrop in the rocky areas, or the fluorescent orange of the Indian paintbrush — hidden among the soft greens of the sage — always give me a special pleasure.

Times like this remind me of Stan Noga and the importance of a nature mentor. He was a wonderful friend for more than twenty-five years, one who helped me to understand what I was seeing. At the time I met him, I was twenty-one and he *was* old, probably fifty. I'd come west to teach horseback riding (be a wrangler) at a summer camp and fell in love with the West. Stan came to the camp a few times that summer and gave nature talks and took walks with the campers. When he found out that I was interested, he often came a couple of hours early, when I'd have a little free time. I can still remember him strolling up to the corral with a grin and saying, "C'mon, let's go learn sm' things." He knew about the plants and the animals, the native Americans and their use of plants, the plants that were edible and which were dangerous, and he was filled with stories that helped me remember what he taught. He didn't seem to mind my nonstop questions and always answered patiently. I worked with the camp for twenty seasons, the last eight as the manager, and still learned from Stan. By that time though I was able to sometimes teach him something, which delighted him. Shortly after Stan passed away, we left the camp and moved to Wyoming. He'd love it here.

I was in a truck with staff and a load of food headed for our lunch cookout, when we passed some riders. They waved at us and pointed toward the river. I stopped the truck and turned off the motor to watch and listen. In a moment there was a clicking of hooves on rocks and a herd of bighorns walked up from the river's edge. There were five ewes and two lambs less than a month old. The adults were fearless, knowing we never disturb them, but the lambs may have been seeing humans for their first time. They sniffed the breeze, which blew lightly from us to them. It was probably a confusing mix of people, perfumes, gasoline, and picnic meat. The lambs bolted and hid behind their mothers, peering at us carefully, one from behind its mother's rump and the other from a safe position under its mother's belly.

Fifty yards further, we found a mother blue grouse with her young. She called softly to keep them together but not bunched. The chicks were the texture of cottony balls and a light tan, almost perfectly matching our soil. Even watching them carefully they disappeared as they stopped for a moment, then appeared again as they picked at a seed head on the grass. I counted two, then watched carefully and spotted another and another until I'd seen five in all.

Another quarter mile brought us Canada geese in the shallows of the river. There were more than a dozen goslings, the size and color of adults but more tentative in the way they looked at us. The youngsters clustered tightly, resting in an eddy behind a boulder, eyes watching us, silent and ready. The four parents floated upstream, their necks and heads low in a boulder imitation. Then the goslings imitated the parents and changed into a little "boulder field" as we continued our wildlife drive.

The *Saratoga Sun*, our local newspaper, had an interesting article that said, "There were no fish in the North Platte River until the early 1870s." The man who first homesteaded this ranch was believed to be the first man to stock fish here. He claimed to have released 120,000 brook trout into Mullen Creek. They eventually moved into the river, too, and reached phenomenal sizes, up to twenty-five inches, until brown trout moved in after being stocked downstream. The browns are more aggressive fish and the brooks died out (or were eaten), except in the smaller streams where they continue to flourish.

This morning, Margie and I decided that we needed a bit of "F&T" (fishin' and togetherness), so we decided to head for our favorite brookie stream. It's a secret spot we never tell anyone about, mainly because we could never describe to someone how to find it. By 8 a.m., we were in our four-wheel-drive pickup, headed into the Medicine Bows, and by 9:30 we'd bounced our way to the bottom of a narrow, green valley with a classic, meandering brook-trout stream. Rushes and sedge grew thick along its narrow banks, and a series of old beaver dams and springtime flotsam created holding water where dozens of silver shadows darted cautiously to safety when any shadow crossed the stream. You have to be a cagey fisherman there.

Margie chose to fish upstream, and I went downstream. Normally we'd crimp the barbs and release anything we caught, but today I'd forgotten my pliers, so the hooks were armed. No problem, we decided, we'll catch lunch and meet at late morning to roast brookies on the coals of a campfire.

Approaching her first pool, Margie crept up slowly, making sure that her shadow never fell on the water, and cast a little #18 Grizzly Adams, onto the surface. It drifted downstream into the eddy for only a moment, then disappeared in a little swirl as a brook trout grabbed it and dragged the line under a branch, snagging the line and trapping the fish. Margie started toward the stream edge to untangle the line and retrieve the fish but slipped on the muddy bank, fell on her back, and slid to the stream edge as the panicked fish broke free. While her front was dry and clean, her back was wet and caked with mud. She'd been fishing for ten minutes.

Meanwhile, I was downstream, pulling in one huge (five-inch to six-inch) fish after another, then releasing them. They weren't going to get any bigger, and I was about to move to another pool but tried one more cast, which caught in a grass clump behind me. Leaning over to free the hook, I accidentally jerked the rod tip.The hook sprang from the grass and into my index finger, curving in then back out, so the barb rested against my skin.

Margie was just recovering from her mud slide when I came up, and we had a good laugh. Then, "Oh yes, have you got a hemostat?" I asked. "No." "How about wire cutters?" "No, why do you need one?" I showed her the hooked finger, and when she realized it didn't hurt, we had another good laugh at our morning's ineptness.

By this time we'd been on the stream less than half an hour. Her back was drying and my finger didn't hurt. We couldn't get the hook out so decided to stay and fish. I continued downstream, tied another fly onto the line, and continued to fish, pointing my index finger daintily as I cast, careful not to tangle the hook in the line.

At lunchtime, we laid out the fish and started a fire. Still needing a couple more, I went back to fishing as Margie stretched out in the sunshine for a quick nap. When I edged to a little pool, I stepped into the stream and sank to my thighs in ooze. The problem was that I'd been walking a bit too fast, and when my legs stopped, my body didn't. Holding both the left hand with its decorated finger and the right with the rod, I couldn't save myself and did a "face plant" in the shallow water.

It was a scene from a movie that might be called, *Laurel and Hardy Go Fishing*. But the adventure continued.

A light breeze had risen, and I was getting cold, so I built up the fire and stripped to my shorts. Hanging the shirt and jeans in a tree, I padded around the campsite in my shorts, long tee shirt, and hiking boots. "Oh, for a camera," my unsympathetic wife said.

After our brookie lunch, we decided to take a little walk, but my jeans were still wet. I put on the shirt and left the jeans in the tree in spite Margie's warning that we might see someone. "Back this far? Not a chance," I countered.

The shirttail was long and hung half way down my thighs, so I was covered as we strolled down the dim trail. We'd gone about half a mile from our camp when Margie exclaimed, "Omigosh, hide. Here comes someone." Too late.

So we held a conversation on the trail with a couple (who, it turned out, were hiking to write a book). I, dressed in what I hoped looked like very short shorts and hiding my finger with its fishhook; Margie trying to hold a conversation and keep from laughing at me. I wondered if they'd write in their book about the crazy couple they'd met on this trail.

The rest of the short hike I led, but there were snickers behind me. Back at the ranch I got a pair of heavy duty clippers and easily removed the hook. From now on, I'll remove the barb as I buy the fly. Maybe we'll even take extra clothes when I go fishing.

I went on a short hike into the Medicine Bow Mountains. After about an hour I found a fast and clear little stream and was following it, looking for brook trout and possible fishing holes for another secret spot. It was an interesting walk that took me alongside a four-feet-deep meandering brook, which wound its way around rocks and fallen tree trunks. It foamed brightly where it fell over some little rock or log dam into a plunge pool, and there were dozens of foamy pools. Most exciting, it was rush hour with the dartings of little brook trout. As I crept along, trying to see the fish without being seen by them, I almost stepped on a toad. I was at 9,100 feet elevation, and it's certainly more rare to find any kind of cold-blooded critter here, so I looked at it closely. This toad was a medium brown, about four inches long, and in a hurry to hide from me, but I still saw its stripe. A thin, yellow stripe stretched full length along its spine, and in my excitement I spooked every fish in the stream — it was a boreal toad! Just last summer I'd talked with a frustrated forest ranger, who was concerned that they might be extinct in our area. Forgetting the trout, I marked the place I'd seen it and drove to the ranger station to report the sighting. By the time we

returned, though, it was nowhere in sight. Still, there must be others.

Territorial rufous hummingbirds are back now, to the frustration of the "trap-lining" broadtails. Our only two hummers, they have very different lifestyles. The broadtails go from flower to flower, sipping nectar over a quarter mile or more of meadow. The rufous prefers to stake out a flower bed, section of meadow, or a hummingbird feeder as its personal property and chases others away.

Taylor B., our gatekeeper and resident artist, told me this story:

The first summer on the job, he was sitting on the porch at Howdy House, watching eight or nine broadtails sharing a full hummingbird feeder. Suddenly, for about the tenth time that morning, they were attacked by a rufous, who chased them all away and began to sip by himself. This had been occurring for about a week. One of the broadtails flew to Taylor. It hovered a foot from his nose a moment, then flew toward the feeder, risking attack. When it returned to his nose and back several times, Taylor realized it wanted help. At first he waved his hands slowly on each side of the feeder. The broadtails knew and trusted him, so they went to the feeder, sheltered by the moving hands, safe from the rufous for a while. In a few days, however, the rufous became more bold until finally Taylor began cupping his hands around the feeder. At that point the broadtails returned to feed in the shelter of his hands while the rufous landed on a branch and sulked. This became a daily ritual whenever the "Red Baron" was around.

Sometimes Taylor would put his hat up, and the broadtails fed inside the crown, perching easily on the "stampede string" when they needed to rest or wait their turn. It became a game to sneak a broadtail or two in for a sip at the feeder without the rufous seeing them.

Taylor returned another summer to welcome guests and feed the hummingbirds. Because the rufous is also back, the broadtails requested and received protection again. But now there's a new level of communication, and he added to last year's story.

A few days ago one of the broadtails flew to Taylor, who was again on his porch, resting with his hand cupping his chin and enjoying the sunshine. When the bird buzzed him, Taylor looked toward the feeder. No rufous was in sight, so he ignored the bird. After several nose buzzings, the broadtail flew to Taylor's hand and gently slipped its beak between each of Taylor's fingers, then ever so gently into his left ear and even his left nostril. Then it flew to the feeder. He thought she wanted his protection so he went to the feeder and, as Taylor puts it, "I responded in a way the bird must have thought incredibly dense." He cupped his hands around the feeder. Instead of feeding, however, she backed out of his hands and went to the next feeder. He cupped that one, and she backed out to the next feeder. "It was as if she wanted to show this dim-witted oaf that none of them were working," he said. Then she repeated the finger, ear, and nostril probe again and still so gently. As he looked back down the line of feeders he focused on them instead of the bird and realized

what she was trying to tell him: they were all empty. "At this point she must have thought that the feeders and my head had a lot in common," he added. As soon as he filled the feeders, the others, which had been waiting patiently, returned.

Places around here are often named for the first white settlers who came to the area. The name remains although they either moved on or died. One of the places we often visit is Slim's Draw, which I've already mentioned. Today, I'm looking for Slim, or at least his house. According to the stories that have come down to us, Slim was an old rancher who lived at the bottom of the draw and raised a few head of cattle. There should be the remnants of his house here, but so far all I've found is an old and decrepit-looking aspen grove.

Juniper sprout in the openings created by fallen aspen and through the jumble of their decaying, gray trunks. I tie my horse to an aspen and walk into the grove. It's normally slough, or at least pretty soggy. There is still plenty of evidence to show where springtime snowmelt meandered through the undergrowth, cutting shallow channels amid the litter. Scattered hummocks are covered with the lance-like, green blades of irises and their drying seedpods, which rattle in the breeze.

Few woody plants cover the undulations of the gullies, more evidence they're normally fly-thigh deep in water. Mosquitoes rise from the rotting muck that remains, drone around my ears, then settle on my sweaty back to probe for food — me. A few birds chitter here and there, but it's mid-afternoon, and most are resting. I'd expected some blue grouse, but the only sign of them is a few down feathers, curling against a drying pussytoes flower. No cows bother to hide in the thin shade, and there are few cloven hoof marks in the dusty ground at the edges. I pause to rest and listen.

The longer one sits the more they can see. A shadow flits across a tiny meadow, and I look up in time to see a pair of golden eagles, soaring upward across the sun. A stiff, tiny caterpillar is drying on an iris leaf he was eating when he died mid-bite. A cinquefoil bush catches my eye, then another and another. This is normally the time for blossoms — tiny, five-petaled, golden — but each shrub is bloomless, so far.

Aspen have more of the white, dead bark cells on their south sides. It rubs off in a gritty, thick flour-like mass when I brush against a tree and looks like flour on my jeans when I clean my hands on them. The cells act like a natural sunscreen that protects the bark from burning in the sun-on-snow light of winter. Of course the trees require more protection on the south side, since that's where the sun is brightest. Is this a good way to tell direction? Moss on the north, thick white layer on the south.

I wonder how the tree protects itself. A fallen tree, still alive and with leaves green and stiff, doesn't have the powdery white. Will it survive the winter? I think of one aspen at the ranch that does very poorly. It's in a path where sprinklers hit it each day of the summer, flushing off the coating. Could that be its problem?

A rustling under a tangle of dead willow leads to another adventure. I creep forward slowly and peer into the mass. As my eyes become adjusted to the strange shapes of the shadows, I see a tiny glint of sunlight on an eye and a cottontail "appears." Neither of us moves. To see if I can get a response from the rabbit, I try a bird's curiosity call, made by kissing the back of my hand loudly, making a high, squeaking sound. While the rabbit is unmoved, a wren, startled or curious, hops from a bush and begins chirring angrily at me from only about two feet away. Then the bird flies off, but Bre'r Rabbit stays hunkered down, safe in his briar patch.

The afternoon wind begins to rise, and I think about a cool ride home. Hurrying across a dry meadow each step stirs up dozens of tiny two-inch-wide butterflies that flutter away from my steps. For a moment they drop their cloaks of invisibility then flutter to the branches and leaves, fold their dusty brown wings, and disappear again.

At the barn yesterday, a hundred or more cliff swallows circled noisily overhead. It's normal for them to be darting about at all hours of the day, but when they are hunting they are well apart from each other. These were gathering in a loose flock, screaming in their little swallow voices at a single northern harrier hawk. The poor hawk was trying to escape but at every flick of its wings it was dive-bombed by another of the blue-black swallows. The tiny squadron drove the hawk back and forth across the barn yard for about five minutes. Then suddenly, the hawk put on a burst of speed, gritted its teeth (beak?), and with a final parting scream of its own, flew away from the flock, looking back over its wing to check if it was being followed. As soon as the hawk was gone, the flock disintegrated and the birds again began bobbing for mosquitoes.

The same hawk was back today. Again I watched as the swallows chased it back and forth across the compound. I was thinking, dumb bird, when suddenly, it turned over in the air and snagged one of the swallows in a talon. With its booty in claw, it made a straight line path away, leaving a cloud of somewhat befuddled swallows.

It's a continuing puzzle, to discover where the trout are hiding. Years ago, when I was writing feature articles for a local newspaper, I had a chance to go with a team from the Game and Fish Department as they did a fish census. For two days we waded up a river, shocking and counting fish. One of the team carried a generator on a backpack and a wooden rod with an aluminum hook at the end. This was attached by a long wire to a second identical rod carried by another man. When they dipped the rods into the river, an electric current passed between them, and any fish in the current was temporarily paralyzed. The rest of us followed with nets and a small, floating cage. When a fish bobbed to the surface, we'd scoop it up carefully and put it into the cage. Every fifty feet or so we'd stop and check out each fish. We'd weigh it, measure its length, evaluate its health, put a wire-like tag in its back, and let it go.

At one point the team passed through a small village. It was a narrow place but with deep water and houses on each side of the stream. We wondered whether there would be any fish in that place. And when a woman came out onto her porch and told us, "You're wasting your time. There are only two fish in this part of the river, and I know them both by their first names," we almost skipped that section. After some discussion we decided to continue. Well, everyone else must have thought the same and never fished that section, because we caught more and bigger fish in town than anyplace else along the stream.

Sometimes we think that a less accessible spot on the river might be better fishing. The fish census taught me that that isn't necessarily the case. Yesterday three families decided to get a box dinner and go as far upstream as they could go, planning to fish until dark. They drove about five miles upriver then waded across the Platte and hiked another mile or two upstream, seeking the perfect hole. The area was beautiful, pristine, and they saw no signs of any other fishermen. Several hours later each had caught *a* fish, but the action they craved just wasn't there. The box dinners became snacks, and they returned to the dining room, where one of the entrees that evening was smoked trout in a flaky pastry shell.

On a hot and dry hillside a few feet above a moist and grassy meadow, a montane vole was creating a safe home. These rodents have gray-brown backs and silvery breasts. They look like mice except that they are a bit larger and have very short tails, only about a third the length of their body

I was sitting rather uncomfortably in the shadow of a red-twig dogwood (at six feet, I'm not overly tall but my mother used to say that I was "all legs and arms." I usually don't "fold up" too well), but I was somewhat hidden and could watch through my binoculars. Only about twenty feet away, the vole filled the field of my glasses, and I was enjoying a close look without frightening her. She would arrive at the entrance and peer out with only those round, slightly bulging eyes and a bit of her silvery breast showing. As it was safe, she dashed out and, with a single motion, nipped a plant at its base then backed up, dragging the whole plant into the den hole. In a few seconds she would return for another until, in twenty minutes, she had cleared virtually all plant material from a two-foot circle around her hole.

Montane voles are usually nocturnal, and I haven't seen them very often, except this year. When they go through their boom-and-bust population cycles they build up to such numbers that only a few at a time can be out looking for food, so some have to be working the day shift. Their population must be booming now.

Voles seem to prefer the wetter areas. Whenever I walk through a bog or damp meadow, I can usually find their covered tunnels, looping through the grass and littered with bits of plant clippings the busy creatures have dropped. Pieces of plywood left lying on the ground make nice tunnel tops, and when one has lain for some time I can pick it up and discover an interstate of tunnels looping through the grass.

One morning I surprised a mother and her family of three when I lifted a tunnel cover. They scurried out of sight quickly but it was more proof that they're in a boom cycle. Voles have an uncommon way of dealing with high populations: they simply have fewer young. In a normal year she might have had six to ten babies.

Other small mammals appear to be doing well too. We have a few new neighbors here in our cottonwood grove, a group of chickarees — small squirrels with pretty brown-gray, brassy-colored hair. They're fairly cheeky fellows in general and not at all afraid of people. I'd stopped at one of the flower beds, to admire the tapestry of color the flower gardener had created, when one of the chickarees came down from a tree about ten feet away and scolded me. I guess I was too close to where he'd hidden some food. To tease him a bit, and to see just how close I could get him to come, I copied his chattering call. His hind legs quivered angrily, as if he were ready to jump, but his front legs were planted firmly, and he tilted his head, listening and confused. We had our little standoff for almost a minute, then he flipped around and scurried up the tree where he picked up something he'd lain on a branch and started eating.

I'm sitting on a rounded boulder in the middle of Mullen Creek, studying how the stream's flow has been affected by a clump of distorted alders. The old tree's branches are full of broken branches and other litter that have floated from upstream and lodged against the alders. Now the pressure from the water has distorted the tree, and many of the branches are bent horizontally. After several years of this pressure they've spread out over the stream and are growing upward again. In the process they created a perfect shelter over a trout hole.

Even now, at the stream's low flow, the water pours over a gravel bar and dives into the litter of sticks. It has cut a deep hole in the stream bed, where it curls around the alders, and four trout, eight to ten inches in length, wait in the darkened shelter. They wait patiently, eating bits of food and insects that float down to them, beneficiaries of those bits of drifting branches that caught on the alders, changing them and their stream.

The population of our village is about 500. One of the joys of living in a small town is to walk down the street or drive down the highway and know most everyone you meet. It's satisfying, and you feel a part of your place. I've felt the same way about being in the forest or the mountains. Over the years, one or two plants at a time, I've learned most of the plants, birds, a few of the rocks, most of the trees, and understand some of the processes that are going on. If I find a plant or a bird I don't know, I feel uncomfortable every time I meet it until I find out what it is and perhaps how it fits into the environment or how it was used by the Native Americans or pioneers. So a walk in the forest is like that walk down the village street, where I meet my friends.

May was cold and wet. Pasque flowers here are normally early May bloomers but came out a full month late. Of course at the time we were a bit depressed. We do look forward to warm weather, and summer's already far too short.

There has, however, been a benefit to our spirits. Those June flowers poised underground and waited for warmth. When it came, they shot from the ground, and today they bloom amid the July flowers, which bloomed on time. Alpine meadows are adrift in colors and textures like I've never seen before. Even a careful hiker must tread on flowers with every step. Even the critters are enjoying them, but in a different way of course. I've watched marmots and deer chomping on scarlet gilias and Indian paintbrushes, and this morning two horses lay in a drift of field daisies like children on a lazy summer day.

One morning I paused at the edge of such a meadow, near a clearing stream that continues its runoff three weeks later than usual. A narrow footpath meandered through the grasses and sedges beside a stream then gently climbed to a drier shelf a few feet above the wetter riparian. There were so many blooms that I decided to see how many plants I could spot in 100 paces. Here's that list:

golden aster	bedstraw
yellow stonecrop	scarlet gilia
Indian paintbrush	wild rose
brome grass	thistle, both musk and elk
chickweed	sky pilot
purple vetch	showy aster
goldenrod	sulphur flower
pink geranium	cinquefoil, flower and shrub
golden aster	harbell
Parry's penstemon	bullrush
purple loco	kinnikinnik
sage, big and silver	purple penstemon
pink clover	yarrow
purple loco	lupine
carex rush	rabbitbrush, both big and little
lichen in green, black, and orange	

As a bonus, there were chickadees, a kingfisher, a western flycatcher, yellow-billed sapsucker, a half dozen song sparrows and many pine siskins. Butterflies? There were tiny mountain blues and yellow sulfurs.

Yours from the life-exploding valleys of Wyoming.

I took a group of guests on a nature stroll yesterday to a little meadow down by the North Platte. We waded through thigh-high grass, talking about riparian areas and how important they are to the overall ecosystem. Yellow and Audubon's warblers twittered in the cottonwoods around the meadow, and cliff swallows darted above the river, snatching up the latest mayfly hatch. A harmless brown garter, our only snake, paused a moment as we surrounded it then slithered easily on its way as our circle parted. The chokecherries are still green but slowly turning bing-cherry red, and I'd just stripped a few from a branch when someone called, "Here's a porcupine!"

It was a footlong youngster, weighing about five pounds and clutching the trunk of a cottonwood at our eye level. As I moved in close, everyone became concerned. "Be careful," they said. "It'll shoot its quills at you." Porcupines don't do that. Catching the long hairs at the tip of its tail, as John E. had shown me, I demonstrated how easily the quills come out. It's when an angry or excited animal bites the porcupine or gets hit by the whipping tail that they get a noseful of quills; it's not a slingshot sort of thing. Using a small branch, I gently pushed the longish gray hairs aside, and we could see how they were interspersed with sharp, white quills that gave a mouthful of pain to any mountain lion, coyote, or dog that tried to bite it. Then, bothered by our intrusions into its privacy, the porcupine continued paw over paw up the tree.

Later in the afternoon there was a rustling outside my window, and I looked out to see a doe and fawn only about ten feet away. The doe browsed on a willow bush then tore off the seed head on a stem of brome grass. A little farther on she sampled a bit of our lawn and then waded into the tall grass at the edge of the mowed section. All this time the fawn was at its mother's hip, watching (although it, too, did try some of the bluegrass). When they stepped into the high grass, all I could see was the mother's head and ears; the fawn disappeared. When they reappeared at the edge of the path, the fawn was behind the doe, trying to nurse between her back legs, but she kept walking. The fawn's muzzle was wet with milk as it got a few sips each time she stopped to tear at a willow branch or flower. Pausing, it raised its black nose and soaked muzzle, sniffing the air, then leaped, bucking down the narrow trail as they wandered into another thicket.

Brown and Mardi C. were fishing when a flight of twenty or so ducks flew upriver toward them. As the ducks passed by, behind them came the sound of a distant jet, with air rushing over giant wings, a golden eagle chasing the ducks. The roar suddenly increased then quieted as the eagle spotted the humans, banked upward, and flew away.

It seems that each larger bird, whether crow or

hawk or eagle, is chased by smaller birds. This morning I watched a golden eagle, perhaps the same one, flying over a peak by the ranch. It was being strafed by a half dozen crows that cawed their laughter at the eagle, which twisted and ducked each time they dove on it and pecked at its head. After ten minutes of chasing, when the poor eagle couldn't get away, it swooped low over the sage and landed. Then it hunkered down and waited. After another ten minutes the crows lost interest and flew off to find other fun. The eagle waited until they were well away, and then it took flight — in the other direction.

Every few weeks the cowboys move the cattle from one pasture to the next, avoiding overgrazing and giving the men a chance to check the cattle and doctor any that need it.

Today, a dozen staff members sat on a deck eating their lunch. They could see a fisherman from New Jersey casting for trout on the North Platte below a cliff. On the hillside above, several cowboys moved a bunch of heifers toward a new pasture. The hillside was gentle, so no one seemed concerned until, suddenly, one of the heifers tried to escape and ran toward the river. Seeing the cliff, she spun but kept sliding toward it, out of control. At the rocky edge, her rear legs went over, and she scrabbled for a moment with her forelegs, trying to get a hold. The staff at the lunch tables was transfixed, the fisherman was unaware of the drama two hundred feet over his head, and cowboys galloped to her rescue, too late. The cow fell backward into the air like a huge, black rock, and splashed upside down in the river only fifty feet from

the startled fisherman. Then she stood and trotted by the astonished fisherman, pausing at the river's edge to shake herself and continue to make her escape.

Our normal humidity is about 20-25 percent but today it's 66 percent.

Two days ago the rain began at about 6 p.m. For an hour it poured, overflowing gutters, muddying the streams, and battering the grass and flowers in the calm air. Rain curtains pulsed over us several times. Huge raindrops pounded the undergrowth and beat their predecessors from the trees and bushes. Then the storm turned gentle, and a fine drizzle fell until about midnight, recollecting on the plants.

At dawn yesterday, the dewdrops joined the raindrops on plants. Of course each droplet weighed less than a thistle down, but soon gallons of water had collected on the willows and grass and trees and flowers, and all drooped under the welcome weight.

Cliff swallows hid under the eaves of barns and were dry, so they began winnowing the air in search of insects, but few seemed to be up and about. I watched a slightly bedraggled yellow warbler probing among the willow stems for damp and slow-moving insects. Each time it landed on a branch, a spray of water drops shook off, and the branch lifted higher.

As the sun rose further, the air heated, and the hillsides of the mountains around the ranch began to fill with evaporation clouds. A few were dense, but most of them were so thin you could see the sage as if through a white veil. As the temperature rose, the clouds picked up more moisture, and the clouds thickened and continued to drift along the hillside on an imperceptible breeze. When the sunlight hit the willows by my office window they began to stir ever so gently, as a baby from a nap, waking then dozing. Within half an hour their leaves were dry, and they again stood erect.

By that evening the clouds had fractured to the point where it was mainly sunny, and we enjoyed our usual Friday-night cookout. The horses stood quietly, tethered together. Guests polished off "just one more" chocolate cupcake, washed down with a steamy mug of cowboy coffee or cold milk. Singers gathered around the campfire, enjoying the melodies and each other. Then the sun dropped below the horizon, and its light bounced off the clouds, creating brilliant colors in them as if afire. At first we looked to the west then realized that the entire sky was orange and red and dove-soft gray and gray-pink. Everyone paused, even the children climbing on the rocks, who were themselves bathed in the colored light. The magic lasted more than ten minutes, and then dusk settled as we started for the ranch.

Yours from Wyoming, where sunset fills the sky.

August

Our chef, Kent T., does an excellent and very creative job but sometimes even he gets stretched. Last night, six-year-old Gordon R.'s parents and he snuggled up at bedtime to read Dr. Seuss's book, *Green Eggs and Ham*. This morning, Gordon went to the dining room and asked to have green eggs and ham for breakfast. The cooks used a bit of green food coloring, and in ten minutes Gordon was happily working his way through a plateful of ham and vibrant green eggs. Sam I Am wouldn't have been happier.

We try to express creativity here and to encourage it where possible. I recently asked one of our staff, an excellent young artist, to do some drawings for us. She asked me what I wanted her to draw. As I thought myself around the ranch, I discovered to my delight that I have a wonderful mental photo album. It's filled with pictures in full color and black and white, with telescopic and wide-angled views. I thought about the Monday-night barbeque with the horses grazing or playing in the meadow by the pool, colored for a moment in golden light, just before sunset. That would be pretty to capture. But then this morning I watched a set of doting parents with their first son on his first pony ride. And a group of six laughing adults, teasing their new rider friend, with his reins too long and his slouched posture, as they forded the river to ride in the forest of Black Cat. Or Mr. B., an alert and charming Birmingham lawyer in his 94th year (54 summers of them here at the ranch), rocking on the office porch, talking with friends and reading the *Wall Street Journal*. Or a throng of children chattering down Main Street, almost dancing in their whirling excitement as one grinning child carries his first fish to the guides for cleaning. (I heard later that he'd surprised his parents by having it served to them for breakfast.) Wonderful, vibrantly colored pictures with plenty of ideas for our young artist.

Cattle and sheep ranchers get along now. Some even raise both kinds of livestock. That wasn't always the case though, and several range wars were fought over the right of "woolies" to graze here in Wyoming or in neighboring Colorado. Even nonranchers often weren't too sympathetic to the sheepmen's cause. An article in the *Saratoga Sun*, dated November 23, 1899, said: "The slaughter of 3,000 sheep in Routt County, Colorado, belonging to the Geddes Sheep Company, is to be deplored, but the owners should have thought of that before invading the cattleman's country."

Most sheep now are kept in pastures, generally guarded by dogs or sometimes llamas, which keep the coyotes away most of the time. But traditions die hard and often a job can only be done in the old ways, a shepherd with his dogs, following and protecting the sheep in high pastures. There are still big flocks of sheep ranging through the mountains, tended by a shepherd and five or six dogs. I met a shepherd today, in a grassy meadow at about 8,500 feet elevation. The broad meadow was filled with perhaps a thousand quiet ewes and busy, blatting lambs. Most shepherds used to be basque, silent and unwelcoming, speaking a language different from any I've heard. But now, more are from Chile or Argentina. This shepherd was a small man with shaven cheeks and a long, dark moustache. He rode a large (perhaps sixteen hands high), muscular

paint horse and sat easily in an ancient and scuffed western saddle. At first the shepherd smiled slightly and reined in his the horse when I walked over. He was more friendly when I talked with him in Spanish, but the friendliness disappeared quickly when he discovered I didn't have a cigarette for him. As we talked, his four border collies lay down facing the flock, totally absorbed in their work.

After a few minutes of strained conversation, he nudged the horse and rode off without a word of farewell. He'd been in the mountain with this flock for six weeks already, with only the dogs for companions. They communicate but don't talk much, and perhaps he just wasn't used to people.

He slowly circled the flock, at a distance of about fifty yards, followed by the dogs. There was a clear two-track road but he avoided it, passing through a grove of aspens and into a sage meadow. I supposed he preferred the rough way over the cultivation of a road. He has a lonely life, perhaps, but one good for contemplation and quiet appreciation for nature and life in general.

I wondered about the shepherd. Does he have a family? In the fall, does he return home to them or go to another flock? Is he a gentle man or does he shed the peace of the mountains and turn abusive? Margie and I lived in New Mexico for a while, and I taught school. A couple of my students had fathers who were shepherds. One family had seventeen children, one for each year the father was home for a few weeks before returning to his other flock. The oldest boy had so few memories of his father that he could barely describe what he looked like. He just recalled the fights, shouting, and drunkenness — and the blessed peace

when his "old man" left, then nine months later another sibling.

A chamber of commerce booklet I read recently described this as an "85 percent sunshine area." I guess that's another way of saying, "semi-arid region." Even though clouds billow by midday, the rain is only in scattered drops that give no real moisture, or it rolls through dramatically, then the sky is clear again. Wildflowers are beginning to dry, and the yellow stonecrop is shriveling, as the moisture it stored is used up.

But there are benefits. Our ranch compound, in the riparian area beside a permanent stream, is a true oasis, and animals gather in our cottonwoods and alder groves and willow thickets. We see birds that normally pass by or stay out in the sage. Goldfinches and western tanagers nest here, and their brilliant oranges, reds, and yellows flash round the groves. At any moment of the day or evening the hummingbird feeders have eight to ten whistling around them. Two does, each with twin fawns, live right by the cabins. They're welcomed even when they have the bad manners to nibble our delphiniums, which they aren't supposed to like.

After a rare week of rainy days and nights, our classic summer mountain weather has returned. Ranchers had waited impatiently, repaired hay equipment, peered at the sky, and gone to sip yet another cup of coffee when it started to rain *again*. Some watched as acres of already-cut hay molded in the lines of windrows. Mice, voles, rabbits, and others moved into the neat "hayways," out of the heaviest weather and well hidden from predators. They lost their houses today though, as the sun dried the grass enough to bale and ranchers unlimbered their balers. In one field, I watched as a rancher rolled up his hay. Two red-tailed hawks and one northern harrier perched, each on its own big bale, and watched as the rancher stirred critters out into the open where the hungry birds waited to pounce on the easy prey. Even crows got into the act. The windrows also hid earthworms, mice, and other delectables, so flocks of the black birds followed the baler and swooped down in dark clouds, following it across the field.

Six friends and I rode up a sage-covered hill with a cool wind whipping our horses' tails and manes, and we squinted as bits of gravel blew into our eyes. As we neared the ridgetop, five kestrels flew low over the sage and beat their way slowly uphill. At the skyline, they launched one by one into the wind, turned, and rocketed downhill again. We stopped to watch as they got to the bottom and started uphill to repeat the maneuver again and again. If birds could smile, I think they'd have been grinning.

The wind creates other interesting events. One of our guests, Roxie H. of San Antonio, Texas, is a stylish and classy lady, even in waders and fishing vest. She just reported a first, for me anyhow. With her son, Walter, she had been fishing on the North Platte, in a riffle near John's Rock. As she cast into the wind her line blew back on itself. She "hooked" a thirteen-incher on the Adams 14, and it put up a good fight, but it felt different.

After a five-minute battle, she worked the fish toward shore and saw that the fly was on *top* of the fish. She thought, "I must have hooked it in the dorsal fin," and landed it with a net. But the fly wasn't in the fin. The line had passed all around the fish behind the gills, and the fly caught its own leader. She'd lassoed the fish! Roxie turned it loose to fight again and returned to her catch-and-release fishing, Wyoming style.

I strolled up a sagey valley and climbed one of the hills to a gravesite we recently discovered. It's atop the ridge, and I imagine the sad, loving care with which the person was laid. The grave orients toward a spectacular, open view the person must have loved.

I sat by a boulder, thinking about who they might have been and enjoying the view myself. After a time a chipmunk came out from the rock carrying a Douglas fir cone and started to take it apart then eat the seeds. She fed under the shadow of a juniper branch, safe from hawks. At the base of her rock lay a pile of old and new cone bits. She'd obviously used this rock for some time, and her relatives before her, because the rock itself was covered with orange jewel lichen, which needs the nitrogen from animals' urination and defecation as fertilizer.

Ants with red heads and thoraxes and black abdomens (known by the creative name of red ants) crawled over the rock, picking up crumbs from the chipmunk picnicker. In the edge of the litter pile was a lost leather glove, a "righty," with just the fingers protruding. They'd been chewed by mice, and most of their fleecy insulation had been carried away to soften and warm their nests.

A nuthatch landed on a branch and, seeing me, gave a "zeet" warning sound. The chipmunk scurried away, and I never saw it again. In a few minutes, though, the nuthatch returned and continued its search for insects between the branches and on the trunk. Two ravens paused in a tree beside me, black silhouettes against the blue sky. Some crows cawed below, and in a moment several flew over with their wings making a soft "woo-woo-woo" sound, like that from a miniature helicopter.

It's a busy place, probably one the person in the grave would have enjoyed.

For some years we've tried to find signs here of the passing of Native Americans, but they are few. Not many miles away though, in springtime or after heavy rains, an arroyo sheds skulls and broken and cut bones of buffalo, bits of sharpened flint and other human-made items. It's the site of a "buffalo jump," where they had been chased over a cliff by the hunters before the U.S. was being formed.

It's calm and cold; in the semi-darkness of false dawn I sit cross-legged in the center of a tipi ring, perhaps two hundred years old. It's the only historic site we've identified on the ranch so far. This ring is about ten feet across and consists of stones half buried in the grass, which some young brave may have used to weight down the edges of a small tipi. Perhaps he was on a vision quest, seeking revelation from the spirits as to the direction for his life. The stones, about ten pounds each, are gradually sinking into the grass.

At the edge of a little tongue of a hill, the ring has a wonderful view in several directions. It seems to have been set in such a way that someone sitting at the entrance could greet the rising sun and, later in the day, bid it farewell for another night. I'm here now, listening to the beginning of day and smelling the cold, moist air. Birds flit busily across the meadow, on their way to the willow thicket behind me. In the silence I easily hear the whir of their little wings. Now the sun peeks over the horizon, and light floods the western hills. The dark shadow of a mountain glides over the dewy grass toward me from the west. I'm always amazed at how fast the sun rises and how quickly the shadow comes toward me, but I always have to sigh in gratitude as the warmth wraps me like a blanket. Now the sun is fully up, gazing down at a light-filled meadow from yet another cloudless sky. I'm ready to start my day, having had my own kind of vision.

Last evening a feeble drizzle began about 7:30. The raindrops were so tiny you could only see them if you looked into the light, toward the sunset. To the east they were invisible, except where they spritzed onto a still pond, creating tiny ripples.

This morning, about 10 o'clock, one of the wonders of the North Platte began to occur. Tiny, white-winged mayflies (tricos) began to hatch, crawling to the undersurface of the river and forcing themselves out into the world of air. For the next two or three weeks a mass will hatch each morning, and millions of them will fill the air over the river, creating a trout feeding frenzy. For fisher-folk with the eyes to tie the tiny size twenty and twenty-two flies onto their lines, the fishing will be spirited, as even the cautious, big, old trout join the feeding frenzy.

Fly fishing is a lifetime sport, for a person can continue to grow and learn about the hatches and the ways of fish, as well as enjoy the experience of being in a stream in the wilderness. We have several ninety-year-olds who take to the streams. Sometimes, though, an older guest might need special help.

A longtime friend called me a few weeks before he and his wife, Nancy, were to arrive. Rod L. told me that Nancy had developed a problem with her eyes, and that she had to wear dark glasses to be outside in the sunlight. Her vision was very poor, but he wondered if I could get her some extra help, so she could still fish. Nancy is in her seventies and has been fishing for a long time, so I knew how much it meant to her. I promised to see what we could do.

The head guide was Maggie G., a dynamic and intelligent young woman who had just graduated from college and was spending her second summer with us, sharing her joy of fishing. When I told her about Nancy, she immediately volunteered to take care of her.

Each morning they met at Nancy's cabin and spent several hours together on the stream. As two dynamic women with many common interests, including fishing, they had much to talk about. Maggie knew that fishing wasn't just about catching fish, so was careful to describe what she was seeing as they drove to the stream. "It's a blue-sky day with only a few little puffy clouds on the horizon. We just passed a doe and a spotted fawn. They were hiding back in the pines, and I almost didn't see them because they were so still....A yellow warbler just flew out of a willow bush out over the stream, to catch an insect and then flew back again....Way, way up above some pale gray, granite rock outcrops there's a hawk or eagle soaring. It's been getting higher each time it makes a circle, and now it's just a dot in the sky....The cottonwood leaves are bright yellow-green and shine brightly with their coat of morning dew....Sunlight on the water flashes like a sequin dress in a spotlight....Let's try this fishing hole. It's about fifty feet long, and the stream here is thirty feet of so wide. At the head of the hole there's a little boulder dam about two feet high, and the water pours through a gap in the rocks making a thick bubble blanket for about ten feet. There are some fish there, hiding under the bubbles, and I can see one feeding right now in fact. When we get to the middle of the stream, we'll be about ten feet from the edge of a big, overhanging willow bush where another fish or two are probably hiding. You can use a regular cast into the bubbles and a side cast under those willows. If you cast above them it looks like the current will carry the fly to the eddy under the bush. There aren't any other willows behind us, so the back cast should be okay and you won't have to worry about catching your line up...."

Then, as Maggie supported her arm, Nancy stepped into the stream, and they began to fish. Each day was a learning experience, as they tried different ways to communicate, never hurrying, just enjoying each other and the days in the stream.

Nancy asked good questions. She felt the wind and its strength and direction but asked what the water surface was like at the moment. "When I cast at 10 o'clock, where is the line landing? Am I using enough power to get the line to the pool, or do I need to allow for more wind drift? Are there any hatches going on that you can see? How about trying a Grizzly Adams?"

At first they nymphed a lot (using a sinking fly), because Nancy could feel the fish on the line and respond to it herself. But she loved to dry fly fish (where the fly floats atop the surface). Although Nancy couldn't see the action, Maggie talked her through the drift of the fly, both poised for a strike, when Maggie would say, "Now!" It was often frustrating, because they missed so many strikes, but it was so satisfying when they did catch a fish that they kept trying. Gradually, they improved their catch rate.

When Nancy hooked one, Maggie watched in awe. Nancy had been fishing for years, and even without seeing she knew by feel how to fight the trout. As she was about to bring it in Maggie would say which side she was on and Nancy would bring the fish in that direction for netting. Before releasing the fish, Nancy would wet her hands (to avoid damaging the protective slime on the fish) and feel the fish in the cold water as Maggie described it. Then the two would work to revive and rest the fish before returning it to the stream.

Saturday was the last day to fish, and they decided to go to The Meadows, a beautiful, natural area with sweeping, open pools and sneaky, native fish. They'd been fishing for a couple of hours when Nancy hooked one. It fought hard, but after about ten minutes it lay in the net.

Maggie told me later: "I couldn't have been more excited! I netted the twenty-two-inch native rainbow and told her, honestly, that it was the biggest native I had seen all summer, not to mention the prettiest. I let her hold the fish and she was amazed at the length. I described the beautiful colors of the fish — its green body with the little black spots, the iridescent red stripe along its sides, and the little white strips along the bottoms of its fins [it looked like the fish had been dipped ever so slightly in some white paint], which means it's a native."

As Nancy told me the story that evening in the lodge, her eyes sparkled, and she put her hands to her chest above her heart. There was a special pride in being able to do something she'd loved for so long, rising above the challenge her eyes were giving her. And there was a connection that had been growing all week with a young college girl who took the time and love to help a grandmother continue to do something she'd always loved.

Yesterday I took an overnight hike through the local wilderness area. The first two hours, I wandered through a jumble of fallen trees and dense vegetation, which made a four-mile walk really more like five. Sometimes I could walk from one tumbled tree to the next for a hundred yards or so. To keep myself to a straight line without a compass, I followed the low sun, which I could see glowing orange through the trees. Camp was beside an open meadow with a fat doe grazing about 100 feet away. I fell asleep with a nearly full moon rising and shining on my face. About midnight a troupe of coyotes serenaded me from across the meadow. Next thing I knew it was morning.

After breakfast I plucked a purple fringed gentian and began to sketch it. I was holding it in my left hand and drawing with my right, when a red-rumped bumblebee flew to the flower, landed, and wriggled right into the blossom. The corolla was so deep that only the tip of the bee's tail showed. After almost ten seconds it backed out and flew away. I finished the drawing and set the flower down. As I was packing to leave, the bee returned. It seemed puzzled when the flower wasn't there, circling in confusion exactly where it had been. Did it buzz to itself, "I'd swear there was a flower right here....Must be getting old."

One very dry summer a couple of years ago, I wrote: "I walk up a gentle slope on the back side of Bighorn Ridge today. It's covered with sage, bitterbrush, and white snowberry (buckbrush). At the bottom of the slope, scattered yellow-flowered rabbitbrush is almost at its height of color. There's a slight breeze, but the only sound at first is the soft burble of a little stream through a gully with a young aspen grove."

Rubber rabbitbrush are low shrubs among the sage. Most visitors fail to recognize them as separate species until this time of year, for now each is covered with a broad crown of golden flowers. They must be sweet and filled with nectar, because each day several varieties of butterflies, dozens of flies and bees share the feast. In the morning or evening light the rabbitbrush glows as if it were lit from within. If I broke a stem in June, it oozed white, rubbery sap. In the '40s, when rubber was in short supply, this dry land plant received a little attention when it was considered as a possible source for rubber, but it grows too slowly to be a commercial product.

The native Americans used the flowers to make a golden yellow dye. Before pots, they would prop a buffalo stomach on a tripod and fill it with water. Nearby, carefully chosen fist-sized rocks would heat in a campfire. The women were careful to use dry stones from the sunshine, not stream rocks, which had water trapped in them and would explode when heated. After these were well heated, she used willow tongs and dropped the hot rocks into the stomach pot, one by one. She removed them as they cooled, and put another heated rock in until the water boiled. Then the rabbitbrush flowers were added and stirred in gently as the water turned golden. After adding a pinch or two of wood ashes, the golden soup was used as a good permanent dye.

At the base of each pale-green, distorted sagebrush is a little scattering of dried sage leaves, which fell off last spring as the new ones came on. They retain a bit of their color and, when I 'crush them in my hand, their scent. Decomposing Douglas fir cones are half buried in the soil, washed down from the last rain two days ago — our third "storm" with less than .2 inches of moisture in each in the last four months. Moss, living in the shadows under rocks and junipers, is half green, half brown as it revives in the long-withheld moisture, little as it was. Patches of soil have washed downhill and created dikes a half-inch high, from the recent "flood." A mountain ball cactus, half buried under a bitterbrush, presents a pale prickly surface; only a few feet away the paddles of the prickly pear share the same bit of thin soil with another bitterbrush. The prickly does have pears, green at the tip, darkening to magenta toward the base, but they are thin and withered.

A squadron of Clark's nutcrackers flies low over me. Their wings pump slowly, giving off a low rhythmic beat, not unlike that of a distant helicopter.

As I walked out last week, the ground was hard, crusted. Today there's a slight springiness, much like the reviving moss. The ground makes a more comfortable seat, and I settle in to watch and listen. Soon the moaning wind dies, replaced by the droning of bee flies and the clacking of the grasshoppers. In my imagination I can almost hear the footfalls of the silent red ants that begin to crawl on my legs. A yellowjacket buzzes in and pauses to sip at the sweat on my leg. When there's a fluttering some inches over my head I turn slowly and enjoy a mountain chickadee on a Douglas fir, standing on tiptoes to see if I pose a threat. It decides not and begins to search for insects, upending itself and dangling like a rock climber on a boulder overhang, but from a shred of dried bark. It strips away another shred and eats an insect that was cringing under it, then leaves with the lightest of wing flutters.

Other critters are less trusting. A flycatcher pauses on a sticky, cone-laden bristlecone pine and watches me with dark, alert eyes, then flies to a juniper at a safer distance. Next, there's a little rustling at my feet and for a half second I look into the striped face of a least chipmunk (Tamias Minimus). It doesn't trust humans, and with a squeak and a twitch of its bristly tail, it disappears around the corner of my boulder seat.

I flick the red ants off my pants, not because they're a bother but because I'm moving on and don't want to take them too far from home. Only then do I look carefully at my backrest.

The boulder is part of an outcrop of multicolored metamorphosed granite schist. Lines of pink quartz and plagioclase feldspar intersperse with a lighter-colored rock that glitters from millions of points of tiny leaves of mica. All this is overlain with ancient, rounded patches of lichen in green, black, yellow, and orange.

Perhaps hundreds of years ago it broke and split in two pieces. Over the hundreds of years, the six-inch crack between them has filled with debris — needles from the firs; manure, discarded nests, and skeletons from mice and chipmunks; cones and seeds from the trees nearby. A juniper is growing from one end of the crack, and at this time of the year, is doing its best to produce seeds. This year they're deflated balls of purple seeds exuding the strong aroma of gin when pinched.

An ageless, gnarled pine grows at the downwind end of a boulder. The wood is splitting, gray, carved by wind and grit that has given it a character like the wrinkled face of an old man, as well as the hard and brittle personality that man might have. Dusty-green lichens grow on the vertical trunks, and bright-orange jewel lichens encrust the crotches, where little animals hide from hawks.

A limber pine, rare here, is very old and mostly dead. A woodpecker has cut a hole *under* one of the dead branches. One branch is very much alive. It's laden with sticky green cones five to six inches long. The dripping sap is pale yellow and clear, but as it dries on the branches below it turns sugary with tiny, clear crystals and preserved ants throughout.

As the moon waxed full, some of the guests began to experience lunacy, at least of a sort. Or perhaps it wasn't just the moon; perhaps it was that they'd just been having a great time together and felt relaxed. I stopped in at the Round Room, our ranch gathering lodge, about 10 o'clock. As usual there were a few people sat by the fire after dinner, talking and enjoying cocktails. One or two were reading about the cowboys and Indians from the area, their feet propped up, enjoying the fire. At the Steinway, Tommy L. played showtunes, and a dozen or so people stood in a circle round the piano singing, including Georgia Mc., a professional opera singer. In the bar Joan K., Roxie H., Henry H., Chris C., and three or four others were gathering. Dressed in their fishing waders, they were preparing to make a midnight foray on the river at John's Rock, if they could find it.

The next morning I asked about their expedition. While the fish seemed to be asleep, the seven humans had a wonderful, wet time.

Summer's beginning to fade a little. There were several cool nights earlier in the month, and although it's warm again, many of the wildflowers have begun to droop and fade as they wither in the late-summer sun. Both the Platte and Big Creek are lower now, and the big trout have gathered in the pools behind rocks and below waterfalls, vying for the floating bits of food and hatching trico mayflies. Of course the fishermen and women are wearing big grins and tell (tall?) tales about their big fish of the day (which of course they released to be caught again, so we have to take their word about the size).

This morning we had our last breakfast ride of the season. As usual, we left with the food truck at about 6:30 and arrived at the ridgetop about 7, just in time for a special treat. It began to rain slightly, actually a drop here and there from a big, gray cloud just overhead. There didn't seem to be any chance it would continue, so we sat on boulders and enjoyed the view. Suddenly, the sun burned its way through a hole in the cloud and streamed down across the meadows and the ranch below. The light through that drizzle gave the

effect of a translucent, silver slide from the cloud. It lasted only a moment or two, because the fast-moving cloud passed on to the west and left us in sunshine.

A very steep trail starts at the edge of the river, snakes its way uphill through the Douglas firs, and finally winds through the sagebrush. I walked up it today at mid-morning.

At the sagebrush area the trail is narrow and shared by people and animals, the narrow arrowheads of deer prints interspersed with the "waffle stomper" shoe prints of humans. Not too long ago I found cat prints and a pile of cougar "scat" (manure) right on the trail. Below me I hear the squeak-honk calls of three separate Clark's nutcrackers, and a chickaree calls like a squeaky door opening and closing slightly. Then one of the nutcrackers begins a continuous call, and gradually the others pick it up. Is it an alarm call? I can't tell, and nothing seems to come of it. Perhaps it's just the equivalent of singing around the campfire.

As I walk downhill toward the trees, the light catches a series of spider filaments. The sunlight appears to slide, one shard of light after another, down the lines. More than ten feet up a fir tree, a two-foot-wide web catches and refracts the light into blues and reds. When I walk back uphill a few feet, the spider's handiwork disappears.

Douglas fir cones, with growths that look like "mouse tails" sticking out, litter the ground. This year's are green, tight. Last year's are still russet brown, with bits of sticky, pale yellow and sugary-looking resin clinging on them. Older ones are gray-brown and brittle. When I sit on a log to sniff at the moldy, pine scent, a mountain chickadee lands nearby and chitters at me. He looks a bit scruffy, as he's in the midst of his molt. At my feet, shiny black ants wander the forest litter and over the gray rock tripe. Most of the grasses are reaching maturity now, still green but brown-edged. Part of the holly grape is turning, its green leaves now edged with red. A golden-mantled ground squirrel scurries onto the log, sees me and leaps away and under another log.

As he climbed into his car to depart the ranch, one of the guests told me this fun story:

He'd gone on a last walk, strolling toward the metal bridge over the river and through the canyon, enjoying the quiet and solitude for the last time until next year. As he jogged toward the ranch, the horses were in the meadow by the road, grazing. He thought to himself that it would be nice to have a last ride, or at least to say goodbye to the horse he'd ridden all week. When he stopped and leaned against the buck-and-rail fence to look at the herd, one of the horses looked up from its grazing and trotted over to him. It was Lightning, the horse he'd ridden all week.

I decided to take a walk and climb one of the cliffsides near the ranch. It's not the kind of cliff where you have to dangle from ropes to make the ascent; rather you must simply pick your way along rock ledges and up grassy slopes. This is the kind of walk I prefer. It challenges me physically, but it also gives me plenty of time and opportunity to see what's happening below my feet, on the rocky foot path I'm following.

I left the road at 7,620 feet elevation and paused beside a five-foot-tall musk thistle. To us they're a prickly, prolific pest. On the other hand, the insects gathering on the purple flowers appear to think they're a special treat. On one, a red-rumped bumblebee probed at the fading blossoms, its hooked feet grasped firmly at each floret, almost as if it were embracing the wind-tossed flower, pushing its way through the flower as a human might through tall grass.

At 7,650 feet, vari-colored lichens encrusted the pale granite rocks. A burnt and a golden sunrise orange lay beside warm yellows, and those beside dead grays and vibrant blacks. The dusty- and Sherwood-forest-green types seem to have cup surfaces, the orange jewel lichen grows in pillow forms. Others looked like blackened, scabby skin. In the bright sunlight, the surface temperature must have been at least ten degrees higher than the already-hot air, but a single, shiny black ant hunted over the nubbled surface.

Reaching 8,000 feet, I sat enjoying the view. Beside me I discovered a micro environment I hadn't expected on this hot, south-facing hillside. A little crevice, created by the overhang of a foot-long rock, was filled with brittle ferns. I supposed the dripping dews of morning and the heavy rock shadows protect them from the dry heat.

Under the shade of a gnarled and splintered juniper, at 8,160 feet, the ground was covered with spiny-leafed holly grape, laden with purple fruit. I paused to reflect in the shade, to soak in the view, and nibble some of the musky grapes, members of the barberry family. Wildlife love the berries, and some of our neighbors still gather them, to make a bit of jelly. Here the plants droop near the ground, but in the forest they seem to grow more upright, perhaps stretching for the sunlight out of the wind. Even as the wind curled round the rocks five feet

away, and into the little hollow, the leaves barely moved, so the wind didn't have a chance to steal the holly grapes' moisture.

As I climbed out of the hollow, I noticed that almost every crevice had a collection of droppings, mixed deer and bighorn. They too must have stopped to enjoy the view.

At 8,040 feet a nighthawk, white wing bars flashing, took off from the rocks at my feet. It flew bat-like, in erratic circles and through a grove of firs, then landed. With its mottled camouflage and its way of perching parallel to the tree branch, it seemed to melt onto the branch. I saw where it landed, but even through my binoculars I could barely discern the bird.

My final reward came at the top, 8,360 feet, where I discovered a small pocket in the rocks. Its granite edges were sculpted and softened by centuries on centuries of wind and water, providing a comfortable backrest. The wind flowed over my rock haven with a high-pitched whistle. A black spider hopped quickly over my shirtsleeve, hunting in silence. A white-breasted nuthatch hunted down the bark of a pine just ten feet away. I dozed in a pool of sunlight, dreaming of soaring eagles and hot and windy, stony hillsides abuzz with life.

Today I visited the burnt-tree site, where we discovered a burning tree this last June. It happened early one night after a lightning storm — no rain. Lydia B., one of the wranglers, was returning from town and saw a light on the hilltop. Instead of ignoring it she reported the sighting to me and Justin, and we started up the mountain with shovels while Laine gathered the crew to help.

With his younger legs and lungs, Justin dashed uphill while I panted along as quickly as I could. The hillside was sagey, and I followed a zigzag route. A single, old ponderosa pine was aflame. We tried to gather the burning bits onto rocks, so they wouldn't spread, and used our shovels to control the fire. This tree grew out of a rock, and the cliff that night appeared to be 25 feet high. (Today I discovered it was more than 100 feet.)

When the other helpers arrived, about eighteen in all, we started a shovel brigade, because the closest mineral soil was 100 feet away, and we needed it to snuff the flames. It took about two hours to stop the fire.

All round now I could see the evidence of our struggle — the pits from which we'd dug the soil, scorched branches we'd pulled from the tree and scraped to put out the coals, a pair of lost gloves lying under some litter. Their fingertips were already mouse-nibbled, and some of the fleece had been carried away to the rodents' dens.

The night of the fire, the smoke poured from the rock on which the tree grew, for the roots were burning, too. We tried to snuff the fire with soil, but each time we covered a place, more thick and yellowish smoke flowed from seemingly solid rock. Today I could see those once-invisible cracks clearly. The heating and cooling had separated them to a quarter inch wide and some rocks were broken into brittle shards.

Inspecting the tree, I savored the delicate scent of charcoal mixed with warm pitch and discovered this wasn't its first brush with fire. In the shiny, squarish blocks of charcoal I could see at least two other healed scars. This time, however, the lightning split the tree into three parts, twisting two of the branches almost full circle; they won't grow again. Or will they? I'll watch it next year, to see how and if it recovers.

(Note: I returned to the tree the next spring. The tree lives, mostly. The branch that was twisted full circle is dead and turning gray. Greenery sprouts from the others.)

A little group of friends hiked to Green Mountain Falls today. The trail was well marked and wound from aspen grove to lodgepole forest and back to aspen. Winter snows are deep here, arriving early and leaving late. One beaver-cut tree, a ten-inch-thick aspen, showed how even the animals have problems with the snow. The beaver must have wanted it very much, because the stump was notched all around in three places. I imagined a beaver starting his first cut standing atop a two-foot layer of snow. Interrupted, he returned when the snow was another eighteen inches deeper then got interrupted again. Perhaps the old fellow muttered to himself, "Ain't never gonna git that thang down." The final, successful, cut was atop five feet of snow.

The flowers here are late, another indication the snow stays a long time. Purple monkshood went to seed at the ranch two weeks ago. In the shadowy groves they are at their prime.

Most people enjoy seeing wildlife but don't take the time that's necessary. Oh, you'll see things if you hurry through the woods, but you'll see more if you go slowly, or even sit. "If you really want to see some wildlife you have to be patient," I told my nature walkers. "Get a book, set your lawn chair under or in a bushy spot, and settle in to read." Animals frighten easily when people walk through the woods. Sometimes it can take more than half an hour for them to return to activity. Sitting quietly you become part of the environment, and the critters come close.

This week a guest took me up on the idea. She read quietly for a while and then was visited by a parade of friends. Birds fluttered in the leafy branches nearby; a dusty black and yellow garter snake slithered by her foot, ignoring her slight cringe; two deer, and more. No sooner had one passed than another took its place.

Rich K. told me this story about a persistent marmot. He and Jim K. had taken a last early-morning drive up Blackhall Mountain knowing they had to leave that day. As they hiked away from the parked car, a marmot climbed into the engine compartment and perched on the warm motor. Rich discovered it there four or five hours and 100 miles later, when he opened the hood to check the oil. It didn't snarl or threaten, but it wasn't about to move. At first Rich's thought was for the safety of the rockchuck. He poked gently, finally knocking the furball onto the ground where it as quickly leapt back onto the engine. After another hour and a half, when all other efforts failed, they decided the safety of the marmot wasn't as important, closed the hood, and drove to Fort Collins, another 100 miles. At the vet school, Rich was joined by three others, two under and one above the car who tried again until finally a tranquilizer put it to sleep. They removed the warm, limp body from the engine and arranged its delivery to a new home back in the mountains near town.

In the earlier days of the ranch, people could ride

a horse to the Friday-night cookout and, if they didn't feel like riding back the horse, it was no problem. The wrangler simply tied the horse's reins to the saddle and let it travel along freely. It could get scarey, because they wouldn't follow in a line, and they'd sometimes kick or bite at each other or even the horses being ridden. Lucinda M. recalled her humiliation one such night. She'd ridden most of the way, but on reaching the top of Devil's Slide, she couldn't muster the courage to ride down. In the darkness she slid off, tied her reins to the saddle, turned it loose and walked down. She claimed to the wranglers that she'd fallen off, but they knew. One wrangler helped her up behind his saddle, to cross the river, and noted, "Funny how as y' was fallin' off'n th' horse y' still had time t' tie up yer ryns."

From June 13 until July 30, we had .2 inches of rain. Perfect "guesting weather," lousy ranching weather. Day followed day of blue skies and warm, tanning sunshine. Every cookout went off on schedule, and we didn't even have to worry about our Friday-night cookout. Normally our mountain weather forecasts are the same throughout the summer: mid-afternoon cloudiness followed by thunderstorms. Early-day heating causes air to rise and clouds to form as the moisture is sucked from the ground. Evening cools the clouds, and they can't hold their moisture, so it rains. Ah, for the normal. Alfred Stieglitz, an early pioneer in photography, called clouds "Songs of the Sky." It's about time they sang to us.

Most of August followed July in its dryness, but two days ago we had an all-night rain. It paused for early morning then started again, a fine mist that soaked into the ground. Riders in yellow slickers left the corral in a spirit of adventure and returned only a bit wet but carrying wide grins and special memories.

This morning, departure day, our valley was filled with fog, a sure sign of a beautiful and clear day. Someone took a last and very early climb up one of the hills and looked out over the valley of clouds. They reminded her of heavy surf crashing in slow motion onto a beach. But she had to look fast for, as the sun rose, the clouds began to evaporate. In minutes the buildings and meadows formed through the mist, like a photo coming out in a tray of developing liquid, and the whole valley sprawled below her, filled with clear, luminescent light.

After breakfast, one of the other guests went to draw the scene. Setting a tablet on her lap, she sat in a shady spot beside Mullen Creek. She began to study the line and texture of the stream and its banks, the dancing reflections of the sunlight on the water, the breeze playing through the branches of the willows. Charcoal pencil poised, she closed her eyes and heard the rustle of cottonwood leaves in the breeze, the chirping of a chickadee from a spruce tree, a deer ripping and chewing at grass tops in a nearby thicket. She sharpened her charcoal and smelled the crushed horsemint where she sat and felt the cool moistness of the earth. Sights, sounds, scents surrounded her, and when the lunch bell rang she realized the morning had passed. Not a single stroke of charcoal had touched her paper, but an indelible image had been impressed upon her heart.

There are still legends about a guest who used to

come in the 1940s and '50s. No one could recall his name, but they remembered his manner of fishing.

Each day he would don his fishing equipment — no boots — and stroll to the corral. A short ride took him up- or down-river, and he rode into the stream to begin his casts. The man was very successful, and I thought this was merely his particular idiosyncracy, until I talked with Tom J. Tom's been coming to the ranch since before he was a teen, and his theory was that the horse's hooves would turn rocks and stir the bottom. Rather than startling the fish, this would actually attract them as mayflies and other larvae were roiled into the water. In their feeding frenzy the fish would be easy to catch. Needless to say, this method of fishing has now been outlawed by the Game and Fish Department.

Each day for the last week, the riders and hikers have been treated to the sight of four buck deer, their antlers in velvet, lounging in an aspen grove just above the ranch. The deer are so aware of our harmlessness that they don't even get out of bed as the humans pass by. Sunday, down by the bridge at the Platte, seven bighorn sheep spent their day greeting our arriving guests. I walked out to see for myself. There was one sleek, sable-colored ram that, judging from its half-curled horns, was about four years old. The others were three, paler brown ewes and their month-old lambs. At first the lambs hid behind their mothers and peered around them curiously. Then, as they discovered that their parents weren't afraid of me, they began to frolic, head-butting each other and hopping from one sage mound to another. I sat down to watch, and in about five minutes one of the more curious lambs eased toward me, sniffing the air and watching its mother for signs of alarm. When she continued to nibble the grass it lost its fear and began to graze about ten feet away. Twenty minutes later the little flock moved on and so did I.

One family has been coming from Texas for years now, three generations in fact, but they haven't met many of the local skunks. That changed this week. Going to dinner tonight, someone left the cabin door slightly ajar. When one of the boys returned later, he surprised a skunk in his mother's open suitcase; it seemed quite at home, barely bristling as several people peered in cautiously. The skunk was well fed. He'd eaten chips, fruit, and cookies from the porch and was in a pretty good humor. Backing slowly away the boys returned to the dining room to tell their story. By the time I got to the cabin the skunk had moved on, leaving a mess but no scent.

We normally don't see or smell them, but this has been a "skunky" month. No one has been sprayed, but our guests have reported one almost every night. They're active even in the mornings. On my way to breakfast I watched one (perhaps the same cabin visitor) amble across the bridge by cabin 1 and down Main Street. In no hurry at all, and not fearing any of the humans who were watching from a safe distance, he poked around rocks and trees, hunting.

A skunk's body (or tail) language is easy to comprehend. This street walker raised his tail from time to time, warning us, then put it down and went along his way. Then he seemed to tire of us, and his direction of travel became more purposeful, until finally he ducked under the Round Room porch.

We set out live-traps and caught about a dozen. But almost immediately another was in its place. At first we thought it was the same one, returning. But when we marked the released skunks with a bit of spray paint (one good spray deserves another), those didn't return. The new animals were probably results of a ripple effect. When we introduced a new skunk into the territory of another, someone had to move, and they moved another in the next territory, until finally one of the animals discovered our unclaimed territory.

They're so brazen that they aren't recognized as stinkers until they're very close. Jack D., from Missouri, was sitting on his porch reading and enjoying a cigar. In walked a skunk. At first Jack thought it was the ranch cat and was about to welcome it to his lap for a visit, when he realized it was a skunk. After a momentary confrontation the skunk turned and silently padded out the door, which Jack quickly shut behind it.

They're generally no problem, though, even when they themselves get startled: The moon was full, casting a bluish light through the small bedroom at A Towers, a staff dorm. Richard D., one of the fishing guides, was asleep when he felt a movement on his feet, as a cat walking over the bed. Then the visitor began licking Richard's feet, which poked out of the blankets. He, too, thought it was Houdini, the black-and-white ranch cat, and shoved it off the bed. The critter scuttled under the bed and began to growl in a very uncatlike way. Richard, now fully awake, stood on his bed and jumped from chair to chair in the darkened room, until he could escape from the room. Then, he peered around the door and flicked on the light. The toe-licker was a skunk. Bristling, but not spraying, the startled animal began to look for an escape route. It easily climbed back onto the

bed and out the open window, disappearing into the night, leaving a slightly shaken Richard and the slightest aroma of *eau de skunk*.

One of our guests, White M., and his daughter, Courtney, told me this story:

They were fishing on the North Platte. Scattered clouds and a hatch of tricos were already making the morning memorable, as both were catching and releasing plenty of trout and enjoying just being together. Suddenly, from the willow thicket nearby, they began to hear a desperate, bleating call accompanied by the scurrying and thumping of animals' hooves on moist ground. It continued for a half minute till a two-month-old fawn leaped out of the willows and into the river. Only a heartbeat behind, two coyotes leaped into the water, like retrievers after a downed duck. The deer was taller than the coyotes and gained ground because it pronked while its pursuers had to "coyote-paddle" through the deep water. The three were about halfway across the river, when the mother of the fawn and a yearling charged after them. Reaching the far shore, the fawn bolted downstream, followed by the sprinting coyotes, followed by the doe (its yearling had paused mid-river and safely watched the drama). Suddenly, the fawn veered into the river just as the doe reached the tails of the coyotes, which realized their danger and ran into the willows. Without breaking stride, the doe followed the pair into the willows. Silence returned, and the two youngsters waited tensely midstream. Several minutes passed, and the yearling turned back, wandering slowly, cautiously, to the riverbank. The fawn trembled with fear and cold but stayed in the river and watched for its mother to return. Several minutes more passed, and the doe returned, waded to her fawn, nuzzled it reassuringly, then led the way back across the river to safety where they joined the yearling, stared around nervously, then faded into the willows.

It's late August, but signs of fall are beginning to show. By cabin 1, a Great Plains cottonwood is already more than ten percent yellow. Last night a dozen robins, mostly young ones with mottled breasts and dull-gray backs, hunted the short grass on the lawns. They'd run along a few feet, pause with heads cocked as they listened/watched, then stab at the grass and pull up a worm. Our hummingbirds will be gone in a few days, and we'll take down the feeders in a day or two. This morning it was twenty degrees, but the flowers continue to bloom, at least for the moment.

A late-afternoon wind turns up the bottoms of the cottonwood leaves, as it soughs gently through the groves and across the grass, like waves on water. Browsing on the purple-black berries and browning leaves of a bearberry honeysuckle, a fawn shows its new independence from its mother, who has wandered around the cabin. The spots he's worn all summer are beginning to fade, except on his rump. Sensing my presence, he turns and sees that I'm looking at him. I expected the fawn to "run to mommy," but he stares for a moment with those huge, soft, liquid brown eyes and returns to eating. He's pruning the new growth on the honeysuckle, much as the rest of his family has been pruning the flowers in our gardens and flower boxes all summer. When a red-shafted flicker gives its sharp call, the fawn startles and walks stiff-legged to its mother; together they walk to the stream for a sip of fresh water before returning to their grazing.

The showy aster already have begun to curl their petals in the colder nights and have turned from lavender to fading red-pink. The light has already begun to change, and with the combination of shorter days and colder nights, we'll notice the change of leaves more each day. In about two weeks the fall color will charm us. By the first part of October and until next June our forests will be bare. I know that some folks around here think of fall as a depressing time, looking ahead to the cold of winter. I prefer to look back on what this past year has brought. Besides, we still get to have another month for our friends to visit.

September

About the first part of this month each year, I notice for the first time that the aspen groves aren't quite as green as they were a few days ago, and a distinct damp-leaf scent drifts gently in the still air. Usually the first to change, my bellwether tree is an old Great Plains cottonwood. While the others pale gently, about the first of September this giant becomes vibrantly yellow-orange. It's already changing.

An early fall storm grumbles and flashes around the hills that surround the ranch. Low, thick clouds and low sun paint gray light and cast a greenish sheen on the clouds, which reflects softly around the ranch buildings. The remaining flowers seem brighter in the somber light. The other, frost-nipped blooms may already have warned the hummingbirds to head south on their journeys. (I often wonder if those flights are lonely journeys because, unlike the blackbirds or ducks, I've never seen a flock of hummingbirds. What a sight that would be.) Within the first week of the month we remove our hummer feeders even though we're told by experts that it's shortened days and not just food supply that moves the tiny birds south. Whatever the reason for their departure, we miss their bright energy.

Fall will arrive soon. By the tenth of the month we'll generally have had three or more hard frosts, and the flowers will throw in their petals, giving up summer for another year, although on the calendar it's another three weeks. Our poor gardener's been working hard to create the special beauty here at the ranch, but those 25-degree mornings were too much. The swallows left weeks ago, headed for South America, but then, they have a long way to go, and they always leave before nights really grow cool. A few days ago I watched as two goldfinches, yellow darting shadows in the willow thickets, looked like they were flying just for the joy of flight.

The bald eagle's juvenile finally left its nest and has been struggling to learn to hunt but is still clumsy. Yesterday it landed on a small bush at the edge of the river and crashed when the bush was just too small to hold its weight. The youngster is, after all, nearly the size of its parents. Both parents continue to feed their offspring, but leave the youthful eagle to learn flying finesse alone, at least for now. By next week the three of them will be soaring on the rising thermals, and the young one may even have a try at trout fishing.

A mink has moved into the bank of Mullen Creek, right beside the foot bridge. It's a small, brown animal about a foot long and looks black when it's wet, which is most of the time. Several people have seen it swimming in the stream, and one even watched as it as he?/she? chased and caught a trout. It then swam to a rock midstream, where it sat upright on its haunches and ate the fish head first, holding and eating it hot dog-like and apparently with as much "relish." Views like this are one of the reasons this ranch is a wildlife sanctuary.

A doe has passed another summer with her fawn in a willow thicket near our dining room. On most sunny days we can watch them grazing or browsing contentedly. Yesterday, Darryl, one of our guests, crept toward them to take a picture. Feeling that he was being followed he turned and found a big jackrabbit. It sat on its haunches like a big cat, only six feet away, and looked up at him curiously. After three more times creeping forward and stopping, the rabbit was still right with him. Darryl turned again, crouched, and from only four feet away he snapped a photo. He continued his deer stalking as the rabbit left him, hopping slowly away to nibble the lawn.

This morning, September 4, we had our first "hard" frost — ten degrees. Preparing for their upcoming flight south, the birds are nervous. Two days ago I watched a dozen barn swallows chasing each other and squabbling over their uncrowded perches. Today every swallow is gone, as the barn swallows follow their cousin cliff swallows south. On Main Street the honeysuckle bushes are laden with their bright-orange berries. I watched a robin trying to pick some, but they were just barely out of reach. As he lunged at the fruit, he continually fell from his bouncing-limb perch. He kept it up for some time, until he heard me laughing and then flew off. I guess I must have embarrassed him.

The brown trout are restless, too, and leaving the river to begin their slow and dangerous trek upstream in Big Creek, Mullen, Savage, Cottonwood, and any other trickle deep enough to wriggle through. We have a small dam on Mullen Creek. Its purpose is to form a small pond and keep the water deep enough to protect a drinking-water pipe that crosses under the stream. So long as the pond is there, and the water is moving, the pipe doesn't freeze.

As I noted, the dam is small, no more than two feet high, but it's an insurmountable barrier for the migrating fish. So we built a ladder for them. It's a sloping plywood piece about four feet across and eight feet long. Planks made from two-by-six timbers are attached perpendicular to the water's flow and alternating halfway across the flow. They slow the water and give the fish a chance to zigzag their way upward. On any day at this time of the year the little pond, no more than twenty feet in diameter, will have a dozen big trout cruising and resting, creating splashes and ripples as they feed on floating bugs. They generally move on by the next day and are replaced by others in their annual autumnal mating parade. The truly large fish generally wait for October, when Mullen's quite low. I've often cheered a 24-incher as it struggled over a logjam's scant inch of water.

It *feels* like September. I think that if I were totally unaware of the date and led outside blindfolded, I could tell fall was coming. Several times each day I find myself sighing happily as I enjoy the mellow air and the subtly changing colors of the trees gently whisking a cloudless blue sky. But it's more. It's cold mornings and warm days and sparkling leaves blowing lightly in the wind, each day glistening with a paler green as the light shines through them. It's animals eating more aggressively and birds flocking, calling with eager gathering-together sounds unlike the melodic songs of May. It's cowboys riding out each morning, dressed in chaps and spurs and heavy coats, returning in the afternoon in chaps and spurs and shirtsleeves, driving cattle before them in bawling black bands, out of the aspen groves and into pastures with brittle but thicker grass. And it's fisherfolk, casting their favorite dry flies onto the reflections of sky and cliff, then bringing a big rainbow in on the smallest tippet possible.

It's still officially summer, but the trees are hinting of autumn. The vibrant green leaves of spring long ago gave way to the deeper tones of summer, and now the trees are sprinkled with bits of gold and copper. At an open window, with a warm breeze on my face and listening to Vivaldi, enjoying the tapestry being woven before me, I wondered, what if each color, value, or chroma produced a different note or chord? What kind of symphony would be played by an autumn or summer day? How would dawn or sunset differ? Or a calm forest from a breeze-tossed treescape?

One of the fishermen returned from Big Creek with a new kind of fish story. He'd "beaten the water to a froth" since about 9 a.m. without a strike and at noon was about to return to the ranch, when he heard rustling in the willows at streamside. As he watched, a mink scampered across the narrow beach and slid into the water about twenty feet away. The creature was curious, apparently young, and unafraid of the fisherman. In fact, it swam in a small circle around his waders, looking up at him curiously. Hungry now, the mink dove where the man had been fishing without luck. Moments later it surfaced with a fourteen-inch rainbow trout held crosswise in its jaws. As the mink returned to the willows with its catch, it paused and looked back at the fisherman as if to say, "Now that's how you do it." The fisherman decided to call it a day. He was, after all, in Wyoming, where even if you don't catch a fish it's still going to be a good day.

It's interesting how our thoughts move from one thing to another so quickly. We flash from present to future to past in the blink of a mind. Today I was looking over our local newspaper (it comes out once a week and keeps us abreast of local doings. It's almost as accurate as the local grapevine.) and came across an auction notice. An older couple was finally cleaning out their barns and sheds. Some of those treasures had been stored there for several decades, so it was time to have a sale. There were boxes of

old books, a smoking stand, an iron crib, an oak commode with oak dowel joints, a computer desk, cabinets, tables, benches, even a Union Pacific shovel. Suddenly I wasn't thinking about the auction; I was helping brand calves.

Back in the early 1960s, when I was first starting out on my own, I went with a group of wranglers to help a local rancher brand his cattle. We drove to the ranch where his hands had already gathered about 250 bawling cows and calves and separated the calves from their mamas. The foreman had given us our jobs, and we'd started to work when I first saw Mr. Mc__, the owner. He was on his horse, riding slowly riding among the cattle, easily settling his rope under the hind feet of the calves and dragging them one-by-one to where we could flank them down for branding, castrating, and vaccinating. Mr. Mc was no youngster; in fact, he was 108 years old, or so I was told. It was impressive that someone could be so ancient yet still vital and strong, mentally alert and in control. He didn't work all day but did put in several hours with us then went back to his house for a nap before dinner (the midday meal). He joined us to eat and helped an hour or so afterward. Then, thanking us heartily, he returned to the house for another nap.

I never saw him again but always wished I could have known him. His foreman, Red, had worked for him for almost fifty years and told me the old man had come to the valley when he was about eighteen, sometime in the 1860s. He homesteaded the ranch and had lived there ever since. One wife died when she was rather young, and he had several more wives over the decades. Each one, of course, wanted to redecorate the house right away, and every few years and he was happy to have her do it. But he was frugal and never threw anything out. So every 10 or 15 years, he'd store the old furniture in a barn, cover it with canvas, and forget it.

A couple of years after the branding, he died, too, and his heirs decided to sell the ranch. Before they did, though, they held an auction. Gathering all the furniture from the barns, they hired an auctioneer and posted a list. Imagine, hundreds of items of furniture dating from the 1870s, used carefully for ten or fifteen years then stored. There were oak bookcases and chests, iron beds, brass beds, oak beds, and walnut beds, brass and copper laundry boilers, wringer washing machines, iron wood stoves, a hybrid wood and gas stove, wood gothic-shaped radios, ancient TV sets, boxes of books about livestock raising, politics, travel, geography, a whole collection of Zane Grey novels, and thousands of trinkets, china, silverware, pottery, cowboy regalia — from saddles and bridles to rawhide lariats and horsehair bridles — carpets and rugs and wall hangings, etc. Margie and I went to the auction to see what we could buy.

We walked through the auction building, feeling like we were in the halls of western history, which in a way we were. Hundreds of people had gathered to see the collection and make some of it their own.

We spotted a beautiful oak lawyer's bookcase. Margie and I decided we could go as high as $500; it started at $800. Prices were high, for everything was in such perfect condition. Besides, most of the buyers had known Mr. Mc and one or the other of his wives and wanted a memento. At the end of the day we'd purchased nothing, outbid on every item.

So when I read an auction notice today, I moved in my mind back to my nineteenth summer, branding cattle, to Mr. Mc, a living relic of the Old West, and to the possessions he left behind that others wished to share.

That same edition of the paper that carried the auction notice had a story about another local fellow, this one a "townie," and the many paths his life had taken. J.D. Paulson's parents were Swedish immigrants, but he left them when he was fourteen and stole away to the West. He'd see hobos riding the metal framework under the boxcars and decided that looked pretty exciting. When he finally stopped, at Walcott Junction, Wyoming, he was in pretty rough shape — hungry and filthy from the soot and dust along the track and the smoke of the steam engine. He met some soldiers, who took him in as a mascot, gave him something to eat, and cleaned him up. Later he learned to cook and drifted to Colorado, where he became a wagon "cookie" for ranches on trail drives and at brandings. On the trail he learned to butcher cattle and returned to Saratoga, Wyoming, where, with the grand investment of $12, he opened a butcher shop. In 1900 he bought the Owl Café. He wanted to make it a saloon, but the teetotaling former owner had stipulated that it couldn't be used as a place to serve alcohol while he lived. Paulson honored the request, but as soon as the man died, Paulson turned it into a saloon with gaming tables. One day, February 8, 1917, to be exact, he got into a poker game with a neighbor, L.S. Stallings, who owned the local paper I'm reading today. Stakes got a bit high, and Paulson walked away from the game with the deed to the newspaper. Not an educated men, he realized the paper's main value for him would be in selling it, which he did a month later. R.I. Martin bought the paper and ran it for fifty years. Paulson used his funds from the sale of the paper and branched out into bottled medicinal water, from the local hot springs probably, selling it out of his saloon.

Not bad for a little kid who ran away to be a hobo in the West.

One morning in mid-September at 10 o'clock, I looked out the office window onto a Main Street so dark that all the automatic lights had come on. People were bundled up and hurried along as if it were winter. By 11 o'clock it began to rain and continued until the next morning, when fall returned, warm and golden, with clear, blue skies. The roads are already getting dusty.

Our fall color reached its height of drama almost overnight, but there have been changes for several weeks. As I've mentioned, the aspen began to turn in late August, and now the ground is a crunchy gathering of brown, tan, and gold leaves. When the wind blows, the dry leaves chase each other across the yards like hundreds of bucking and running miniature sheep. Some trees are bare, but most cling to their treasure and provide golden canopies on our horseback rides. One of the fishermen "confessed" to spending his morning sitting beside the river, not once even wetting his line. As a friend noted, "Fall does that to you."

Each morning the black Brangus cattle gather atop the highest ridges, their dark coats soaking up the new sun, and they are warmed sooner, well above the cooler air that flowed into the valley below (where we are). Coyotes sing from those same hills, calling into the crisp, sage-scented morning. The dew is heavier now than in August, and each morning lays thick coats of icy crystals on the grass. Delicate lines with cloven hoofmarks punched at intervals end at the flower beds, where does and fawns nibble at the dying flowers. We'll close this week and turn the ranch over to the winter critters, which never really left anyhow.

Our first snowfall greeted us on September 18, dropping in huge snow clumps that fell straight down in the still air. They settled in damp, silvery clusters on the leaves and grass. Margie, and I decided to take a horseback ride.

Soon, the flakes filled the cup-like grooves on leaves and packed into the pale, dusty green sagebrush. The exposed soil retained some heat from yesterday and melted the snow, which became soft and muffled the hoof beats, which thumped rather than clopped over the trail. Although it was snowing, the air was warm, and so were we.

Crows had been flocking for several days and took flight from a snowy meadow in a dark, vibrating cloud. A lone hummingbird searched for nectar at a snow-covered flower and was probably making plans for a southern departure after a quick breakfast.

Along the trail, dozens of shredded spider webs hung from the serviceberry and chokecherry bushes. Without the snow, they'd have been almost invisible. Some had gathered crystals of snow, and they looked like strings of rock candy.

A doe stood poised in the sage, her hair blotchy as she begins a change from rich summer brown to winter silvery gray. Then a marmot startled, dashed across a rock outcrop, and dove behind a rock. Seconds later a little masked face peered back over the rock at us, like a bandito checking on the pursuing posse.

An hour away from the ranch the weather began to change. At first, only a slightly elevated wind shook little showers of snow onto our cheeks and shoulders.

173

Then our feet became colder as snow from the bushes packed into the stirrups and soaked the boots.

Macho style, I was cold but didn't say anything because Margie seemed to be having such a great time! Margie was cold but hesitant to say anything, macha style. I seemed to be having a great time, and besides, the ride was her idea. Finally, one of us, I don't recall who, asked the other if they were cold, and we laughed to discover what each had been thinking.

By this time, the wind was up and our finger and toe temperatures down. As we turned toward the corral the horses were glad to trot, and this warmed us, so we again enjoyed the ride. Back at the ranch we gave them grain and hay; we had hot chocolate and Grand Junction peach sandwiches.

Next day the snow was gone, and warmth and clear, blue skies returned. Nature's dramas continued. Mayflies were hatching, swimming to the surface of the river and shedding their old skins then crawling onto the top of the water. The mayfly didn't see the brown trout until it became its supper. The trout didn't see the bald eagle bearing down on it, and the eagle didn't see the prairie falcon stooping on it from a thousand feet overhead. As the eagle's talons yanked the startled trout from the water the bird spread its wings and quickly rose fifty feet over the river. Then it caught sight of the falcon bearing down on it. The eagle folded its wings slightly and turned upward to face the falcon, which sideslipped and shot upward. The dead fish fell from the eagle's talons and splashed into the river where it drifted on the current until it lodged in an eddy. The mischievous falcon rose on an updraft and slowly disappeared, to all that is but the eagle, which sat hunched on a bare cottonwood branch and glared at the slowly disappearing speck then retrieved its dinner.

Our local coyote pups are about full grown now. They've begun wandering more often by themselves, hunting rather clumsily yet learning from each failure. This morning I came to a meadow about half a mile from the main ranch. I'd paused to watch the morning sun skimming over the grass just as three gray and brown pups bounced into the light. When they saw me, one of them turned and ran. The others merely circled the outer edge of the meadow. Noses to ground, they were intent on finding mice, voles, or even a big grasshopper. As I said, they were clumsy in their attempts. In fact, one of them froze then leaped at something eight times before I finally saw it chewing a catch. Like young siblings everywhere, they were more intent on causing each other mischief than in the job at hand. More than ten minutes passed as they hunted and romped their way around the meadow and into the good mousing grounds of an aspen grove.

The frost has killed off most of the flowers now, but the aspen gold continues to fill the mountainsides. Like the pioneers who first came here, I've spent a few hours gathering winter-cress roots. Back in those lonely frontier days, there were no freezers or fresh produce shipped in from distant, warm places. To get winter greens the ladies were very creative. They could wait until the warm days of late winter and gather the new leaves of winter-cress, but they needed vitamins in January. I'm using their technique.

Yesterday, I built four wood boxes five inches deep and six inches wide, about a foot long and with a loose-fitting lid. This morning I took a dandelion digger and searched around the edges of the nearby meadows and streams, digging up the long, tapered winter-cress roots. A couple of months ago the plants were covered with yellow flowers. Those are gone now, and the leaves are brown and wilted but still recognizable. Their shape is unmistakable — several leaflets along the stem with one large lobe at the top. When I'd gathered a bagful, I trimmed off the dead stems right down to the crown but was careful not to cut into the root crown itself. Then I packed them in my boxes, side by side, like sardines standing up, filled the spaces between with moist sand and set the lid on it. All four boxes are stored in our house's crawlspace, where it's cold but not freezing.

This winter, when we'd like some greens, I'll put an opened box in a sunny window, water it again, and wait. In a few days we'll have greens to eat either fresh or cooked like spinach, just like the pioneers.

Sometimes our guests have to deal with a spouse that's so involved in the quest for fish that the nonfisher gets ignored. Joan B. told me this story about one such evening for her.

She was a fishing widow. When the hatch was on, her husband, Ron, often stayed on the stream well into the evening, leaving her to have dinner by herself. One night, she was walking to the dining room, alone again, and paused at the office. "Joe" (a mannequin) sat in his usual place on the porch, legs crossed casually and with one hand on his lap, enjoying the sunset.

"How about going to dinner with me?" Joan asked. When he didn't answer she giggled and whisked him off to the dining room. Of course in walking he wasn't any help at all and she carried him much as one would a drunken friend. People startled, then grinned as Joe and Joan came into the dining room together, arm-in-arm. After all, they were a striking couple: she, a pretty little Italian lady, and he, a dark-skinned and tall (that is, he would have been tall if he could stand) Native American. She ushered her guest to her table and helped him into a chair.

Actually, he wasn't hungry (what mannequin ever is?), and so she ordered and ate as he watched. Although he didn't talk much, Joe was an excellent listener, and they enjoyed a lively one-sided conversation most of the evening. She was pretty, an excellent conversationalist, and gave him her utmost attention, so Joe was thoroughly enjoying himself. From time to time one or two other guests stopped by to visit and pay their respects to the chief on his visit to the dining room. He was sad when Joan escorted him back to his porch. Of course, being a tough man(nequin), he didn't show it.

She settled him back onto his bench and arranged his legs comfortably, turning him so he could watch the stars. The streetlights were just turning on when she pecked him on the cheek, thanked him for the nice evening, and hummed her way back to her cabin. As other guests walked by, they, too, bid him good night. He was still his usual, stoic self, but his hat appeared to be worn at a bit more jaunty angle. Later, when Joan's husband, Ron, returned from fishing and walked by, Joe secretly grinned. He wasn't sure how the fishing had been, but he'd had a perfect evening.

Each summer the sow bears chase their two-year-old cubs away. For a month or two, the young bears wander, looking for food, probably scared, but still curious about everything. One cub discovered the ranch, and we found it in various places around the buildings

— wandering by the boys' dorm, sauntering across the little bridge by the laundry, sitting atop a dumpster, even checking out the compressor room. In fact as it thumped around in the compressor room, it had company — about a dozen staff members who sat atop cars and roofs outside the door. The only one who really decided to check it out closer was Morris, the yellow cat. As the ranch cat approached, the bear poked its head out of the room, and when it saw the Morris it took a half-hearted swipe at him then stepped out into the night again. The next day, the Game and Fish Department sent out a trailer with a culvert trap on it. The next time the bear was seen it was 12:30 a.m. We heard a loud clang-clump sound as the door on the culvert trap slammed shut. By the time we arrived to have a look, the bear was already eating, making slurping sounds and apparently unconcerned about the people shining flashlights in his face. By 6 o'clock in the morning the trap, with bear inside, was rolling toward the back side of Blackhall Mountain, to a safe home in a less peopled area.

September is a dangerous time in the forest, because wildfires flash easily in the dry leaves. When that happens a thin cloud of smoke fills our valley. We don't like the pollution, but it creates a progression of beautiful sunrises and sunsets where even a cloudless sky is pink or violet. Many times our guests leave Slim's Draw to ride into the magnificence of a sunset that fills the sky, not just the horizon.

Then the end of September comes, and the ranch closes. It's suddenly very, very quiet. Quiet, that is, but for the horned owl that squawks at me each evening as I walk home and the coyotes that sing to each other from Overlook Hill and across the valley, up in Black Cat Forest. Mornings are cool, sometimes cold, and on most days a light fog drifts down river. It gradually dissipates when the sun rises and the valley floor warms.

Yesterday several friends and I rode horseback along Mullen Creek and into the aspen. It was cool when we left the corral, but we quickly shed our jackets as the sun rose. In about 45 minutes we paused atop a ridge to soak in the color, breathe the scent of crisping fall leaves, and listen to the high-pitched "scree" call of a golden eagle as it wheeled in a perfectly blue sky. To some folks, fall is a sad time, the passing of yet another summer, and time for cold and struggle. That may be, but the journey from summer to winter seemed pretty good today.

Last night the Milky Way sprinkled through the sky like a celestial yellow-brick road, so I walked out to a hill to stargaze. An hour later, I returned home and noticed the lightning. I don't know why I hadn't seen it before, except perhaps I was so busy stargazing. All along the outlines of the mountains to the north and west, flashes of colored light strobed continually. When I called Margie, who was on business in Denver, I sat in a chair outside with the long cord of the phone extended through the open door. We said good night, and I stayed to watch the show. An hour later I went inside. It was still flashing in the warm air, and I dozed. At about 11:30 I was awakened suddenly, when a gust of wind shook the house. At the dorms it blew Karissa L.'s window in, throwing broken glass over her room. Jennai and Matt heard her scream and ran to her dorm to help. All were soaked before they had the window covered with plastic. Meanwhile at our house, the anemometer registered 39 mph, and the rain was blowing horizontally, almost a half-inch in a little more than twenty minutes!

Then the wind stopped. All this was dramatic, but the real gift came in the morning. Again the sky was completely cloudless, but the air was frigid, and the hills, trees, and grass were covered with a two-inch layer of icy snow. Aspen leaves have flat stems that make them tremble in the slightest breeze or brush of a snowflake. They trembled all night in the wind, and this morning, while the pines are black with white snowdrifts covering them, the aspen are golden and snow-free. The rising sun poured through the groves at meadow's edge and switched on the aspens' gold. It's calm now. The only sound is a little flock of chickadees knocking snow from branches in their search for seeds and groggy bugs. They're so hungry that one landed on the rim of the cup I was using to fill the bird feeder. I suppose the snow will be gone by tonight, but for now . . .

One of the horses learned a new trick: opening a wire gate. About fifty of the horses took the opportunity and made a break for it, into one of our big meadows. As I rode through the willow bushes, looking for strays, I saw a movement at the base of one and paused to watch. It was a female coyote. Her coat, a mixture of gray and russet, helped her blend into the dry grass and dying leaves. As she slunk around the willow and away from me, her left hind leg swung uselessly, broken. When I rode around the willow, I found her with a huge, German shepherd-sized male, which stood protectively over her. He glared at me, unafraid and unthreatening, for a full minute. Then he leaned down and nuzzled her decisively. She dashed across the meadow, still holding up the injured leg. He didn't move but watched me carefully. Then, when she was safe, he calmly trotted across the grass, pausing to turn and watch my reaction. When she was well into the sage he loped slowly after her, and I continued looking for my lost horses.

Even the wildlife seem to realize that summer's about over and winter's on its way. They're relaxing and enjoying the warm sun while they can. I had some errands in town today, and when I drove back into the ranch at mid-afternoon, there was a coyote dozing *in the middle of the road*, just below our airstrip. It woke, yawned and stretched, then strolled off the road as I drove by only a few feet away, then to the warm road bed.

This morning I went to the river. Reflections from the changing cottonwoods fell onto the water, creating riffles of molten gold. Aspen leaves floated over the riffles like gold foil boats, then continued their journey onto the blue-sky river. Then, a bighorn ram strolled out of the willows and into the water. He was a tawny tan, almost the same color as the dying brome and rustling Great Plains rye grasses that he paused to nibble as he splashed back onto shore and melted into the willows, not far from a fisherman out on his last trip of the season, casting into a pool of iridescent color.

Appendix A

Finding the Beauty: learning to make the world more meaningful to yourself and your family and friends.

One of my favorite orchestral pieces is by Claude Debussy, "Afternoon of a Faun." It's a lovely, flowing piece that musically depicts the meanderings of a faun (the half-man, half-goat kind) through a forest. He makes discoveries, lies by a brook, probably does a bit of mischief, but generally has a peaceful, inward kind of day. Whenever possible, I like to hike off that way, with no particular place in mind, just the goal to experience what I find, not just to see it fleetingly. Even that which happens quickly, I try to perceive in slow motion, to get the details, or as Sherlock Holmes would have said, "Don't just see. Perceive."

What things do I take with me when I go into the woods? It's easy to get loaded down with lots of fancy equipment, but I travel light. Too much weight is a hassle, and too many things get between you and the experience. I take those tools that allow me to look closer. Here's my list. Together they fit into a couple of pockets.

Binoculars. Mine are waterproof and small enough to fit into my shirt pocket. I like the eight-power size, because I can hold them steady and they still bring the birds in very close. They're even useful to help you look closer at a nest, an interesting rock or tree branch, petroglyph, etc., in places where you can't inspect it first hand.

Most of the time a person thinks of binoculars as a way to bring distant things closer. One day I startled a Nuttall's cottontail and it froze in place only 15 feet from me. I wanted to get closer but knew that if I tried it would frighten her away. When I discovered that my binoculars would focus at that close range I slowly scanned the little creature. Through the lenses I could peer into its eyes, see the whiskers quivering slightly, even the slightly trembling muscles under the multi-brown-colored hairs. Now I use the binoculars often, to reach out visually, even when an animal or plant is fairly close.

If I've forgotten my pocket microscope (see below), I can turn the binoculars around and look through the big end of one tube. When I hold an insect, leaf, or rock in my hand, or lean against a rock or dead log, and put the small end up close, I get a hugely magnified view.

Pocket Microscope. Mine looks like a futuristic pen, fits into my shirt pocket, and gives me a 30x magnification. Some go as high as 50x. There's a reflector at the end, which makes it a bit difficult to teach someone else to use, especially a child. Once you learn to use it, however, you'll enjoy "getting into" the parts of a flower or looking at a pinch of soil.

Fresnel Lens Magnifier. A Fresnel lens acts like a magnifying glass but is flat and made of plastic. Mine is a bookmark/lens, made for people like me who sometimes need a bit of help seeing the print. It tucks nicely into a shirt pocket, and I can study a mouse dropping, a flower, or a bit of lichen without having to squint. If I want to look closer yet, I can use the pocket microscope.

Camera. They are wonderful for recording visual details, and I usually carry a very small one, but often I return without taking a single picture. Most photos I take are of my friends traveling with me. If you take a camera, be careful that it doesn't take over the focus of your hike. My advice, for what it's worth, "Don't figure you'll take the picture and look at the scene later. It won't ever be the same, even if you're a great photographer."

Short-legged Beach Chair. While I don't generally use this on longer walks, it's nice if I'm planning a longer time sitting in one place. Animals, as I noted earlier, will usually accept you sooner if you're sitting quietly for at least twenty minutes. My favorite place to use the chair is by a stream. I set the chair as close as I can to a willow or under an alder, anything to break up my body outline in a shadow. If I sit quietly for twenty minutes or so, moving only to make notes and even then doing it slowly, the animals begin their parade past me.

Notebook and Pen. For me, these are the most important. Even a word or two or a short sentence can bring back a flood of memories, if they contain a few sensory clues. Learning to write more pictorially will help the pen and notebook become the power tools they are. If I've forgotten the notebook, I use anything I can write on — even a folded piece of paper or the back of a credit-card receipt.

Appendix B

Observing and Writing What You See

Don't worry about writing eloquently, at least at first, but you should try to look for details. You have to get past the tendency to write only, "I saw a bird eating on a branch of a tree in my yard." It's far longer but a better memory-maker to note, "A mountain chickadee perched on a pencil-sized pine branch. It stood on a sunflower seed, hammering at it with its bill until the seed cracked and the bird ate the kernel, dropped the husk, then flew down for another seed."

Often it takes very few words to make a phrase more meaningful later. It helps to choose the right words. "A mountain chickadee hammering on a sunflower seed as it sat on a thin, bare pine branch." Your mind will fill the blanks. Don't worry about writing fine literature, or even in sentence or paragraph form.

My notebook has waterproof paper, and I use a permanent type felt-tip marker. Yours might be anything from a folded piece of paper to a spiral notebook or a leather-bound volume with paper for both writing and sketching. I've used them all.

If I think about it, the day after I return from a walk I'll review my notes. Usually I think of other details I want to add, or I might change a word or two. My goal isn't great literature (as you know from reading Yours...), but to add more to my notes, my memories of the experience. Sometimes I'll use the notes to write the things in detail and in a finished form. However, that's not at all necessary and depends on what I feel like I want to do.

Look with the eyes of a child. In fact, if you have one yourself, are a grandparent, or can borrow one, take them for a walk in the woods, your yard, a park. Be a kid yourself. Lie down in the grass, look at things from a bug's eye view, get muddy or dirty if need be. As we get taller, it moves us further from the neat things we saw as a kid.

Or take a friend. Everyone not only sees the same thing differently, but sees different things. Three people can look at the same patch of ground, bug, or bird, and experience different parts of it, because we each see and interpret from our own experience. That's great.

You have five senses, or more; use them.

The hardest part for most people is to focus on the natural event. Some want to see things instantly. Others keep thinking of work they must do later. Focusing is a form of meditation, and there are plenty of things your mind wants to consider that you have to put aside for a while. Animals will need at least twenty minutes to begin to accept you as a harmless part of the forest, but you may need that amount of time to quiet your mind anyhow.

One day when I was living in the city, I went to a little park to ease the tensions I was feeling but couldn't really identify. I found a nice place near a little stream and sat down by and slightly under a cluster of young ash trees. It was a lovely scene, but the freeway was nearby. At first the rushing cars and the noise of their motors and tires were all I could hear. Somewhere nearby, a gas station

had stored old tires, and their smell drifted into the woods. Ten minutes passed, and my mind was still confused. After twenty minutes the sounds continued to disturb me.

Then, gradually, almost imperceptibly, I began to relax. A movement below a bush turned out to be a towhee, and I became fascinated by its technique of leaping forward then pulling back with both feet, stirring the soil so it could harvest the seeds and scurrying insects. It passed a cottontail rabbit, which sat motionless, watching me. I began studying the trees near the cottontail, looking out of the corner of my eye at the fearful creature, so it would relax. It did and went about its nibbling. Soon I began to hear the stream as it flowed over the rocks. A light breeze soughed through the copse, ruffling the leaves on the trees and the short hairs on the bunny. Other birds came and went, several fingerling fish flashed like silver needles in the stream, and a walking stick three inches long stepped from the bush beside me onto my arm. It walked slowly up to my shoulder, then stepped off to another bush.

Although the day was hot, I felt the coolness of the moist ground. With each breath more scents came to me, including the leaves I sat on, already on their way to becoming compost. After about twenty minutes, I realized that the human sounds and smells around the forest were less disturbing. Although focusing on them turned up the volume in my mind, I was still enveloped by nature. If I'd given up after that first twenty minutes, I never would have had the memory I now treasure. Patience is a key, and love.

Appendix C

Forest and Range Fire

Late July-Early August, Year One

A single lightning bolt crashed onto the base of Overlook Hill at about 1:30 in the afternoon. In a few minutes, flames and yellowish smoke began to climb up the hill. By the time our crew arrived, half an hour later, the flames were ten feet high. At the ridge top, the wind blew toward the northeast, and the line of fire was headed from the sage into the lodgepole and aspen forests.

We fought it until the firefighters arrived, some of the hottest, hardest work I've ever done. In the reduced wind after sunset, the flames licked lower but wound sinuously, glowing orange in the darkness and eerily beautiful as the shadows of the fighters worked just beyond the light. In eighteen hours more they had it under control, and a few days later I walked the smoking hillsides.

Blackened sagebrush stems poked up from the hot and dusty gray soil, but beyond that it was a desert. Everything burnable had been reduced to ash, including an old buck-and-rail fence. Since the fire, we'd had little wind, and the ash from the burned rails lay in straight lines exactly where the poles had fallen. Some of the soil and many of the rocks were reddened by the heat of the fire.

The animals were fairly unaffected, except, of course, any that had nests in the grass or trees. A badger, who had lain safe in his cool den, under the heat, was up and turning out brown soil atop the grayed soil, and so were some of his neighbor Wyoming ground squirrels. Overhead a kestrel hovered, watching for something to move across the desert.

When I sat at the edge of a scorched aspen grove, the ground actually warmed my seat. In many places the ground was too hot for comfortable walking. At this grove the outer parts had mostly been spared, but the center was still hot and smoking, creating an atoll of trees. At mid-grove, the roots were smoldering, and when I tried to walk across it I fell through to mid-calf, into the empty spaces once filled by the trees' support system. The smell of smoke, burnt and burning grass and hot rocks filled the air, and orange embers glowed where I'd fallen through. The place was obviously still in danger and I called the forest service to report it.

Overall about 150 acres had been burned.

One week later a high wind fanned those hidden embers to flame, then blew the coals into the lodgepole pine forest. That fire took another 1,200 acres.

In the heat of mid-afternoon, I watched as the flames ate their way toward a huge ponderosa pine in an open meadow. There wasn't as much duff deposited in the meadow but the flames raced across it anyhow, devouring grasses, sage, and buckbrush. Surrounding the tree, the flames heated the trunk, which began to smoke. As the pitch on the bark heated, it caught fire, and the flames flew to the top of the tree. I expected the flames to engulf the tree, but it went out as suddenly as it had begun, and the rest of the fire passed on by, leaving it scorched but alive. The old giant may have been attacked like this before.

Each morning and evening our sunsets were glorious orange and pink and magenta as the sun burned its way through the thin smoke in our valley. It created an eerie feeling, as the "volcano" continued to burn so close to us, and a slurry bomber flew only a few hundred feet overhead, and I thought of how people must feel who live next to truly huge natural disasters or war zones. At least this isn't a true destruction. When I return in other years, I know I'll see regeneration and growth that the fire made possible.

August, Year Two

It's not been a wet summer, and as I walk to the places I visited last year I notice that the regrowth hasn't been as fast as I'd expected. The open hillsides are still pale, scorched brown. Even the rain doesn't want to come. Rabbitbrush and buckwheat and bitterbrush are the first colonizers. The fire was so hot and the season so dry that the grass doesn't seem to be taking hold well. The bitterbrush crowns are greenest and already show tooth marks from the bighorn sheep. The yellow mules-ear flowers grew well this spring. Now they've passed their prime, and their wilted leaves lie on the soil, pale sage-green. Scattered among them, puffballs — like lost golf balls waiting for the next drive — wait to be gathered for a morning's omelette. Yarrow is the most surprising. It's normally about ten inches tall here, but these — perhaps from the flush of minerals from the ashes, lack of competition, more sunshine, or all the above — are two feet high. Along with the rabbitbrush, this is the most common flower.

I stop at the atoll aspen grove, where the center was smoldering, and find a wreck. The center is dead and sunken with semi-burned trunks akilter as if stirred. At the edge of the grove, where I sat last year, however, there are hundreds of seedlings about two feet tall, none with stems larger than a pencil. They blanket the ground, and under them a few blades of a half dozen kinds of grasses are beginning to grow.

Walking through the burned lodgepole forest, at the edge of the national forest, is a treat to the eyes and nose; flowers by the hundreds grow among, surprise, thousands of aspen, also two feet tall! And millions of tiny lodgepole seedlings two inches high.

The buck-and-rail fence line is still visible, especially where the rails lay on the ground and burned with such heat. No longer the pale gray of last year, the soil there is now pale brown. Even the few rains we've had left small arroyos in the dust and the start of erosion on the steep hillside, but there is growth.

August, Year Three

The atoll aspen grove is still gray at its center but more of the trees have fallen and are beginning to rot. At the edge of the grove, where I sat the year before, the thousands of aspen seedlings are now hundreds. The deer and elk did their part and thinned them out, eating the smaller seedlings for winter food. Those remaining are thick-stemmed, growing heartily from a field of knee-high grass.

Crawling up the hillside, the dusty remains of the buck-and-rail is still visible but finally fading as grasses, mules-ear, and bitterbrush fill in the empty spots. Most of the original fire site in the sagebrush is still easily visible, greener than the surrounding area. The bighorn sheep have abandoned their traditional grazing and lambing grounds across the river and have moved to this open area, rich with winter and summer food.

August, Year Four

At the atoll grove, the center is slowly filling in with trees and vegetation. There are dozens of aspen sprouts at the edge now, only six inches tall but all of them robust and with thicker stems that are less desirable to browsing deer and elk. Most of them have leaves two to three times the size of an adult tree. The extra size is fairly common on younger aspen and probably helps them to perform photosynthesis more readily, making more food for them to use in their growth. Bighorns spend much of their winter in this area, nibbling at the thicker grass on the south slopes and pruning back the new, more nutritious, sprouts of bitterbrush.

The lodgepole forest floor is covered with thick grass and nodding wildflowers in two dozen varieties. Blackened trees point upward from a carpet of green with purple, pink, and blue accents. Eight-inch-tall seedlings of lodgepole and three-foot aspen are scattered throughout the grass. Yes, the forest is well on its way to recovery, a slightly different forest and one even more filled with animals than before, ready to leap or wander or graze or burrow or play where we can see them and create new memories as they share their lives with us.

A Parting Shot

One of our guests, Mike H., went to buy a cowboy hat. He was raised in Colorado, and from the age of four he'd worn cowboy boots and a cowboy hat. Then he grew up and moved to a place where adults don't usually wear those kinds of things. After a long time away, he returned to Colorado and decided that forty years without a cowboy hat was too long. Besides, he was coming to Wyoming, where the old and new West is the same. Stopping at a western store, he made friends with a salesman. The man was very helpful. He showed Mike Resistols and Baileys and Stetsons; hats with narrow and wide brims; hats with tall and short crowns; explained the benefits of 4x or 5x beaver over 2x beaver; helped Mike to decide the best shape and style for his face and build. Then he left Mike to try on hats. He put on and rejected several, using a three-sided mirror, so he could check them out from all angles. Finally, he chose a black hat with a stockman's crease. It was a good hat, and he looked great in it. Stepping up to the cash register, Mike showed it to the salesman who agreed. "That hat fits great and is just right for you," the man said. "There's only one thing. You might want to turn it around because you've got it on backwards."

Yours from Wyoming, where we hope your hat's pointed our way.

Robert Howe

Bob was born in his father's beloved Texas and passed a year or two among its grass and bluebonnets. Then the family moved to his mother's home on the Illinois prairies. There he grew up playing in the cornfields and oak forests near town. Those were wonderful places, but in 1961, when he first saw the soaring, gray Rockies, he knew he was home. Since then, although his body sometimes has had to be elsewhere, his heart and soul have never left the mountains.

After college, when he was a teacher, his classes included science and math, history and government, psychology and sociology. In life as in teaching, his interests have been eclectic.

Unwilling, and perhaps unable, to live in a suburb or city, he and his wife, Margie, have spent most of their adult lives and raised their children in remote country. For a quarter of a century, they worked at or ran summer camps and for the past two decades have managed a guest ranch.

Bob is an amateur ethno-botanist, an interest that has taken him to South America and Africa. There he passes his time in the jungle with various forest tribes, learning how they live in what most people see as wilderness. In this pursuit he's learned Spanish and Portuguese, even a little French and Swahili.

He loves to ski but has about given up the downhill variety, preferring the quiet of cross country. There were just too many people on the slopes, and he never saw animals, only the lines of tracks below or an occasional chickaree squirrel that scolded the lift-riders. Many of the stories he tells in *Yours, from Wyoming* are of those solitary trips — on skis, on horseback, or on foot.

The ranch he operates is quite remote — the driveway is eight miles long — and Bob can cross-country ski, hike, ride his horse all day and never see anyone. Yet, he's no hermit, and in each week of the summer he gets to share this land with 180 of the nicest, most interesting and vibrant people imaginable. Since the ranch is not advertised, and since most of the guests are returners, they're friends who are anxious to share the experiences and see how everyone's kids have grown. Some have returned for three generations now and bring their children and grandchildren. Bob and Margie are grateful to be a part of their family histories.

We instinctively reach out to natural experiences. Almost everyone has a treasured memory of moments in which they connected with animals, plants, a particular view, etc. Many Americans do, however, feel a disconnection from nature and often fear it. One of Bob's goals for *Yours, from Wyoming* is to help the reader to perceive their world more closely and to love the natural world we hope to protect.

Vel Miller

Vel Miller's home/studio is a chestful of treasures. It sits atop a series of rolling Central California hills that end at the Pacific some twenty miles away. The house, like the artist, is filled with memories of the most important things in life . . . people . . . mementos of family, friends, and mentors who have enriched her life. Paintings cover the walls, and sculptures perch on cowhide-draped antique tables. Each corner is filled with richly patinaed artifacts of the Old West. These are the things of which Vel's life is made.

In her painting and her sculptures, Vel concentrates on the emotional view of the West. Vel says, "The most rugged and strong people I've known have also been the kindest and most loving. This is what I try to portray. I want the person who views my work to see something they have personally experienced or to feel something in the work that brings them happiness."

Vel was born in Nekoosa, Wisconsin, but moved to California before she was five. She spent most of her childhood outdoors, where she grew to love and respect nature and animals.

Her extensive travel has helped her gather the backgrounds for her work, including the years that she and her husband, Warren, spent managing Walter Brennan's ranch in Joseph, Oregon. There were heavy demands on her days — ranch work and cooking for her family and six ranch hands — but she's always found time to express her wonderful, creative talents.

While a student at the Art League of Los Angeles, studying anatomy, composition, and color, she taught up to six painting classes a week.

On their ranch at Atascadero, California, Vel and Warren raise Texas longhorns and quarter horses, and she captures the West. Vel's paintings and sculptures grace homes and museums throughout the world. Both Vel and her artwork have been featured in Contemporary Western Artists, Southwest Art and Art of the West. She is currently listed in Who's Who in American Art and Who's Who in the West.

Vel feels that the West lives, not just in the heart of the cowboy roping a calf or an Indian chasing a buffalo. It lives in all of us. She says, "I see it in a child with his or her animals or a mother or father with their children. It's the wonder of the latest crop of calves and colts, or in the evening light skimming across a darkening meadow. I hear it in the creak of a new saddle, the crowing of a rooster as dawn approaches, and the soft nicker of a mare to her newborn foal."

Living as we do has been a wonderful way to raise our family. The children learn early how to handle responsibility and hard work. But the best benefit has been that Margie and I are usually nearby, so we can sneak in a few minutes with our children, even in the workday. We've created traditions that bind us emotionally to our offspring. Some of those traditions continue despite the fact they have their own families.

When Heather was in about fifth grade she got her first horse. Hanni was a pretty bay, a Morgan-Arab mix with the classic head of her Arab mother. Each day after school Heather and her friends would brush their horses, bridle them, and head off bareback to explore the nearby forests. Saturday mornings, though, were our time for long rides together. Hanni's gone now — she lived to a very ripe old age — and Heather's the mom of two boys. They live away from the ranch, so we don't get to do our rides as much. Still, when she does come to the ranch, we love to ride out like we used to, just the two of us for a couple of hours. A visit wouldn't be complete without a ride together. They're coming this week, and I've found a new area to explore with her.